DEFENSE, SECURITY AND STRATEGIES

INTELLIGENCE, SURVEILLANCE AND RECONNAISSANCE: ACQUISITIONS, POLICIES AND DEFENSE OVERSIGHT

DEFENSE, SECURITY AND STRATEGIES

Additional books in this series can be found on Nova's website
under the Series tab.

Additional E-books in this series can be found on Nova's website
under the E-books tab.

DEFENSE, SECURITY AND STRATEGIES

INTELLIGENCE, SURVEILLANCE AND RECONNAISSANCE: ACQUISITIONS, POLICIES AND DEFENSE OVERSIGHT

JOHANNA A. MONTGOMERY
EDITOR

Nova Science Publishers, Inc.
New York

Copyright © 2011 by Nova Science Publishers, Inc.

All rights reserved. No part of this book may be reproduced, stored in a retrieval system or transmitted in any form or by any means: electronic, electrostatic, magnetic, tape, mechanical photocopying, recording or otherwise without the written permission of the Publisher.

For permission to use material from this book please contact us:
Telephone 631-231-7269; Fax 631-231-8175
Web Site: http://www.novapublishers.com

NOTICE TO THE READER

The Publisher has taken reasonable care in the preparation of this book, but makes no expressed or implied warranty of any kind and assumes no responsibility for any errors or omissions. No liability is assumed for incidental or consequential damages in connection with or arising out of information contained in this book. The Publisher shall not be liable for any special, consequential, or exemplary damages resulting, in whole or in part, from the readers' use of, or reliance upon, this material. Any parts of this book based on government reports are so indicated and copyright is claimed for those parts to the extent applicable to compilations of such works.

Independent verification should be sought for any data, advice or recommendations contained in this book. In addition, no responsibility is assumed by the publisher for any injury and/or damage to persons or property arising from any methods, products, instructions, ideas or otherwise contained in this publication.

This publication is designed to provide accurate and authoritative information with regard to the subject matter covered herein. It is sold with the clear understanding that the Publisher is not engaged in rendering legal or any other professional services. If legal or any other expert assistance is required, the services of a competent person should be sought. FROM A DECLARATION OF PARTICIPANTS JOINTLY ADOPTED BY A COMMITTEE OF THE AMERICAN BAR ASSOCIATION AND A COMMITTEE OF PUBLISHERS.

Additional color graphics may be available in the e-book version of this book.

Library of Congress Cataloging-in-Publication Data

Montgomery, Johanna A.
 Intelligence, surveillance and reconnaissance : acquisitions, policies and defense oversight / Johanna A. Montgomery.
     p. cm.
  Includes index.
  ISBN 978-1-61470-900-8 (hbk.)
 1. Military intelligence--United States. 2. United States. Dept. of Defense--Procurement--Evaluation. 3. United States. Dept. of Defense--Appropriations and expenditures--Evaluation. 4. Military surveillance--United States. 5. Military reconnaissance--United States. I. Title.
  UB251.U5M64 2011
  355.3'4320973--dc23
                          2011027349

Published by Nova Science Publishers, Inc. † *New York*

CONTENTS

Preface		vii
Chapter 1	Intelligence, Surveillance, and Reconnaissance (ISR) Acquisition: Issues for Congress *Richard A. Best Jr.*	1
Chapter 2	Actions Are Needed to Increase Integration and Efficiencies of DOD's ISR Enterprise *United States Government Accountability Office*	25
Chapter 3	Counterinsurgency (COIN) Intelligence, Surveillance, and Reconnaissance (ISR) Operations *Department of Defense*	51
Chapter Sources		151
Index		153

PREFACE

Increasing calls for intelligence support and continuing innovations in intelligence technologies combine to create significant challenges for both the executive and legislative branches. Intelligence, Surveillance, and Reconnaissance (ISR) systems are integral components of both national policymaking and military operations, including counterterrorism operations, but they are costly and complicated and they must be linked in order to provide users with a comprehensive understanding of issues based on information from all sources. These complications have meant that even though many effective systems have been fielded, there have also been lengthy delays and massive cost overruns. This new book explores the uncertainties about the long-term acquisition plans for ISR systems that persist even as pressures continue for increasing the availability of ISR systems in current and future military operations and for national policymaking.

Chapter 1- Increasing calls for intelligence support and continuing innovations in intelligence technologies combine to create significant challenges for both the executive and legislative branches. Intelligence, Surveillance, and Reconnaissance (ISR) systems are integral components of both national policymaking and military operations, including counterterrorism operations, but they are costly and complicated and they must be linked in order to provide users with a comprehensive understanding of issues based on information from all sources. Relationships among organizations responsible for designing, acquiring, and operating these systems are also complicated as are oversight arrangements in Congress. These complications have meant that even though many effective systems have been fielded, there have also been lengthy delays and massive cost overruns. Uncertainties about the long-term acquisition plans for ISR systems persist even as pressures continue for increasing the availability of ISR systems in current and future military operations and for national policymaking.

Chapter 2- The success of intelligence, surveillance, and reconnaissance (ISR) systems in collecting, processing, and disseminating intelligence information has fueled demand for ISR support, and the Department of Defense (DOD) has significantly increased its investments in ISR capabilities since combat operations began in 2001. In fiscal year 2010, intelligence community spending —including for ISR—exceeded $80 billion. Section 21 of Public Law 111-139 mandated that GAO identify programs, agencies, offices, and initiatives with duplicative goals and activities. This report examines the extent to which: (1) DOD manages and oversees the full scope and cost of the ISR enterprise; (2) DOD has sought to identify and minimize the potential for any unnecessary duplication in program, planning, and operations for ISR; and (3) DOD's ISR Integration Roadmap addresses key congressionally directed management elements and guidance.

Chapter 3- MG Flynn's comments come at a time when Department of Defense (DoD) resource constraints and challenges are becoming more evident, even as the Department faces a wide range of prospective COIN operations in the future. As a result, the Department must take into account what it has learned in recent and current COIN operations, the need to continue supporting current operations as effectively as possible, and the challenges of preparing for the future. This report represents an effort to understand the balance that will be required to meet these challenges, and to plan accordingly.

Chapter 1

INTELLIGENCE, SURVEILLANCE, AND RECONNAISSANCE (ISR) ACQUISITION: ISSUES FOR CONGRESS[*]

Richard A. Best Jr.

SUMMARY

Increasing calls for intelligence support and continuing innovations in intelligence technologies combine to create significant challenges for both the executive and legislative branches. Intelligence, Surveillance, and Reconnaissance (ISR) systems are integral components of both national policymaking and military operations, including counterterrorism operations, but they are costly and complicated and they must be linked in order to provide users with a comprehensive understanding of issues based on information from all sources. Relationships among organizations responsible for designing, acquiring, and operating these systems are also complicated as are oversight arrangements in Congress. These complications have meant that even though many effective systems have been fielded, there have also been lengthy delays and massive cost overruns. Uncertainties about the long-term acquisition plans for ISR systems persist even as pressures continue for increasing the availability of ISR systems in current and future military operations and for national policymaking.

These challenges have been widely recognized. A number of independent assessments have urged development of "architectures" or roadmaps setting forth agreed-upon plans for requirements and acquisition and deployment schedules. Most observers would agree that such a document would be highly desirable, but there are significant reasons why developing such an architecture and gaining an enduring consensus remain problematical. First, ISR technologies are not static; whereas it is possible to plan for aircraft, ships, or tanks that can be used for decades, it is doubtful that today's inventory of satellites, unmanned aerial vehicles, and manned aircraft will still be the right mix a few years hence. Some believe that a "cast-in-concrete" plan would inhibit the ability to take advantage of new technologies or techniques as they emerge. Secondly, achieving consensus on such a plan would be greatly affected by the separate priorities of different

---

[*] This is an edited, reformatted and augmented version of a Congressional Research Service publication, CRS Report for Congress R41284, from www.crs.gov, dated January 20, 2011.

parts of the intelligence community, the Defense Department, and Washington policymakers. The needs of policymakers and military commanders are different and are usually reconciled only on a case-by-case basis. Furthermore, different congressional oversight committees may also have different perspectives on priorities and some may seek to emphasize funding for specific systems.

The Director of National Intelligence could be given authority to reach across current organizational boundaries to define requirements and priorities. Some propose establishing a position for a separate "ISR Czar" to do this. Few observers believe that ISR programs could be carved out of the intelligence budget and/or the defense budget, and placed under the control of a single officer or lead agency. There is a strong likelihood that separate needs and concerns that effect the current systems will not disappear; even if one official has a new and expansive charter. Similar concerns would exist in regard to the jurisdictions of congressional oversight committees.

A fundamental question is not whether a long-term plan can be agreed upon and implemented, or whether the current disparate bureaucratic arrangements can be transformed, but whether the conflicting priorities and budgetary realities can be at least recognized and addressed in approximately the same timeframe by all responsible officials. ISR systems can be viewed as providing a test case for the interagency cooperation that observers believe will be increasingly important throughout the federal government.

INTRODUCTION

Intelligence, surveillance, and reconnaissance (ISR) systems are matters of great congressional interest. These systems can provide policymakers with information on the military capabilities of foreign countries, the location of key defense and industrial sites, indications of the presence of weapons of mass destruction, and information on the plans of foreign leaders and terrorist groups. National-level ISR is essential for both defense planning and for arms control negotiations. Military commanders rely on intelligence systems for information on enemy positions and activities; tactical ISR has also been essential for precise targeting in counterterrorism operations while minimizing civilian casualties. At the present time major ISR systems—national and tactical—are used by both military commanders and Washington policymakers to follow developments in combat areas in great detail. ISR systems include reconnaissance satellites some of which have been operational for decades, Unmanned Aerial Systems (UAS)[1] of various sizes, as well as manned aircraft and other sensor platforms. In practice, some ISR systems acquired for one purpose are regularly used for other missions that may have been unanticipated when the systems were designed.

Acquisition of ISR systems presents particular challenges to the intelligence community, the Department of Defense (DOD), and Congress. Agencies responsible for national systems are usually separate from those that design and acquire tactical systems. The costs and complexity of individual systems, continuing changes in technologies, and the difficulties involved in linking disparate systems together to serve a variety of consumers require different acquisition approaches than those often used for ships, tank, and manned aircraft. Moreover, since the establishment of the United Launch Alliance in late 2006,[2] ISR satellites rely on launch platforms and other technologies used by non-intelligence satellites; thus, there is a necessity to coordinate intelligence satellite developments and launch schedules with elements of the national space effort that is managed by federal agencies outside DOD and the intelligence community.

UAS have demonstrated that on occasion they can provide data at a fraction of the costs of multibillion dollar satellites, but UAS acquisition efforts have been anything but simple. There has been a tendency to introduce new and untested capabilities to unmanned platforms causing production delays and cost growth. Some policymakers would centralize UAS acquisition efforts under an executive agent (an initiative that Congress at one point mandated but then abandoned), but, in practice, the four services have been intent on acquiring different UAS that meet their perceived unique requirements. The result has often been excessive costs required for different systems with duplicative or overlapping capabilities. Other platforms for ISR collection such as manned aircraft continue to have important functions, but often they compete for agency funding with non-intelligence aircraft rather than with unmanned intelligence systems and intelligence requirements may not receive the highest priorities. Acquisition efforts are further complicated by the fact that Congress addresses ISR programs through a number of committees, principally Armed Services, Intelligence and Appropriations.

Such factors taken together have often led to piecemeal acquisition efforts, major cost overruns, and an inability to ensure that disparate systems can be linked effectively to yield a comprehensive intelligence picture. There have been production delays and only recently have UAS been available in adequate numbers to support the pace of operations in Iraq and Afghanistan. Observers argue—and a number of key members of Congress have concurred—that the drawbacks inherent in past and current ISR acquisition efforts are serious enough to indicate that consideration should be given to the preparation of an agreed-upon multi-year plan or "architecture" that provides production schedules for currently planned ISR systems and the introduction of new platforms. If such a plan were agreed upon, advocates argue, it would be possible to restrain cost growth, ensure that all requirements had been considered, and establish the best possible mix of satellites and unmanned and manned systems. On the other hand, skeptics suggest that dynamic technologies and the changing international environment would nevertheless necessarily limit what can be done in terms of multi-year procurement efforts.

EVOLVING REQUIREMENTS FOR ISR SYSTEMS

A key consideration underlying efforts to acquire, deploy and operate ISR systems is the way or ways that they will be used. The need to gain insights into Soviet military capabilities during the Cold War provided the principal impetus for the sizable investments in global signals intelligence and overhead reconnaissance capabilities. These systems were considered "national"; they were acquired primarily to support the President and key cabinet members. A number of "national" organizations—especially the National Reconnaissance Office (NRO) and the National Security Agency (NSA), along with the Central Intelligence Agency (CIA)—were established to gather and analyze information for senior policymakers. The ability of U.S. leaders to gauge the extent of Soviet strategic capabilities was essential to defense planning and arms control negotiations, but there was less capability to support military commanders in ongoing combat operations.

Beginning with Desert Shield in 1991, however, these national-level systems began to be adapted to tactical use in Iraq, Bosnia, Kosovo, Afghanistan, and elsewhere. Wherever U.S. forces have been deployed for combat there have been requirements for intensive intelligence support that called upon national systems that were not originally intended for tactical uses. In peacekeeping/peacemaking/stabilization operations, the overriding need to minimize attacks on civilians has led commanders and national-level leaders to seek ever more precise target data from all available sources of information.

In addition to adapting older systems to the demands of current modes of warfighting, newer ISR systems have also been employed with considerable success. In particular, UAS have proven their value as relatively low-cost systems that can be routinely used by ground commanders to acquire tactical intelligence. In regular use since the early 1990's, UAS range in size and sophistication from very small systems that can be launched by an individual soldier for short-range tactical operations to the high-altitude Global Hawk that can acquire much of the same information as reconnaissance satellites. The potential overlap, or possibility of close coordination between UAS and national satellites has, however, called into question the separate organizational and congressional oversight structures that have been established or have evolved over the past decades.

In Spring 2009, Secretary of Defense Robert Gates argued in *Foreign Affairs* that the nature of U.S. strategic planning has unalterably changed. His comments summarize the evolution of defense and intelligence planning that guided the Administration's budget proposals for FY2010.

> for far too long there was a belief or a hope that Iraq and Afghanistan were exotic distractions that would be wrapped up relatively soon—the regimes toppled, the insurgencies crushed, the troops brought home. Therefore we should not spend too much or buy too much equipment not already in our long-range procurement plans or turn our bureaucracies and processes upside down.... As a result of these failed assumptions, the capabilities most urgently needed by our warfighters, were for the most part fielded ad hoc and on the fly, developed outside the regular bureaucracy and funded in supplemental legislation that would go away when the wars did—if not sooner."
>
> . . .
>
> [G]iven the types of situations the United States is likely to face ... the time has come to consider whether the specialized, often relatively low-tech equipment well suited for stability and counterinsurgency missions is also needed. It is time to think hard about how to institutionalize the procurement of such capabilities and get them fielded quickly.[3]

Secretary Gates was addressing issues of defense acquisition in general and not ISR systems in particular. It is clear, however, from the text of his speeches and his actions as Defense Secretary that he sees ISR support to warfighters as a major example of the challenge facing policymakers in both the executive branch and Congress. Military operations have increasingly come to depend upon the availability of copious amounts of real-time ISR. As a result of the commitment to Iraq and Afghanistan, requirements for ISR and the actual use of ISR data have grown exponentially in the past decade. The military priorities of both the Bush and Obama Administrations have established priorities for particular kinds of intelligence and thus particular types of intelligence collection systems.

The February 2010 Quadrennial Defense Review (QDR) Report reflected Secretary Gates' earlier statements.

> The wars we fighting today and assessments of the future security environment together demand that the United States retain and enhance a whole-of-government capability to succeed in large-scale counterinsurgency (COIN), stability, and counterterrorism (CT) operations in environments ranging from densely populated urban areas and mega-cities, to remote mountains, deserts, jungles, and littoral regions.
>
> Stability operations, large-scale counterinsurgency, and counterterrorism operations are not niche challenges or the responsibility of a single Military Department, but rather require a portfolio of capabilities as well as sufficient capacity from across America's Armed Forces and other departments and agencies. Nor are these types of operations a transitory or anomalous phenomenon in the security landscape. On the contrary, we must expect that for the indefinite future, violent extremist groups, with or without state sponsorship, will continue to foment instability and challenge U.S. and allied interests.[4]

The QDR indicates that DOD has placed special emphasis on "certain capabilities that have been in consistently high demand and have proven to be key enablers of tactical and operational success."[5] These enablers include manned and unmanned aircraft systems such as the Predators and Reaper UAS.[6]

ISR ACQUISITION PROCESSES

ISR systems are acquired in very different ways; the process is conducted in classified channels and there is no overall ISR package that is developed by the executive branch and forwarded to Congress for its consideration. Rather, different systems are treated separately and requests come to Congress in different ways. Funds are also authorized and appropriated in different legislative measures. As might be expected, the result can be disjointed, with duplicative coverage in some areas and shortfalls in others. The most important ISR category is the National Intelligence Program (NIP) that includes systems designed for the use of national policymakers—the President and the National Security Council (NSC). Other important ISR systems are designed for and operated by military commanders and are grouped in the Military Intelligence Program (MIP). However, NIP systems can also be used to support tactical operations, and MIP systems can collect information of interest to senior policymakers. Traditionally, satellites are acquired as part of the NIP, but some are now included in the MIP. Most UAS have been MIP systems as have manned aircraft in recent decades. The composition of annual NIP and MIP budget submissions are classified and available only to members of Congress and appropriate committee staff.

"National" Space

The most expensive ISR system has been surveillance satellites, the development of which is perhaps the greatest accomplishment of U.S. intelligence. For many years the NRO—an agency created in 1961 with no public acknowledgement of its existence for over thirty years—was able to develop and acquire cutting edge reconnaissance systems. Early systems were placed into orbit only after many failures; costs were relatively unconstrained, and work proceeded in secret and with minimal oversight from either DOD or Congress. Reconnaissance satellites, in being able to delineate Soviet capabilities—and the absence thereof—made a major contribution to U.S. defense policies during the Cold War and, most observers would acknowledge, essentially justified their costs. The end of the Cold War reduced the need for satellite reconnaissance of foreign military forces; the "open-checkbook" approach to satellite acquisition ended. A reduction in intelligence budgets in the 1990s coincided with the beginning of the retirements of many in the generation of scientists and engineers that launched the satellite program.[7]

It is widely acknowledged that there is inherent tension between efforts to acquire new satellite technologies and the need to maintain and/or replace existing capabilities. Acquisition of systems using currently available technologies can yield stability and contained costs; while trying to push the technological envelope to acquire cutting-edge or "exquisite" systems can be more disruptive. In addition, the tendency to prefer large Cold War-era systems has drawbacks. A senior DOD official acknowledged:

> we have attempted to buy large monolithic systems that produce a capability that is one size fits all, i.e. a single system that satisfies all customers, without evaluating the full set of alternatives....
> This model is a Cold War relic, when space systems were needed to satisfy only the strategic policy decision maker and events unfolded in a fairly static timeline. Today's reality is that one size does not fit all.[8]

Further, the operational tempos in all of the Areas of Responsibility (AOR) diverge greatly and require different timeliness of access, volume, or fidelity. Developing a system that can satisfy all users all of the time is unsustainable, if not impossible. ... deploying architectures with constellations of just a few satellites leave[s] the nation incredibly vulnerable and invites our adversaries to target our systems."[9]

Satellite acquisition is complicated. First, satellites overlap to some extent with airborne systems in terms of reconnaissance capabilities; there are potential trade-offs. Secondly, the acquisition and operations, (especially the launching) of reconnaissance satellites is closely related to other types of satellites used for meteorology and communications that are not intelligence systems. As one report has noted:

> The U.S. space sector, in supporting commercial, scientific, and military applications of space, is embedded in our nation's economy, providing technological leadership and sustainment of the industrial base. To cite one leading example, the global Positioning System (GPS) is the world standard for precision navigation and timing, directly and indirectly affecting numerous aspects of everyday life. But other capabilities such as weather services; space-based data, telephone and video communications; and television broadcasts have also become common, routine services. The Space Foundation's 2008 Space Report indicates that the U.S. commercial satellite service and space infrastructure sector is today approximately a $170 billion annual business.[10]

Thus, the potential that high-altitude UAS have for meeting the same requirements as satellites may suggest that funds for satellite programs be shifted to UAS acquisition (leaving aside the issue of whether satellites actually provide better coverage and whether satellites are potentially less vulnerable to attack.) On the other hand, if fewer reconnaissance satellites are to be launched, economies of scale among all satellite programs along with the "space intelligence base" might be affected.

Another program, the Space Based Infrared System (SBIRS) consisting of infrared sensors that can detect incoming missiles demonstrates the cost risks inherent in satellite acquisition; according to one media account the program exceeded its original $3 billion cost estimate by some $7.5 billion. The SBIRS program, centered on a space-based missile warning satellite, "originally pegged at around $3 billion, in now in the neighborhood of $10 billion; launch of the first satellite, originally targeted for 2002, is now expected anywhere between late 2010 and spring 2011."[11]

Satellites have always been costly. In earlier decades their unique ability to peer behind the Iron Curtain justified substantial investments that were known only to a few members of relevant congressional committees. National satellites remain costly, reportedly over $1 billion for each satellite not counting considerable associated ground support and analytical efforts. The effort to acquire new technologies or to exploit available cutting-edge technologies results in highly expensive systems. Many observers argue that costs of satellite systems are unnecessarily inflated by too great a commitment to innovative technologies when others are adequate for likely missions; others point to a tendency to add unnecessary requirements ("bells and whistles") that increase complexity and delay production. Others maintain that opportunities for technological breakthroughs should not be passed up and innovative technologies usually pay for themselves eventually. The growth of program costs, however, is beyond doubt.

Since passage of the Land Remote Sensing Policy Act of 1992 (P.L. 102-555), commercial imaging satellites have been launched and federal agencies were the first major customers. Arguably, commercial imagery saves the government money since purchases can be limited to meet particular requirements. In large measure, however, imagery companies have become highly dependent on government contracts and changes in imagery procurement can have great implications for the commercial industry. In many cases, government satellites can produce more detailed information but at higher costs and the government has to cover both acquisition and operating costs over a multi-year period.

The end of the life-cycle for the current satellites was foreseen well ahead of time. Although plans for follow-on systems were, and remain, classified there has been considerable public commentary about one approach, known as the Future Imagery Architecture (FIA) in which billions were invested only to have funded canceled in 2005 when it became apparent that delivery schedules and budget limitations could not be met. Most observers credit the FIA debacle as a result of choosing an inexperienced contractor, imposing excessively tight deadlines and cost controls without an adequate government oversight mechanism.[12]

In April 2009, Dennis Blair, newly appointed as DNI, announced a plan to modernize the satellite imagery architecture by having the NRO build and operate "satellites" (no number specified) and significantly increasing the acquisition of imagery produced by U.S. commercial providers. He noted that commercial "less-complex satellites, which are based on technologies already in production by U.S. vendors, would be available sooner than the much more capable NRO developed and acquired systems."[13] Media accounts indicate that efforts would be made to avoid the problems associated with FIA and that independent cost estimates and tougher assessments of technological maturity would be involved for the new systems that are due to operational before 2020.[14] Some members, especially Senator Christopher

Bond, the Vice Chairman of the Senate Intelligence Committee, have criticized the plan, arguing that there is an opportunity to take advantage of potential technological breakthroughs and proposing a different, but as yet untested, satellite technology.[15] The Administration proposal would provide a few highly sophisticated satellites that have the advantage of being based on available, proven technologies; Senator Bond's proposal which was reportedly included in the FY2010 Intelligence Authorization bill, S. 1494, would include larger numbers of smaller, less expensive satellites that are based on cutting edge technologies that have not yet been tested and approved. Media accounts indicate that defense authorization (P.L. 111-84) and defense appropriations measures (P.L. 111-118) for FY2010 included funding for the acquisition of at least one of the larger satellites with funding beginning in FY2011.[16]

Several attempts have been made to provide overall direction to space surveillance acquisition efforts. In 2004 the National Security Space Office (NSSO) was created to develop and coordinate national security space strategies, architectures, plans, programs, and processes on a continuing basis. The NSSO remains, however, essentially an advisory body and has not had the authority to define programs and monitor implementation. According to GAO the NSSO developed a National Security Space Strategy in 2004 but it was never issued.[17] In 2003 an Executive Agent for Space was established with the Secretary of the Air Force designated to fill the position.[18] The Executive Agent would have a wide range of responsibilities for planning and programming DOD's space systems including Milestone Decision Authority. The persistence of space acquisition problems, however, led to the abandonment of the position in 2005 with procurement responsibilities returning to the office of the Assistant Secretary of Defense for Acquisition, Technology, and Logistics. In 2009, however, the Defense Appropriation Act, P.L. 111-118 provided $7 million for a Space and Intelligence Office (SIO) within the Office of the Under Secretary of Defense for Acquisition, Technology (USD(AT&L)). The new office is to serve as the DOD space architecture planning office; it is to provide a roadmap to Congress in mid-2010 on how it will be used in future space system architecture planning.

"Tactical" Space

Although considerable efforts have been underway for many years to make information collected available for tactical use, collection priorities for NRO satellites are established by the DNI. Although military commanders may have the opportunity to request coverage of a given target they cannot be certain that their requirements will be considered more important than those of other agencies. The inability of combatant commanders to obtain what they consider as adequate support from national satellite programs led to efforts for DOD to acquire satellites independently of the NRO for the primary support of the warfighters. Some saw significant advantages to be gained by moving beyond "the sclerotic national programs [that] simply cannot maintain the pace required for future operations."[19] The goal was to build new, less expensive, less sophisticated satellites that could meet the critical requirements of combat commanders. Under the program, known as Operationally Responsive Space (ORS), military commanders would have access to an inventory of relatively unsophisticated satellites that could be launched when needed to provide information for limited durations. ORS would complement information from national satellites and other collection programs.

Some observers have raised concerns that this program to some extent duplicates or at least overlaps the capabilities of NRO satellites and may have been established simply to avoid the organizational complexities of national satellite procurement and the need to coordinate collection management with Washington agencies.[20] The GAO concluded in 2008 that "the [ORS] concept is in the early stages of development and not commonly understood by all members of the warfighter and national security space communities." In addition "DOD has not clearly defined key elements of the ORS concept and has not effectively communicated the concept with key stakeholders." Furthermore, GAO believes that "officials from the intelligence community were concerned about DOD's lack of consultation and communication with them regarding the ORS concept." These officials "also raised concerns about the importance of using their current processes and architecture so as not to create unnecessary duplicative processes to get data to the war fighter." [21]

Other observers maintain, however, that new systems could be built from the bottom up using available technologies including those used in the commercial sector and that ORS could provide a useful capability for commanders whose requirements will always be subject to adjustment or derogation when collection priorities of national systems are established and implemented.[22] ORS provides a just-in-time capability that can be tailored for missions of limited duration. The ORS concept has gained support in the Defense Department and Congress has funded the ORS in defense authorization and appropriations legislation, albeit not to the extent envisioned by the Air Force. For FY2010 the Administration requested $112.9 million, an increase over the FY2009 appropriations level of $83.7 million, but over $100 million that was originally envisioned by ORS planners was included in an Air Force list of unfunded priorities.[23] The conference report reflected an agreement to provide only the $112 million requested, but not to provide the additional funds.[24] However, Defense officials believed that further ORS satellites will be approved if the first one can be built "within the kinds of very aggressive parameters that we've set up."[25] As the Administration requested only $93 million for the ORS program for FY2011, some observers suggest that the limited funds may ultimately jeopardize the program.[26] Nevertheless, support for ORS remains strong in both chambers; the House version of the FY2011 defense authorization bill (H.R. 5136) would add an additional $40 million to the Administration request and the Senate Armed Services Committee in its bill (S. 3454) would add an additional $20 million. The ORS satellite currently planned for launch at the end of 2010 is intended to meet specific needs of Central Command.

In April 2009, testimony of Josh Hartman, a long-time proponent of ORS, set for the rationale for what he termed "a balanced architecture":

> The solution is a change in our business model that will enable employment of an architecture distributed to multiple nodes and layered to provide right level of capability to the right geographic regions at the right times, while leveraging commercial systems and multiple sensors from different sizes of space craft and non-space platforms.
>
> This model would provide for a balanced architecture where a foundational capability would be provided from medium or large systems. At the same time, small and agile, less complex systems would be "layered" to augment in optimized orbits, with additional capability in high demand areas, and niche capability for special operations, irregular needs or crisis situations." As recommended by the GAO, evolution of capability would be a hallmark and key tenet of this model. Systems would be purposely be designed to live shorter lives to reduce the system complexity, synchronize on-orbit

life with developing time, increase industry volume, and take advantage of rapidly advancing technology.[27]

DOD is assessing other satellite systems besides ORS. Some hope to realize significant savings over NRO-led efforts. One media report suggests that one company believes it can deliver a halfmeter-resolution imagery satellite for $6 million-$7 million a satellite.[28] ORS remains a work-in-progress. Efforts to take advantage of new technologies to produce relatively inexpensive satellites to support military commanders could usefully supplement intelligence gathered from other sources. At the same time, however, the ORS effort appears to have been undertaken in isolation from the organizations that have been responsible for launching satellites over many years. Observers suggest that the extensive expertise available in the NRO and NGA have not been fully accessed, possibly risking waste and duplication of effort. Alternately, some might argue that long-existing organizational relationships tend to become sclerotic, potentially inhibiting the development of innovative technologies that can serve operating forces at reasonable costs.

Unmanned Aerial Systems (UAS)

UAS have become essential parts of military operations.[29] Although first deployed during the Vietnam conflict, their use was limited until 1990-1991 when they supplied exact locating data during Operations Desert Storm that was used in targeting precision guided munitions (PGMs). Their use expanded during operations in Iraq and Afghanistan when great emphasis has been placed on avoiding inadvertent attacks on civilians. Increasing availability of UAVs especially the MQ-1 Predator with a range of 454 miles and the follow-on MQ-9 Reaper with a range of over 3600 miles and a flight time of over 20 hours, has made them tactical weapons of choice. In addition to the Predators, longer range Global Hawks which fly at much higher altitudes have also been employed in combat operations. Communications have improved to the point where information intercepted by UAVs can be forwarded not only to the local commander but also to intelligence centers at various echelons where it can be combined (or "fused") with data from other sources to produce a more complete intelligence picture.

The history of UAV acquisition has been complicated. A crucial step was taken during the Reagan Administration by Navy Secretary John Lehman who, having witnessed Israeli use of the systems over Lebanon, procured commercially built Israeli UAVs for the U.S. Navy. Later, the Defense Airborne Reconnaissance Office (DARO) was established by DOD to manage UAV acquisition throughout the Defense Department; this effort did not, however, endure and in the FY1998 Defense Authorization Act (P.L. 105-85, sec. 905), Congress directed the transfer of relevant DARO functions to the separate military departments. Since then, some consideration has been given to designating one service as an executive agent for UAV acquisition, but this approach has never been accepted in the face of significant opposition from other services determined to ensure that their unique requirements can be met.

In recent years the use of UAVs has proliferated in Iraq and Afghanistan where they helped in meeting the objectives of identifying elusive enemies and avoiding civilian casualties. According to DOD, "the number of deployed UAS has increased from approximately 167 aircraft in 2002 to over 6,000 in 2008, while defense investment in UAS capabilities has dramatically grown from $284 million in Fiscal Year 2000 to $2.5 billion in Fiscal Year 2008."[30] The FY2011 request was for $4.1 billion. Responding to continuing needs for tactical systems, in the first months of the Obama Administration, Secretary of Defense Gates realigned DOD's budget priorities to emphasize tactical ISR systems including UAVs. Funding was recommended to field and sustain some 50 continuous orbits for Predator or Reaper-class UAVs along with manned ISR platforms such as the turbo-prop aircraft that have been used by Army brigade-level commanders in Iraq. Although additional funding for ISR systems was included in the FY2009 supplemental, Secretary Gates indicated his intention to ensure that ISR programs are incorporated into base budgets rather than in supplemental appropriations measures. He also indicated plans for more extensive research and development efforts on ISR systems with emphasis on those systems that link warfighters and national systems.[31]

The most commonly used UAV systems, Predators and Reapers, are designed for tactical use. The Predator flies at altitudes up to 25,000 feet; the Reaper 50,000 feet. Both have an endurance of 24 hours. Some UAVs such as the Global Hawk have capabilities that rival those of reconnaissance satellites. They can fly higher, over 60,000 feet—and longer—28 hours. There is potential overlap between Global Hawk capabilities and those of reconnaissance satellites. Development costs of UAS have tended to exceed initial estimates by significant amounts. Development costs of the Air Force's Global Hawks grew by 284%; the Reaper by 97%; the Shadow by 80%, and the Predator by 60%.[32] In some cases (especially with the Global Hawk) the increases resulted form immature technologies and fundamental restructurings; in others it was simply a matter of increasing the number of platforms to be acquired.

ISR acquisition requirements extend well beyond satellites and launch vehicles. The increasing use of large numbers of UAS and other mobile ISR systems requires different and more varied communications support. In particular, the commands using such tactical systems may not have access to major DOD communications networks based on fiberoptic cables and must instead rely on communications satellites. According to one assessment the latter are essential for "reach back" from tactical units to intelligence centers at higher echelons or in the U.S. where processing and analytical support can be obtained.[33] The increased use of tactical ISR systems increases requirements for the acquisition of communications satellites and for other systems to facilitate tactical communications with an increasing emphasis on Internet-based systems. As the study noted: "While small units may not require large quantities of ISR data, their needs are focused, immediate and critical when engaged with the enemy."[34]

UAS are procured by the four services although efforts have been made to encourage shared use. An Air Force initiative in 2007 to be designated as executive agent for medium and high-altitude unmanned aerial vehicles was ultimately not approved, but efforts to make use of technologies developed for another service continue. For instance, the Marine Crops determined that the Army's Shadow system could meet its requirements and by procuring an existing system saved the costs of development and obtained systems that could be rapidly be made available to the operating forces.[35] Similarly, the Navy has taken advantage of various components of both Global Hawks and Reapers that were developed for the Air Force in acquiring its Broad Area Maritime Surveillance UAS.

Despite such initiatives GAO has argued that DOD should undertake a "rigorous and comprehensive analysis" of the requirements for UAS to identify commonalities and develop a strategy for making systems and subsystems more common and that the services should demonstrated that they have explored potentials for common platforms and sensors and are taking an "open systems approach" that will permit use of interchangeable sensors.[36] GAO further expressed concerns about cost growth in UAS programs, indicating that "development cost estimates for the 10 [UAV] programs we assessed, collectively, has increased more than $3.3 billion (37% in 2009 dollars) from initial estimates—with $2.7 billion attributed to the Air Force's Global Hawk program.[37] The GAO underscored the advantages it believes can be gained by designing compatible unmanned systems that are effectively linked together especially using commercially available open sources.[38] On May 18, 2009, the Air Force announced its "Unmanned Aircraft Systems Flight Plan, 2009-2047." The Plan describes a family of UAS ranging from man-portable vehicles to larger, "tanker sized" platforms. The goal is to acquire "a common set of airframes within a family of systems with interoperable, modular 'plug and play' payloads, with standard interfaces."[39]

Manned Airborne Systems

The military services remain committed to the use of manned surveillance aircraft that can be configured for a variety of different missions depending upon specific requirements. Some systems still in use were originally designed for Cold War missions, but they continue to serve as platforms for use in tracking insurgents and improvised explosive devices. Eventually the older systems have to be retired; the Navy is currently acquiring over 100 P-8 Poseidon maritime surveillance aircraft to replace aging P-3s. The Air Force is considering P-8s as a possible replacement for the E-8 JSTARS aircraft which has played a major role in supporting combat operations in Iraq and Afghanistan although the E-8s are scheduled to have new engines to extend their service life. The P-8 is a modified Boeing 737-800 aircraft of proven reliability and can be fitted with various sensor systems depending on the particular mission. Its predecessor, the P-3, first entered service in the 1960s; P-8s are also expected to be available for decades. A recent media report indicated that the Army is even considering the development of intelligence-gathering airships.[40]

In comparison to the complex acquisition history of UAS, the process for acquiring manned aircraft, although not without challenges, generally follows well established procedures. Congressional oversight in the House is shared between the Armed Services and Intelligence Committees and in the Senate is primarily the responsibility of the Armed Services Committee with input from the Intelligence Committee.

ASSESSMENTS OF ISR ACQUISITION PROCESSES

ISR acquisition efforts, given their size and cost, have generated significant public controversy, but public discussions are hampered by the absence of relevant information that is unclassified. However, there have been a number of recent outside reviews conducted by properly cleared outsiders. In general, these assessment have faulted organizational arrangements for the acquisition of ISR systems. A 2008 study conducted by the congressionally chartered Independent Assessment Panel on the Organization and Management of National Security Space (sometimes described as the Allard Commission after a key congressional sponsor, former Senator Wayne Allard) described the current organization for space systems used for national (as opposed to tactical) purposes:

> Authorities and responsibilities are spread across numerous organizations, including many within the Office of the Secretary of Defense (OSD) [Under Secretary of Defense (USD/Intelligence], USD/Acquisition, Technology and Logistics; USD/Policy; and the Assistant Secretary of Defense (ASD/Networks & Integration], USAF, USN, USA, USMC, DARPA [Defense Advanced Research Projects Agency], MDA [Missile Defense Agency], and NRO. Furthermore:
>
> - There is no standing forum or mechanism below the level of the President to coordinate efforts among the agencies responsible for NSS or to adjudicate differences over requirements and resources.
>   - The predominant capability providers are NRO and SMC [Space and Missile Systems Center, a component of the Air Force's Space Command], which today have parallel requirements and funding paths within the IC and DOD.
>   - Space capability providers in NOAA [National Oceanic and Atmospheric Administration], NASA [National Aeronautics and Space Administration],, and other federal agencies have their own requirements, funding, and reporting chains.
> - Within DOD, there is no common authority below the Secretary of Defense to integrate space acquisition programs and resources, or to adjudicate differences
>   - There are separate requirements and funding chains within the Pentagon for the Air Force, NRO, DARPA, MDA [Missile Defense Agency], Navy and Army, commercial satellite communications, and commercial imagery.
> - A structure for coordinating space operations between DOD and the intelligence community is emerging and is thought to be on target.[41]

The Independent Assessment Panel argued that the President should establish and execute a National Space Strategy and establish a National Security Space Authority who would be jointly responsible to the Secretary of Defense and to the DNI and charged with defining the space budget for DOD and the intelligence community and executing the program with milestone decision authority. There would also be an effort to improve the qualifications of Air Force and NRO acquisition professionals. Most controversially, the Panel would create a National Security Space Organization which would combine several Air Force space offices with the NRO under the National Security Space Authority. Arguably, this official might be perceived as a security space "czar" with a role subordinate to one Cabinet officer and the DNI.[42]

In 2008 the House Permanent Select Committee on Intelligence (HPSCI) undertook its own assessment of U.S. space capabilities. The resulting report reflected the conclusions of the committee's majority, that the U.S. is "losing its preeminence in space." The report focused on the need for an "integrated overhead roadmap" or "architecture." By "architecture," HPSCI meant

- A problem-driven approach that is based on securing prioritized, well-defined national security interests;
- A comprehensive solution that balances the financial investment against the overall risk to national security;
- A realistic delivery schedule that meets the defined timeline that in many cases must be flexible and updated against the risk; and
- A plan to migrate from a requirements-based acquisition approach towards a capabilities-based strategy, with the proviso that a purely capabilities-based approach could introduce additional challenges.[43]

Although the report acknowledged that executive branch officials believed they had provided a plan, committee members disagreed, maintaining that "there is no comprehensive space architecture or strategic plan that accommodates current and future national security priorities, DOD and intelligence community capability requirements."[44] The committee suggested that the practice has been for requirements to be added during the acquisition process resulting in added costs and delays and the need to resolve repeatedly the differing priorities of DOD and the intelligence community. When cutting-edge—and not yet available—technologies are chosen, the committee suggests that uncertainty and need for further testing complicate acquisition.

The report alluded to the interest of some to develop space systems solely for operational commanders in isolation from the NRO. Presumably reference was being made to the ORS; HPSCI suggested that "it is not in the best interest of country to pursue separate national and military space architectures."[45] The House report recommended that R&D be treated as a national security priority and protected against from diversion to immediate operational needs.[46]

The HPSCI report raised concerns about programs jointly funded in the National Intelligence Program (NIP) and the Military Intelligence Program (MIP). The NIP is designed to provide intelligence systems that can supply information primarily of interest to national-level policymakers; the MIP supports combatant commanders. Although there is pervasive overlap between the two sets of systems, there is also concern that, in some instances, funds from the NIP have in effect been used by DOD to fund what are essentially MIP projects.

The committee report also addressed use of commercial imagery and statutes and regulations governing space commerce. members of the committee's minority criticized several aspects of the report and maintained that it failed to "address the importance of integrated ground systems for tasking, processing, exploitation and dissemination."[47]

In November 2008 a Joint Defense Science Board and Intelligence Science Board task force on integrating sensor-collected intelligence produced a report looking at various flaws in current ISR efforts that extend beyond acquisition issues. It argued that ISR efforts can be better improved by integrating data from multiple sensors rather than by improving the design and performance of single sensors. In making this argument the task force pointed to structural issues that complicate such data integration. To accomplish this goal the task force recommended ensuring the inclusion of meta-data (or tags that describe specific data that can in turn be searchable whereas the data itself may not be) that can allow identification of information of specific interest. The task force's emphasis on better ways to access and analyze data is influenced by the vast expansion in data available and in many cases never exploited. It tended to favor a larger number of less sophisticated systems and achieve increased performance by integrating data from multiple sensors and platforms.[48]

Significant problems derive from limitations on the dissemination of collected data. Currently, meta-data are not consistently applied and tags are not consistent from agency to agency. Military commanders demand much larger quantities and more sophisticated types of intelligence (especially tactical imagery), but in many cases are unaware of and incapable of accessing data available throughout the intelligence community. "The number of images and signal intercepts are well beyond the capacity of the existing analyst community so there are huge backlogs for translators and image interpreters and much of the collected data are never reviewed. Further, decision makers and intelligence analyst have difficulty knowing what information is available."[49] Although an enormous number of full-motion video missions in support of tactical commanders has been conducted in Iraq and Afghanistan, the task force suggested that surveillance has often been episodic and continuing coverage of a given region had not always been possible.

The task force report emphasized that the ISR concept encompasses more than platforms for collection. It noted that DOD has developed the Global Information Grid which includes a highspeed communications network of various ground, air and space components. There is a need, according to the task force, for better ways for tactical commanders to access this information "on the move" and thus it emphasized the advantages of assured and accessible communications as would be made available by the redundant and complementary communications capabilities— terrestrial fiber, government and civilian communications satellites, networks built and maintained by specific agencies. (The task force advocated the Transformational Satellite System (TSAT) to provide links to the fiber network to mobile and fixed theater commands. TSAT was subsequently killed by DOD because it was considered duplicative.) A key goal should be, according to the Task Force, to ensure that future communications systems adhere to interoperability standards to ensure that they can support joint and international operations as well as "reach back" to U.S. agencies for analytical support. The essential concern of the task force was to ensure that the ongoing proliferation of platforms and sensors be matched by sufficient communications capabilities to enable their use. Currently, they found that "Our rapidly growing airborne ISR collection capabilities are not in balance with supporting communications."[50]

Furthermore, the task force noted that even though the Office of the Under Secretary of Defense for Intelligence (USDI) is double-hatted as Director of Defense Intelligence under the DNI, his judgment on space programs is affected by decisions of the Under Secretary of Defense for Acquisition, Technology and Logistics (AT&L) whose mandate encompasses all DOD programs and is not limited to intelligence programs.

The report reflected a concern that DOD requirements, including to some extent tactical ISR requirements, are being met at the cost of supporting national needs, echoing HPSCI's concerns. The task force found that there is a perception that intelligence officials may not be empowered to balance national and tactical requirements. The report noted the decline in the number of trained and experienced government program managers who are able to conduct extensive acquisition initiatives over a multi-year period. The report criticized short tours of duty for acquisitions personnel that precluded the development of deep expertise in specific systems and over-reliance on advisory contractors. The lack of expertise was criticized as contributing to delays and costly changes in specifications. More broadly, the report noted declining numbers of students pursuing engineering degrees and a reluctance of some to seek careers in the satellite area where work can be repetitive and sporadic. The tendency in recent years to focus on satellites that can fulfill current missions may discourage students who are most interested in "cutting-edge" R&D.

The Government Accountability Office (GAO) has assessed ongoing space systems acquisitions issues over a number of years. In a May 2009 report it recommended that a formal space plan based on a national security space strategy is essential for managing the acquisition and deployment of space systems. Without a strategy (and a plan to implement it) "the defense and intelligence communities may continue to make independent decisions and use resources that are not necessarily based on national priorities, which could lead to gaps in some areas of space operations and redundancies in others."[51]

In March 2009 GAO testified to the Senate Armed Services Committee in regard to challenges facing DOD in space acquisitions. Echoing the views of other assessments, GAO found

- on a broad scale, DOD starts more weapon programs than it can afford, creating a competition for funding that encourages low cost estimating, optimistic scheduling, overpromising, suppressing bad news, and, for space programs forsaking the opportunity to identify and assess potentially more executable alternatives;
- DOD has tended to start its space programs too early, that is, before it has the assurance that the capabilities it is pursuing can be achieved within available resources and time constraints—in part a result of the tendency to favor acquisition programs over efforts to ensure that new technologies are reliable;
- DOD has tended to prefer fewer but heavier, larger and more complex satellites than larger constellations of smaller satellites
- several more recent space programs began in the late 1990's when contracts were restructured in ways that reduced government oversight and shifted decision-making responsibilities to contractors, a situation that magnified problems relating to requirements creep and poor contractor performance.[52]

GAO generally recommended a number of best practices of the commercial sector to separate technology discovery from acquisition, follow incremental paths to meet user needs, match resources and requirements at program's start and use quantifiable data and demonstrable knowledge to decide when to move to a new program phase. GAO acknowledged that DOD was attempting to implement some of these practices and noted legislative initiatives that were later enacted.[53] GAO also went further to underscore the difficulties resulting from the fact that requirements, resource allocation, and acquisition processes are led by different organizations and the need to strengthen coordination of military and intelligence space efforts. As noted above, GAO has been skeptical of the Operationally Responsive Space effort due to its separation from other intelligence space programs even though it envisions smaller satellites built with available, proven technologies.

In January 2010 GAO forwarded another report to the Subcommittee on Air and Land forces of the House Committee on Armed Services that expressed concern about the ability of the services to share information within combat theaters.[54] GAO recommended that DOD establish a concept of operations to provide direction and priorities for sharing intelligence information across the defense intelligence community. GAO also urged the services to develop their own implementation plans and set timelines for sharing data with the rest of DOD.

THE OBAMA ADMINISTRATION'S APPROACH

Although outlines of the Obama Administration's overall approach to longer-term ISR acquisition issues have not been publicly detailed, the Administration has taken an initial approach based on acquiring additional reconnaissance platforms that are based on currently available technologies. In April 2008, Defense Secretary Gates, having been frustrated by reports from the field regarding inadequate numbers of UAVs, established an ISR Task Force, that eventually made a number of recommendations to maximize the availability of systems in the inventory and to acquire adequate numbers of additional systems.[55]

Based on these findings, in April 2009, Secretary Gates forwarded the Administration's plans for ISR programs in the FY2010 budget based on his determination to "to rebalance this department's programs in order to institutionalize and enhance our capabilities to fight the wars we are in and the scenarios we are most likely to face in the years ahead, while at the same time providing a hedge against other risks and contingencies...."[56]

"First, we will increase intelligence, surveillance and reconnaissance (ISR) support for the warfighter in the base budget by some $2 billion. This will include

- Fielding and sustaining 50 Predator-class unmanned aerial vehicle orbits by FY11 and maximizing their production. This capability, which has been in such high demand in both Iraq and Afghanistan, will not be permanently funded in the base budget. It will represent a 62% increase in capability over the current level and 127% from over a year ago.
- Increasing manned ISR capabilities such as the turbo-prop aircraft deployed so successfully as part of 'Task Force Odin' in Iraq.
- Initiating research and development on a number of ISR enhancements and experimental platforms optimized for today's battlefield."[57]

The administration proposal apparently does not include efforts to acquire "exquisite" satellite technologies that are at best still in the research and development stage. Congress essentially endorsed this approach in FY2010 defense appropriations and authorization legislation (P.L. 111- 118 and P.L. 111-84).

Media reports indicate that the Obama Administration ordered a thorough review of existing national space policy, including national intelligence assets, originally intended for completion by October 2009, but has not been made public.[58]

In May 2009 Defense Secretary Gates indicated that he and the DNI had agreed that a new charter for the NRO is needed given that the original one is decades old. A committee headed by retired Air Force General Trey Obering was asked to look at the NRO's roles and missions, and reportedly recommended that the NRO structure should not be altered. In March 2010 the DNI and the Secretary of Defense endorsed a set of organizing principles for the NRO that is intended to serve as a foundation for a revised NRO charter.[59]

Information on the ISR component of the Administration's FY2011 budget request is mostly classified, but DOD did state that an additional $2.6 billion was added for contingency operations in Afghanistan and Iraq at the recommendation of DOD's ISR Task Force, including nearly doubling procurement of the MQ-9 Reapers.[60] ISR funding requested for ongoing combat operations rose from $5.9 billion in FY2010 to $7.0 in FY2011.

CONGRESSIONAL INITIATIVES

Congressional oversight of the acquisition of surveillance systems has its own challenges. ISR systems are overseen by the armed services, intelligence, and appropriations committees. Most aspects of the ISR program are necessarily secret. Historically, the "national" systems were overseen by the intelligence committees whereas the tactical systems were usually overseen by the armed services committees (although the House Intelligence Committee had jurisdiction over both tactical and national systems). Public statements by some members indicate, however, that important differences among committees exist in regard to current plans for satellite programs and there has been considerable differences in regard to UAS programs as well. There is widespread frustration about cost growth of ISR systems, unnecessary duplication of effort, and the possibility of inadequate collection.

A significant factor has been the absence of intelligence authorization legislation for over five years. This suggests that the congressional role has been primarily exercised by the appropriations and armed services committees. Some observers believe that these committees may tend to focus on ISR systems as components of larger defense programs whereas the intelligence committees might have focused more on support to national policymakers.

In addition to authorizing and appropriating funds for specific ISR systems, Congress has repeatedly emphasized the need for a more comprehensive approach to ISR as a whole. The October 2008 report by the House Permanent Select Committee on Intelligence noted that "members of Congress have repeatedly expressed their disappointment that no architectural plan exists, and have repeatedly asked the Administration for the plan. The lack of an integrated architecture was one of the first issues to face the DNI after the office was established in 2005. The frustration has continued to this day, and many believe that the nation is no closer to having a clearly defined plan than it was three years ago."[61] The HPSCI majority recommended that the DNI and the Secretary of Defense "should develop a common architecture for all space-related systems (imagery, signals, communications, etc.) that supports prioritized national and military needs and takes into consideration budgetary constraints. Organizations proposing new satellites should demonstrate how their proposals fit into the architecture." The committee further recommended that the Office of Management and Budget "carefully consider what space programs it recommends for funding until both the DNI and [the Secretary of Defense] agree on an architecture."[62] Some observers suggest the goal of a "dynamic architecture" that will permit judicious investment in existing technologies to acquire adequate numbers of systems for current needs while intentionally providing windows of opportunity for the introduction of new technologies and adaptations to new military or diplomatic requirements.

The Duncan Hunter Defense Authorization Act for FY2009 (P.L. 110-417), enacted on October 14, 2008, directed that the Secretary of Defense and the DNI jointly conduct a comprehensive review of U.S. space policy, including space-based intelligence and surveillance and reconnaissance from space. The review was to describe current and planned space acquisition programs.

This policy review by DOD was to have been undertaken in conjunction with the national-level review of space policy. When the overall space policy review is complete DOD's Space Posture Review will be issued. At one point there were plans to issue an interim report that would detail current posture and programs.[63]

The FY2009 Defense Authorization Act, section 144, also required "the Secretary of Defense in consultation with the Chairman of the Joint Chiefs of Staff establish a policy and an acquisition strategy for intelligence, surveillance, and reconnaissance payloads and ground stations for manned and unmanned aerial vehicle systems. The policy and acquisition strategy shall be applicable throughout the Department of Defense and shall achieve integrated research, development, test, and evaluation, and procurement commonality."

The 111th Congress

In the explanatory statement accompanying the FY2010 Defense Appropriations Act (P.L. 111-118), DOD was directed to provide a classified report that describes the deployment of additional ISR capabilities, particularly tactical signals intelligence and full motion video, to support combat operations in Afghanistan ...[and] address the adequacy of these capabilities to support troop commitments to Afghanistan as well as the plans to correct any shortfalls."[64]

In 2009 the House Appropriations Committee (whose annual bill includes the great bulk of intelligence funding) directed that DOD and the DNI prepare a long-range plan for space system investment, including research, development, test and evaluation as well as procurement, including schedule and funding profiles, for all national security space systems for the next thirty years. The report is to include estimated levels of annual funding to carry out the programs.[65] The bill, H.R. 3326, was eventually enacted as P.L. 111-118; it mandated that DOD deliver a 15-Year Space System Investment Strategy by May 2010.

There are indications that ORS funding issues have led to broader questions about efforts to use space platforms to support national security goals. In its October 2008 report on the need for a space architecture, the House Intelligence Committee recommended that the DOD and the DNI "develop a common architecture for all space-related systems" and urged that "[o]rganizations proposing new satellites should demonstrate how their proposals fit into the architecture."[66] In May 2009 the Senate Appropriations Committee reported the defense appropriations act for FY2010 with an expression of concern that

> the committee is concerned about the tendency of temporary, single-issue acquisition initiatives to grow into persistent, stovepiped bureaucracies with increasingly ambiguous mandates. This tendency is often the result of deficiencies in the acquisitions process, in which urgent joint requirements are too often not effectively addressed.[67]

Section 911 of the FY2011 Defense Authorization bill, P.L. 111-383, by the President on January 7, 2011, requires that the Secretary of Defense and the DNI shall develop an integrated process for national security space architecture planning, development, coordination, and analysis." The effort is to include both defense and intelligence efforts, to provide mid-term to long-term recommendations to guide acquisitions, and is independent of but coordinated with efforts by the military departments and intelligence agencies. The accompanying report to an earlier version of the legislation (H.R. 5136) by the House Armed Services Committee indicates a determination to provide a clear mandate to conduct integrated space architecture planning in order to avoid isolated, stove-piped, efforts by the services and intelligence agencies. The committee added, nevertheless, that, "This section would not be intended to limit rapid acquisition efforts such as Operationally Responsive Space (ORS); however, the committee does endorse efforts that expand user access to ORS capabilities and data."[68]

The various reviews requested are likely to be forward in classified channels and it is not known if summaries will be publicly available. Nor is it known how consistent the studies will be with budgetary requests, but they will clearly provide a benchmarks for Congress as consideration of annual legislation proceeds.

CONCLUSION

Many consider the desirability of a long-range plan or architecture for the deployment of surveillance assets is a given, but suspect it is almost unobtainable. Future intelligence requirements may change from the those recently indicated by Secretary Gates. The policies and military capabilities of sophisticated nation states may again become the highest collection priorities of the intelligence community, rather than terrorist groups that are currently the chief concern. Similarly, there are no indications that technological capabilities of ISR systems have reached a stabile plateau, and basing future plans on current technologies may prove to be shortsighted. There are inherent challenges involved in establishing plans for acquisitions over a multi-year span, even if they are arguably outweighed by the limitations of annual planning cycles.

Ultimately, most recognize that there are limitations on what Congress can do to shape the international environment or the emergence of new technologies. Congress can, however, alter the roles and missions of the organizations involved in ISR programs acquisition, as well as authorize and appropriate funds for ISR systems acquisition. Some observers have suggested a number of steps internal to Congress that might improve the acquisition process for ISR systems. The 9/11 Commission, for instance, recommended that the intelligence committees be provided with responsibilities for both authorization and appropriations.[69] Others have recommended a separate annual intelligence appropriations act and subcommittees for intelligence within the two appropriations committees. Such initiatives would allow greater concentration on intelligence programs as separate and distinct from defense programs. On the other hand, such separation could complicate the close linkages and desirable duplication between some intelligence and defense programs. Congress could also set up special panels to look at ISR programs with representatives from current intelligence, armed services, homeland security, and appropriations committees.

Nevertheless, many of the complications involving ISR systems derive from the organization of the executive branch and current policies. The ability of the ODNI and DOD (including both the USD(I) or the USD (AT&L)) to establish an agreed-upon acquisition plan is inevitably a key factor. The role of the staffs of the National Security Council and the Office of Management and Budget in overseeing and monitoring acquisition plans and their implementation is also important.

Some observers conclude that, ultimately, there must be some form of an overhead surveillance architecture, even if it cannot be set "in concrete" for a multi-year period. In this view, it must include not only the collection platforms, but also associated communications, and data processing and analysis systems. In ongoing legislative dialogue, the Executive and Legislative Branches will be challenged to design and fund systems that maximize adaptability to new missions while accepting reasonable cost constraints. Such a goal will require not only careful interagency and inter-branch coordination, but also a willingness by all involved to accept decisions that do not fully meet the goals of each and every agency. Observers suggest a key role for congressional committees in minimizing the role of initiatives launched by "special interests" that ultimately could add significant unnecessary costs, and do not deliver maximum collection contributions. The unique perspectives of the armed services, intelligence and appropriations committees, if considered together, arguably could provide the comprehensive oversight that has occasionally eluded the executive branch.

ISR has revolutionized military operations in the past half-century; it is today an essential component of national security planning and operations. At the same time, experience shows that not all the billions of dollars that have been invested have resulted in useful systems. Acquiring and using ISR systems is likely to remain a substantial challenge for the U.S. government in coming decades and one that will depend on effective cooperation among the intelligence community, the Defense Department, and Congress.

End Notes

[1] According to the Defense Department, Unmanned Aerial Systems (UAS) refer to systems whose components include the necessary equipment, network, and personnel to control an unmanned aircraft. An Unmanned Aerial Vehicle (UAV) refers to a powered aerial vehicle that does not carry a human operation, uses aerodynamic forces to provide vehicle life, can fly autonomously or be piloted remotely, can be expendable or recoverable, and can carry a lethal or nonlethal payload. Thus UAS is a broader term that includes equipment, networks, and personnel in addition to the UAV; in practice the terms UAS and UAV are often used interchangeably. See Department of Defense, Dictionary of Military and Associated Terms, Joint Publication 1-02, 12 April 2001, updated through April 2010.

[2] See http://www.ulalaunch.com for information on the cooperative effort by Lockheed Martin and Boeing to provide space launch services to federal agencies.

[3] Robert M. Gates, "A Balanced Strategy: Reprogramming the Pentagon for a New Age," *Foreign Affairs*, January/February 2009, pp. 34-35.

[4] U.S. Department of Defense, Quadrennial Defense Review Report, February 2010, p. 20.

[5] Ibid., p. 21.

[6] Ibid., p. 22. It is noteworthy that the QDR does not specifically address satellite surveillance systems although it makes reference to the fact that "[f]orces in Iraq, Afghanistan, and elsewhere have developed new and more effective means for rapidly processing, exploiting, and fusing information from a wide array of sources and disseminating this information to operators at the tactical level." Pp. 22-23. The "wide array" undoubtedly includes national satellite systems.

[7] See Joshua Boehm and Craig Baker, "A History of United States National Security Space Management and Organization," Prepared for the Commission to Assess United States National Security Space Management and Organization [2001].

[8] Testimony of Josh Hartman, Senior Advisor to the Under Secretary of Defense (Acquisition, Technology & Logistics) before the House of Representatives, Committee on Armed Services, Subcommittee on Strategic Forces, April 30, 2009.

[9] Ibid.

[10] Institute for Defense Analyses, *Leadership, Management, and Organization for National Security Space: Report to Congress of the Independent Assessment Panel on the Organization and Management of National Security Space*, July 2008, p. 2.

[11] Turner Brinton, "Software Fix Adds $750M to SBIRS Price Tag," *Space News*, July 27, 2009, p. A3.

[12] See Philip Taubman, "In Death of Spy Satellite Program, Lofty Plans and Unrealistic Bids," *New York Times*, November 11, 2007.

[13] Office of the Director of National Intelligence, "DNI Blair Announces Plan for the Next Generation of Electro-Optical Satellites," ODNI News Release No. 12-09, April 7, 2009.

[14] Andrea Shalal-Esa, U.S. Plans New Government Owned Satellites," *Washington Post*, April 8, 2009.

[15] See Tim Starks, "Senate Intelligence Bill Would Conflict With Wishes of Obama, Other Panels," *CQ Today*, July 14, 2009. Earlier, some observers concluded that differences over satellite acquisitions had doomed efforts to passed an intelligence authorization bill for FY2009. See Tim Starks, "Did a Satellite Dispute Knock Intelligence Bill From Orbit? *Congressional Quarterly*, March 31, 2009.

[16] See Warren Ferster, "Lawmakers Near Agreement on White House Spy Satellite Plan," *Space News*, October 19, 2009.

[17] See Davi M. D'Agostino, Director, Defense Capabilities and Management, Government Accountability Office to the Hon. Bill Nelson and the Hon. Jeff Sessions, Subcommittee on Strategic Forces, Committee on Armed Services., *Defense Space Activities: National Security Space Strategy Needed to Guide Future DOD Space Efforts*, GAO-08-431R, March 27, 2008, p. 10.

[18] Department of Defense Directive 5101.2 of June 3, 2003.

[19] Arthur K. Cebrowski and John W. Raymond, "Operationally Responsive Space: A New Defense Business Model," *Parameters*, Summer 2005, p. 70.

[20] See Turner Brinton, "ORS Office's Success May Hinge on Its Ability to Skirt the Bureaucracy," *Space News*, May 11, 2009, p. A6.

[21] Ibid., p. 18; U.S. Government Accountability Office, *Defense Space Activities: DOD Needs to Further Clarify the Operationally Responsive Space Concept and Plan to Integrate and Support Future Satellites*, GAO-08-831, June 2008, p. 4.

[22] See GAO-08-831.

[23] Letter from Norton A. Schwartz, General, USAF, Chief of Staff to the Hon. John M. McHugh, May 18, 2009, available at http://www.afa.org/grl/pdfs/AirForceFY10UnfundedRequirementsList.pdf.

[24] U.S. Congress, 111th Congress, 1st session, House of Representatives, Committee of Conference, *National Defense Authorization Act for Fiscal Year 2010*, October 7, 2009, H.Rept. 111-288, p. 1015.

[25] Testimony of General C. Robert Kehler, Commander, Air Force Space Command, before the Strategic Forces Subcommittee of the House Armed Services Committee, May 21, 2009.

[26] See John T. Bennett, "USAF Surprised OSD by Putting Small Sats on Wish List," *Defense News*, June 8, 2009, p.6. For additional background on Air Force funding priorities, see James B. Armor, Jr., The Air Force's Other Blind Spot, *Space Review*, September 15, 2008.

[27] Statement of Josh Hartman, Special Advisor to the Under Secretary of Defense (Acquisition, Technology and Logistics) to the House Armed Services Committee, April 30, 2009.

[28] Turner Brinton, "Uncertainty Looms Office Amid Declining Budget Projections for 3-year-old ORS," *Space News*, April 23, 2010.

[29] UAS, especially the larger platforms such as the Global Hawk, can also have "national" missions.

[30] Department of Defense, *Quadrennial Roles and Missions Review Report*, January 2009, p. 25.

[31] U.S., Department of Defense, Defense Budget Recommendation Statement, April 6, 2009.

[32] See U.S. Government Accountability Office, *Defense Acquisitions: Opportunities Exist to Achieve Greater Commonality and Efficiencies among Unmanned Aircraft Systems*, GAO-09-520, July 2009, p. 8.

[33] See U.S. Department of Defense, Office of the Under Secretary of Defense for Acquisition, Technology, and Logistics, Report of the Joint Defense Science Board/Intelligence Science Board Task Force, *Integrating Sensor-Collected Intelligence*, November 2008, p. 86.

[34] Ibid., p. 89; the report strongly recommended the Joint Tactical Radio System and the Transformational Satellite System.

[35] GAO-09-520, p. 3.

[36] Ibid., p. 4.

[37] Ibid., p. 2. It is noteworthy, however, that per unit costs for the widely deployed Predator have actually declined by 41%; see p. 10.

[38] The limitations of commercial systems were, however, revealed when reports surfaced that enemy fighters were downloading unencrypted information from Predator communications links; see Pauline Jelinek, "Pentagon: Insurgents Intercepted Drone Spy Videos," *Washington Post*, December 18, 2009.

[39] U.S. Air Force, *United States Air Force Unmanned Aircraft Systems Flight Plan, 2009-2047*, May 2009.

[40] Walter Pincus, "Military Seeks an Intelligence-Gathering Airship," *Washington Post*, February 16, 2010, p. A11.

[41] Institute for Defense Analyses, *Leadership, Management, and Organization for National Security Space: Report to Congress of the Independent Assessment Panel on the Organization and Management of National Security Space*, July 2008, pp. ES-4, 14. Senator Allard endorsed most of these recommendations in a floor speech in which he indicated the need for "a top-to-bottom overhaul to restore the vitality of our space programs." *Congressional Record*, November 19, 2008, pp. S10636-10637. Similar conclusions were also reached by the Committee for U.S. Space Leadership, a group of industry leaders; see Turner Brinton, "Nonpartisan Group Urges Obama to Tackle Systemic Space Problems," *Space News*, February 23, 2009, p. 6.

[42] See testimony of Secretary of Defense Gates, Hearing of the House Armed Services Committee, May 13, 2009, Federal New Service Transcript.

[43] U.S. Congress, House Permanent Select Committee on Intelligence, *Report on Challenges and Recommendations for United States Overhead Architecture*, 110th Cong., 2nd sess., October 3, 2008, H.Rept. 110-914 (Washington: GPO, 2008), p. 8.

[44] Ibid., p. 2.

[45] Ibid., p 9.

[46] Ibid., p 14.

[47] Ibid., p. 27.

[48] U.S. Department of Defense, Office of the Under Secretary of Defense for Acquisition, Technology, and Logistics, Report of the Joint Defense Science Board/Intelligence Science Board Task Force, *Integrating Sensor-Collected Intelligence*, November 2008, p. 63.

[49] Ibid., p. 65.

[50] Ibid, p. 26.

[51] U.S. Government Accountability Office, *Defense Space Activities: National Security Space Strategy Needed to Guide Future DOD Space Efforts*, GAO-08-431R, March 27, 2008. See also GAO, *Space Acquisitions: DOD Needs a Departmentwide Strategy for Pursuing Low-Cost, Responsive Tactical Space Capabilities*, GAO-06-449, March 2006.

[52] U.S. Government Accountability Office, *Space Acquisitions: DOD Faces Substantial Challenges in Developing New Space Systems*, GAO-09-705T, May 20, 2009, pp. 8-9. The last point has also been made by Scott F. Large, the Director of the NRO, "National Security Space Collaboration as a National Defense Imperative," *High Frontier*, August 2008, p. 4.

[53] These initiatives included P.L. 111-23, the Weapons Systems Acquisition Reform Act of 2009.

[54] U.S. Government Accountability Office, *Intelligence, Surveillance, and Reconnaissance: Establishing Guidance, Timelines, and Accountability for Integrating Intelligence Data Would Improve Information Sharing*, GAO-10-265NI, January 2010. In May 2010 the House Armed Services Committee endorsed GAO's recommendations and asked for a report from DOD indicating implementation plans. U.S. Congress, 111th Congress, 2d session, House of Representatives, Committee on Armed Services, *National Defense Authorization Act for Fiscal Year 2011*, H.Rept. 111-491, May 21, 2010, p. 339-340.

[55] The ISR Task Force was not designed to be permanent but a congressional requirement was established (in S.Rept. 111-20) for DOD to report on the strategy chosen to transition its responsibilities by October 1, 2009. This deadline was apparently not met. (See explanatory statement accompanying the Defense Appropriations Act, *Congressional Record,*, December 16, 2009, p. H15043.)

[56] Robert M. Gates, Defense Budget Recommendation Statement (Arlington, VA), April 6, 2009

[57] Ibid. For background to Gates decision making, see Greg Jaffe, "A Single-Minded focus on Dual Wars," *Washington Post*, May 15, 2009.

[58] Amy Klamper, "President Orders Sweeping U.S. Space Policy Review," *Space News*, July 6, 2009, p. 6.

[59] Statement for the Record, Betty Sapp, Principal Deputy Director, National Reconnaissance Office, before the House Armed Services Committee, Subcommittee on Strategic Services, April 21, 2010.

[60] Department of Defense, Overview – FY 2011 Defense Budget, March 2010, pp. 4-2.

[61] *Challenges and Recommendations for United States Overhead Architecture*, H.Rept. 110-914, p. 8.

[62] Ibid., p. 9.
[63] U.S. Department of Defense, DOD News Briefing with Undersecretary Flournoy and Vice Adm. Stanley, February 1, 2010.
[64] *Congressional Record*, December 16, 2009, p. H15043.
[65] U.S. Congress, 111th Congress, 1st session, House Committee on Appropriations, *Department of Defense Appropriations Bill, 2010*, to accompany H.R. 3326, July 24, 2009, H.Rept. 111-230, pp. 278-279.
[66] Ibid., p. 3.
[67] U.S. Congress, Senate Committee on Appropriations, *Making Supplemental Appropriations for the Fiscal Year Ending September 30, 2009, and for Other Purposes*, Report to accompany S. 1054, 111th Cong., 1st sess., May 14, 2009, S.Rept. 111-20, p. 15.
[68] U.S. Congress, 111th Congress, 2d session, House of Representatives, Committee on Armed Services, *National Defense Authorization Act for Fiscal Year 2011*, H.Rept. 111-491, May 21, 2010, p. 342-343.
[69] National Commission on Terrorist Attacks Upon the United States, Final Report, Washington: GPO, 2004, p. 420.

In: Intelligence, Surveillance and Reconnaissance ...
Editor: Johanna A. Montgomery

ISBN: 978-1-61470-900-8
© 2011 Nova Science Publishers, Inc.

Chapter 2

ACTIONS ARE NEEDED TO INCREASE INTEGRATION AND EFFICIENCIES OF DOD'S ISR ENTERPRISE[*]

United States Government Accountability Office

WHY GAO DID THIS STUDY

The success of intelligence, surveillance, and reconnaissance (ISR) systems in collecting, processing, and disseminating intelligence information has fueled demand for ISR support, and the Department of Defense (DOD) has significantly increased its investments in ISR capabilities since combat operations began in 2001. In fiscal year 2010, intelligence community spending —including for ISR—exceeded $80 billion. Section 21 of Public Law 111-139 mandated that GAO identify programs, agencies, offices, and initiatives with duplicative goals and activities. This report examines the extent to which: (1) DOD manages and oversees the full scope and cost of the ISR enterprise; (2) DOD has sought to identify and minimize the potential for any unnecessary duplication in program, planning, and operations for ISR; and (3) DOD's ISR Integration Roadmap addresses key congressionally directed management elements and guidance.

WHAT GAO RECOMMENDS

GAO recommends that DOD compile and aggregate complete ISR funding data, establish implementation goals and timelines for its efficiency efforts, and give priority to examining efficiency in ISR collection activities. DOD agreed or partially agreed with these GAO recommendations. GAO also suggests that Congress consider holding DOD accountable to address required elements of the ISR roadmap.

---

[*] This is an edited, reformatted and augmented version of the United States Government Accountability Office publication, Report to Congressional Committees GAO-11-465, dated June 2011.

WHAT GAO FOUND

The Under Secretary of Defense for Intelligence (USD[I]) has the authority to oversee DOD's ISR enterprise; however, the broad scope and complex funding arrangements of DOD's ISR enterprise make it difficult to manage and oversee. The scope of the ISR enterprise and capabilities include many different kinds of activities conducted by multiple agencies. As a result, ISR activities may be funded through any of several sources, including the Military Intelligence Program, the National Intelligence Program, overseas contingency operations funding, and military service funds. To manage DOD's large ISR enterprise, the USD(I) serves as DOD's senior intelligence official, responsible for providing strategic, budget, and policy oversight over DOD's ISR enterprise. However, the USD(I) does not have full visibility into several budget sources that fund DOD's ISR enterprise, such as national intelligence capabilities, dual use assets, urgent operational needs, and military personnel expenses related to ISR. The USD(I)'s inability to gain full visibility and clarity into all of DOD's ISR financial resources hinders efforts to develop an investment strategy for ISR and to achieve efficiencies.

DOD has developed general guidance in directives and other documents emphasizing the need to identify efficiencies and eliminate duplication or redundancies in its capabilities, which provides a foundation for further action. In August 2010, the Secretary of Defense directed that the department begin a series of efficiency initiatives to reduce duplication, overhead, and excess. However, the scope of the review pertaining to ISR was limited to analysis activities and excluded activities associated with collecting ISR data—one of the largest areas of growth in ISR spending. Additionally, two ISR efficiency initiatives are in the early stages of development and do not have implementation goals and timelines. Without goals and timelines, it will be difficult to determine whether these initiatives will make progress in achieving efficiencies.

The National Defense Authorization Act for Fiscal Year 2004 required DOD to develop a roadmap to guide the development and integration of DOD ISR capabilities over a 15-year period and report to Congress on the contents of the roadmap, such as goals and an investment strategy to prioritize resources. DOD responded to both of these requirements by issuing an ISR roadmap. GAO's review of DOD's 2007 and 2010 ISR roadmaps found that DOD has made progress in addressing the issues that Congress directed to be included, but the 2007 and 2010 roadmaps did not address certain management elements identified by Congress. In 2008, Congress restated the 2004 requirements and provided additional guidance to the USD(I). However, the 2010 roadmap still does not represent an integrated investment strategy across the department because it does not clearly address capability gaps or priorities across the enterprise and still lacks investment information. Until DOD develops an integrated ISR investment strategy, the defense and intelligence communities may continue to make independent decisions and use resources that are not necessarily based on strategic priorities.

ABBREVIATIONS

DOD	Department of Defense
DNI	Director of National Intelligence
IED	improvised explosive device
ISR	intelligence, surveillance, and reconnaissance
JIEDDO	Joint Improvised Explosive Device Defeat Organization
ODNI	Office of the Director of National Intelligence
USD(I)	Under Secretary of Defense for Intelligence

June 3, 2011

Congressional Committees

Intelligence, surveillance, and reconnaissance (ISR) systems have proved critical to the combatant commanders to plan and execute military operations in Iraq and Afghanistan by providing them timely and accurate information on adversaries' capabilities and vulnerabilities. The success of ISR systems in collecting, processing, and disseminating useful intelligence information has fueled growing demand for more ISR support, and the Department of Defense (DOD) has increased its investments in ISR capabilities significantly since 2002. In fiscal year 2010, intelligence spending across the national and military intelligence communities— which includes ISR—exceeded $80 billion. As demand for ISR has increased and DOD has moved quickly to develop and acquire new ISR capabilities, integrating and managing DOD's ISR enterprise has become more complex and challenging. In September 2010, the Deputy Secretary of Defense acknowledged that the growth of intelligence organizations within DOD has not been centrally directed or managed and there is a high probability that inefficiencies exist. In January 2011, Congress expressed the need to continue with oversight over certain ISR efforts given the growth and demand of ISR.

Since 2004, Congress and we have reported on the need for greater integration and efficiencies across DOD's ISR enterprise. In the National Defense Authorization Act for Fiscal Year 2004,[1] Congress required DOD to develop a fully integrated ISR roadmap and coordinate activities across the military services, defense agencies, and combatant commands. In 2008, a congressional committee provided additional guidance stating the need for an ISR investment strategy. We have also reported that ISR activities are not integrated and efficient; effectiveness may be compromised by lack of full visibility into operational use of ISR assets; and agencies could better collaborate in the acquisition of new capabilities. Although DOD has designated the Under Secretary of Defense for Intelligence (USD[I]) to manage ISR investments as a departmentwide portfolio, the Under Secretary of Defense for Acquisition, Technology and Logistics has been designated to lead the task force responsible for oversight of issues related to the management and acquisition of unmanned aircraft systems that collect ISR data. We have concluded that DOD has not articulated a clear vision of the ISR enterprise and a unified investment approach to manage the enterprise.[2] A new statutory requirement mandates that GAO identify federal programs, agencies, offices, and initiatives with duplicative goals and activities within departments and governmentwide.[3] Under that mandate, this review examines the extent to which: (1) DOD manages and oversees the full scope and cost of the ISR enterprise; (2) DOD identified and minimized the potential for any unnecessary duplication in program, planning, and operations for ISR; and (3) DOD's ISR Integration Roadmap addresses key management elements required by law or directed by congressional committees.

To determine the full scope and cost of DOD's ISR enterprise we assessed DOD's ISR funding and budget elements reported in the Military Intelligence Program, analyzed DOD's ISR spending plans in the Future Years Defense Program, and conducted discussions with DOD, military service, and intelligence agency officials regarding ISR funding and capabilities. To determine the extent to which DOD manages and oversees the full scope and cost of this enterprise, we reviewed DOD directives regarding the capability portfolio management, the role of the USD(I), and the Military Intelligence Program and compared information found in DOD strategy and briefing documents along with relevant meetings and discussions with USD(I), military service, and intelligence agency officials against the directives. We met with three of DOD's combat support agencies—the National Security Agency, the National GeospatialIntelligence Agency, and the Defense Intelligence Agency—to obtain information on how they use Military Intelligence Program funds and their role in DOD's ISR enterprise. We discussed national intelligence funding and efforts to assess duplication, fragmentation, and overlap in the National Intelligence Program with an official in the Office of the Director of National Intelligence (ODNI). ODNI also provided us classified information on the extent to which the National Intelligence Program budget funds each of the combat support agencies, excluding the National Reconnaissance Office. We also determined that the data contained in both the Future Years Defense Program and Military Intelligence Program along with data received from the military services were reliable for our purposes by conducting a data reliability assessment. To evaluate the extent to which DOD has identified and minimized the potential for unnecessary duplication, we assessed the progress of DOD efforts to identify and implement efficiencies. We reviewed directives and budget guidance documents to assess to what extent the need to eliminate unnecessary duplication and fragmentation was emphasized as a priority. We evaluated DOD's guidance to determine to what extent it incorporated best practices we previously identified, such as developing performance metrics, timelines, and goals for implementation of efficiency efforts. We evaluated the extent to which DOD took actions to resolve instances of fragmentation and duplication they identified by reviewing ISR capability assessments and recent ISR efficiency initiatives. Finally, to assess the extent to which DOD's ISR Integration Roadmap addresses management elements required by law or directed by congressional committees, two of our analysts independently evaluated the 2010 ISR Integration Roadmap against key elements of congressionally directed actions. We also compared the 2010 ISR Integration Roadmap to the 2007 ISR Integration Roadmap to determine what progress DOD has made in addressing these elements.

We conducted this performance audit from August 2010 through June 2011, in accordance with generally accepted government auditing standards. Those standards require that we plan and perform the audit to obtain sufficient, appropriate evidence to provide a reasonable basis for our findings and conclusions based on our audit objectives. We believe that the evidence obtained provides a reasonable basis for our findings and conclusions based on our audit objectives. More detailed information on our scope and methodology is provided in appendix I.

BACKGROUND

GAO has conducted various assessments related to DOD's ISR enterprise including efforts assessing (1) unmanned aircraft system development, acquisition, and operations; (2) how new ISR requirements are generated; (3) the intelligence information processing, exploitation, and dissemination processes; and (4) other intelligence-related topics.[4] DOD's ISR enterprise consists of multiple intelligence organizations that individually plan for, acquire, and operate manned and unmanned airborne, space-borne, maritime, and ground-based ISR systems. The Under Secretary of Defense for Acquisition, Technology and Logistics oversees the space and unmanned aircraft systems acquisition programs. In addition to the intelligence branches of the military services, there are four major intelligence agencies within DOD: the Defense Intelligence Agency; the National Security Agency; the National Geospatial-Intelligence Agency; and the National Reconnaissance Office. The Defense Intelligence Agency is charged with providing all-source intelligence data to policy makers and U.S. armed forces around the world and provides defense human intelligence. The National Security Agency is responsible for signals intelligence and information assurance and has collection sites throughout the world. The National Geospatial-Intelligence Agency prepares the geospatial data, including maps and computerized databases, that are used by ISR systems necessary for targeting for precision-guided weapons. The National Reconnaissance Office develops and operates reconnaissance satellites. As figure 1 shows, DOD's ISR enterprise is related to other elements of the U.S. national intelligence community.

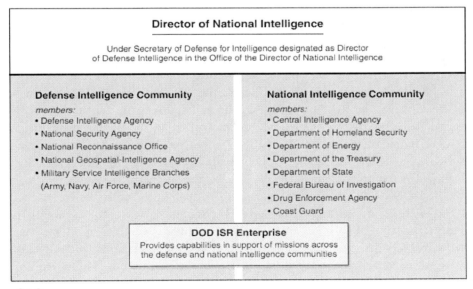

Source: GAO.

Figure 1. DOD's ISR Enterprise Relationship to the U.S. Intelligence Community.

Spending on most ISR programs is divided between the defense intelligence budget, known as the Military Intelligence Program—totaling $27 billion in fiscal year 2010—and the national intelligence budget, known as the National Intelligence Program—totaling $53.1

billion in fiscal year 2010. The Military Intelligence Program encompasses DOD-wide intelligence programs and most intelligence programs supporting the operating units of the military services. The USD(I) is responsible for compiling and developing the Military Intelligence budget and issuing detailed procedures governing the Military Intelligence Program process and timelines associated with budget development. The agencies, services, and offices that are included in the Military Intelligence Program are: the Office of the Secretary of Defense, the military departments, the U.S. Special Operations Command, the Defense Intelligence Agency, the National Geospatial-Intelligence Agency, the National Reconnaissance Office, the National Security Agency, the Defense Threat Reduction Agency, the Defense Information Systems Agency, and the Defense Security Service. Each office, agency, and service designates a manager who is charged with responding to guidance from the USD(I) and managing programs and functions within the budget, among other things. The USD(I) guides and oversees the development of the Military Intelligence Program in coordination with the Under Secretary of Defense (Comptroller), Under Secretary of Defense for Policy, Under Secretary of Defense for Personnel and Readiness, Chairman of the Joint Chiefs of Staff, and the Director of the Office of the Secretary of Defense's Office of Cost Assessment and Program Evaluation.

The national intelligence community, which primarily provides support to national decision makers, also supports DOD ISR activities. The line between military intelligence activities and national strategic intelligence activities has blurred as DOD's tactical ISR supports strategic decisions and national intelligence collection informs military operations. The National Intelligence Program, which funds national intelligence activities, also funds a portion of DOD's ISR activities to support military operations. The Director of National Intelligence (DNI) is responsible for compiling and reviewing the annual National Intelligence Program budget.

To encourage integration of DOD's ISR enterprise, in 2003 Congress required the USD(I) to develop a comprehensive plan, known as the ISR Integration Roadmap, to guide the development and integration of ISR capabilities. The law also required the USD(I) to report back to congressional committees on this effort. In response to this requirement, DOD issued an ISR Integration Roadmap in May 2005 and updated it in January 2007. However, we reported that this 2007 roadmap still did not meet all the management elements the USD(I) was required to address.[5] In 2008,[6] the House Committee on Armed Services restated the need for the USD(I) to address these requirements and provided the USD(I) with additional guidance for the roadmap. The USD(I) issued an updated roadmap in March 2010.

In 2008, DOD began an effort to manage ISR capabilities across the entire department, rather than by military service or individual program. Under this capability portfolio management concept, DOD intended to improve the interoperability of future capabilities, minimize capability redundancies and gaps, and maximize capability effectiveness.[7] The USD(I) was designated as the civilian lead office for the portfolio of ISR activities, which is known as the Battlespace Awareness Portfolio. As the portfolio manager for ISR investments, the role and authorities of the USD(I) are limited to two primarily advisory functions: (1) reviewing and participating in service and DOD agency budget deliberations on proposed ISR capability investments, and (2) recommending alterations in service or agency spending to the Secretary of Defense as part of the established DOD budget review process. Also in 2008, the Secretary of Defense established the ISR Task Force to increase ISR capacity in Iraq and Afghanistan, as well as improve operational integration and efficiency of ISR assets across the services and defense agencies. The ISR Task Force's primary focus was on regional capabilities and capabilities that could be delivered more quickly than in the standard DOD acquisition cycle. The task force is currently assisting the USD(I) and the services in deciding how to integrate into the long-term base budget more than 500 ISR capabilities that were developed to meet urgent operational requirements in Iraq and Afghanistan.

We have previously reported on DOD's challenges in improving the integration of ISR efforts, including difficulties in processing and sharing information that is already collected and developing new capabilities. We reported in 2010 that DOD's efforts to make intelligence data accessible across the defense intelligence community have been hampered by not having integration of service programs and a concept of operations for intelligence sharing.[8] The services have each pursued their own versions of a common data processing system to share information, the Distributed Common Ground/Surface System, which was initiated in 1998. Although the services can share limited intelligence data, their progress toward full information sharing has been uneven. Moreover, as we reported in March 2011,[9] although DOD created the Joint Improvised Explosive Device (IED) Defeat Organization (JIEDDO) to lead and coordinate all of DOD's counter-IED efforts, which include some ISR capabilities, many of the organizations engaged in the counter-IED defeat effort, such as the Army, Marine Corps, and Navy, continued to develop, maintain, and expand their own IED-defeat capabilities. Even though urgent operational needs include ISR capabilities, the USD(I) does not have a direct role in determining urgent operational needs.

THE COMPLEXITY OF DOD'S ISR ENTERPRISE FUNDING PRESENTS CHALLENGES FOR MANAGING AND OVERSEEING THE SCOPE AND COST

The USD(I) has the authority to exercise oversight responsibility over DOD's ISR's enterprise; however the broad scope and complex funding arrangements of DOD's ISR enterprise make it difficult to manage and oversee. The scope of the ISR enterprise and capabilities include many different kinds of activities—from collection of information through dissemination of analysis compiled from multiple sources—conducted by multiple agencies. As a result, ISR activities may be funded through any of several sources, including the Military Intelligence Program, the National Intelligence Program, overseas contingency operations funding, and service appropriations, or by a combination of these sources. To manage DOD's large ISR enterprise, the USD(I) serves as DOD's senior intelligence official, responsible for providing strategic, budget, and policy oversight over DOD's ISR enterprise.[10] However, the USD(I) does not have full visibility into several budget sources that fund DOD's ISR enterprise, such as national intelligence capabilities, capabilities used for ISR and non-ISR purposes, urgent operational needs, and military personnel expenses related to ISR. Figure 2 illustrates that the USD(I) does not have full visibility into many capabilities included in DOD's ISR enterprise. The USD(I)'s inability to gain full visibility into all of DOD's ISR financial resources may hinder efforts to develop an investment strategy for ISR, to consider tradeoffs across military services and programs, and to address potential duplication, fragmentation, and overlap.

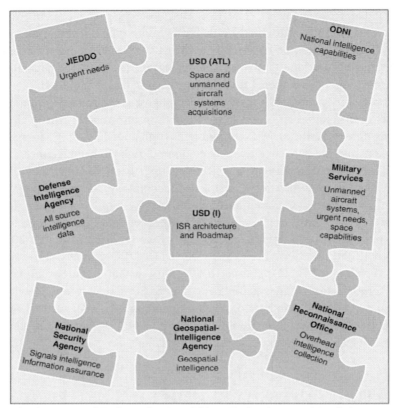

USD (ATL): Under Secretary of Defense for Acquisition, Technology, and Logistics
USD (I): Under Secretary of Defense for Intelligence
ODNI: The Office of the Director of National Intelligence
JIEDDO: Joint Improvised Explosive Device Defeat Organization
Source: GAO analysis of DOD's ISR structure.

Figure 2. Offices That Oversee Various DOD ISR Capabilities.

DOD's ISR enterprise comprises many organizations and offices from both the defense intelligence community and the national intelligence community, which represents a challenge for DOD in integrating capabilities across the ISR enterprise. DOD relies on both its own ISR assets and national ISR assets to provide comprehensive intelligence in support of its joint warfighting force. DOD organizations are involved in providing intelligence information using their respective or joint ISR assets to both the defense and national intelligence communities. Determining the scope of the ISR enterprise precisely is difficult because the intelligence agencies and military services include different activities in discussing their ISR missions and priorities.

Within DOD's ISR enterprise, multiple organizations conduct strategic planning, budgeting, and data processing and analysis across intelligence disciplines in accordance with their own priorities. Within the Office of the Secretary of the Defense, the USD(I), and the Under Secretary of Defense for Acquisition, Technology and Logistics have responsibilities for aspects of ISR that may overlap. Specifically, DOD has designated the USD(I) to manage ISR investments as a departmentwide portfolio. However, as the ISR portfolio manager, the

USD(I) has only advisory authority and cannot direct the services or agencies to make changes in their investment plans. Moreover, the Under Secretary of Defense for Acquisition, Technology and Logistics has been designated responsible for heading a task force related to the management and acquisition of unmanned aircraft systems that collect ISR data and are part of the ISR portfolio. The services and defense agencies also conduct ISR activities. The military services each have their own ISR plans and roadmaps that focus on their respective ISR activities and are not integrated with other services' plans. For example, the Air Force maintains its own ISR plan and metrics separate from DOD's ISR Integration Roadmap and the other service roadmaps, and the other services have developed several roadmaps outlining ISR priorities and capability gaps.

Because of the broad scope of ISR and the multiple agencies involved, DOD's ISR enterprise is funded through several budgetary sources, including both DOD and non-DOD organizations. These multiple sources of funding complicate the USD(I)'s role as the office that develops and oversees DOD's ISR enterprise, according to DOD officials. In particular, USD(I) officials noted that the USD(I) does not have complete information on ISR funding by these organizations and that it is difficult to manage planning for ISR funding. As figures 2 and 3 show, the Military Intelligence Program, the National Intelligence Program, and military service budgets are the various sources of funding. Moreover, some ISR programs are funded through combinations of these funding sources. For example, the USD(I) does not have full visibility into space acquisitions, urgent warfighter needs, and unmanned aircraft systems acquisitions and does not routinely collect data regarding funding information. In fiscal year 2010, DOD's ISR enterprise was funded by the entire Military Intelligence Program budget totaling $27 billion, along with a portion of the National Intelligence Program[11] budget of $53.1 billion. In 2008, we reported that DOD and the Office of the Director of National Intelligence (ODNI) work together to coordinate funding for programs that support both military and national intelligence missions, but determining how costs for joint ISR programs will be shared can be difficult.[12]

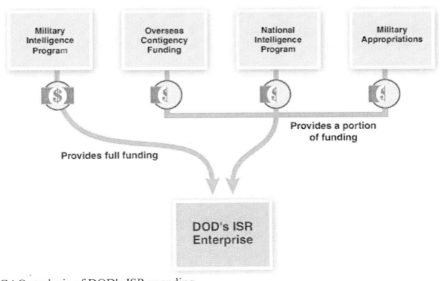

Source: GAO analysis of DOD's ISR spending.

Figure 3. Examples of the Multiple Sources That Fund or Partially Fund DOD's ISR Enterprise.

According to DOD Directive 5143.01,[13] the USD(I) is responsible for developing, coordinating, and overseeing the implementation of DOD policy, strategy, and guidance related to ISR. This directive also provides the USD(I) with the authority to obtain reports and information as necessary to carry out assigned responsibilities and functions. The USD(I) also has responsibility for ensuring that policies and programs related to the acquisition of ISR capabilities are designed and managed to improve performance and efficiency. GAO's Internal Control Standards[14] state that managers, such as the USD(I), need accurate and complete financial data to determine the effective and efficient use of resources. However, the complexity of DOD's ISR enterprise may make the USD(I)'s management and oversight responsibilities difficult to fulfill because it is not receiving complete information and does not have full visibility over DOD's entire ISR enterprise.

The USD(I)'s lack of full visibility into the full scope of ISR capabilities, programs, and budget sources, makes it difficult for the USD(I) to receive, collect, and aggregate reports and information necessary to carry out its oversight responsibilities. We identified four areas for which the USD(I) does not have complete information on ISR spending: (1) military assets that are used for both ISR and non-ISR missions—that is, dual use assets; (2) DOD's urgent ISR warfighter capabilities; (3) budget items funded from multiple sources; and (4) military personnel funding related to ISR missions and capabilities.

- **Dual use assets**—DOD officials stated that certain assets fulfill both non-ISR and ISR missions. Such assets are funded primarily through appropriations for the military services and may not always be reported to the USD(I) as Military Intelligence Program capabilities, which limits the USD(I)'s oversight of such capabilities and ability to make trade-offs or shift resources across the department. According to the USD(I), specific examples of dual use capabilities include the Air Force's airborne ISR Reaper program, the Navy's P-3 Orion land-based maritime patrol aircraft, and DOD's biometrics program.
- **Urgent ISR warfighter capabilities**—As we reported in March 2011,[15] GAO estimated that between fiscal years 2005 and 2010 DOD spent $6.25 billion on urgent ISR capabilities sponsored by the ISR Task Force, as well as a portion of the $19.45 billion sponsored by the JIEDDO to field new ISR capabilities. However, we also reported that DOD cannot readily identify all of its urgent needs efforts or associated costs, including spending on ISR, because it has limited visibility into the totality of urgent needs submitted by warfighters.
- **Capabilities funded from multiple sources**—DOD officials have also cited capabilities funded from multiple sources as a cause of delays in tracking and reporting ISR data. For example, many ISR capabilities are funded jointly by the Military Intelligence Program and National Intelligence Program. In addition, capabilities that have both ISR and non-ISR uses receive funding from different appropriations. For example, capabilities with both ISR and non-ISR uses can be supported by services' operation and maintenance and personnel funding. In 2010, according to a DOD financial regulation[16] the Under Secretary of Defense (Comptroller) and the Director of the Cost Assessment and Program Evaluation Office are to work with the USD(I) to create and maintain whole, distinct budget items within each component of the intelligence community. The military services and defense agencies are required to show measurable and steady progress towards

completing this effort. On the basis of information we received from the military services, the services reported making varying progress in developing whole Military Intelligence Program budget items for some of its ISR capabilities. The services estimated that this effort will be completed sometime after 2012 and they have cited challenges in creating whole budget elements. For example, a Navy official said that it is very difficult to determine individual Military Intelligence Program and non-Military Intelligence budget portions for some capabilities at the program level.

- **Military intelligence personnel funding related to ISR**—DOD, military, and intelligence officials cited challenges in identifying exact costs associated with military personnel conducting ISR activities. In a change from previous years, DOD's fiscal year 2012 Military Intelligence Program budget submission did not include military personnel costs. According to a USD(I) official, military personnel funding was removed from the Military Intelligence Program because: (1) military personnel expenses are not reported in the National Intelligence Program; and (2) the USD(I) does not have oversight authority for military personnel funding. Some of the military services cited military personnel costs as an example of a budget item that is split between ISR and non-ISR programs. For example, the Air Force estimates that it has approximately 200 budget items that contain at least some funding for military intelligence personnel. Additionally, Army officials reported that military personnel funding accounts for approximately 62 percent of their budget items that are funded from multiple sources.

Without accurate and complete financial resource data, the USD(I) may not be able to fulfill its responsibility to develop, coordinate, and oversee the implementation of DOD's ISR enterprise policy, strategy, and programs and manage the Battlespace Awareness capability portfolio from an informed perspective. Until the USD(I) gains more clarity over DOD's ISR funding, DOD efforts to integrate ISR, recommend tradeoffs within the Battlespace Awareness capability portfolio, determine the effective use of ISR resources, and address potential fragmentation, overlap, and duplication will continue to be impeded.

DOD HAS ESTABLISHED INITIATIVES AND PROCESSES TO ACHIEVE EFFICIENCIES, BUT ADDITIONAL STEPS COULD IMPROVE ACCOUNTABILITY

DOD has developed general guidance in directives, a manual, and memorandums emphasizing the need to identify and eliminate duplication or redundancies in its capabilities, which provides a foundation for further action. ISR activities are explicitly included as an area for possible efficiency improvements. However, current ISR efficiency studies have limited scope, initiatives are in the early stages of development, and implementation plans, including resource requirements, have not been fully developed.

DOD Has Emphasized the Importance of Efficiency in ISR Activities through Broad Guidance, but Efficiency Initiatives Have Limitations

DOD's broad guidance highlights the need for the services and defense agencies to work together to eliminate duplication in ISR activities. DOD's directive *Functions of the DOD and Its Major Components*[17] instructs the services to coordinate with each other in eliminating duplication, to equip forces that can work closely with each other, and to assist other components by providing intelligence. Similarly, DOD's *Capability Portfolio Management*[18] directive charges portfolio managers with identifying resource mismatches, including redundancies, and providing recommendations on integrating capabilities. In addition, DOD's requirements process guidance instructs the services and defense agencies to identify overlaps and redundancies when proposing the development of new capabilities and to assess areas of overlap and unnecessary duplication that could be eliminated to provide resources to address capability gaps.

In response to the emphasis on efficiencies, DOD, as a departmental official indicated, has recently completed one efficiency study and is developing two tools to help identify efficiencies and promote integration in its ISR enterprise; however, these efforts have limited scope or are in the early stages of development. Further, it is not clear whether the tools will result in improved efficiencies because DOD has not established implementation goals or timelines with which to establish accountability, measure progress, and build momentum. As we have previously reported, successful management efforts use implementation goals and timelines to identify performance shortfalls and gaps, suggest midcourse corrections, and build momentum by demonstrating progress.[19]

In August 2010, the Secretary of Defense directed that the department begin a series of efficiency initiatives to reduce duplication, overhead, and excess. The ISR portion of the review focused on streamlining organizations that primarily analyze intelligence information. The review group's assessment recommended cost savings of approximately $29 million in intelligence personnel costs for fiscal year 2012 by consolidating some intelligence centers and streamlining certain intelligence organizations. However, the scope of the review was limited to ISR analysis activities and excluded ISR activities associated with collecting ISR data, which represents one of the largest areas of growth in ISR spending. ISR officials were unsure whether or when ISR collection activities would be studied for efficiencies.

Two other DOD efforts are intended to address impediments to integration of the ISR enterprise management that we reported in March 2008.[20] In our assessment of DOD's 2007 ISR Integration Roadmap, we noted that DOD had improved its ability to look across its ISR enterprise by compiling a useful catalog of capabilities. We have previously identified a set of desirable characteristics for defense strategies such as the ISR Integration Roadmap, which are intended to enhance their usefulness in resource and policy decisions and to better assure accountability. These characteristics include laying out goals and objectives, suggesting actions for addressing those objectives, allocating resources, identifying roles and responsibilities, and integrating relevant parties.[21] However, we reported that the 2007 Roadmap did not provide (1) a clear vision of a future integrated ISR enterprise that identifies what ISR capabilities are needed to achieve to DOD's strategic goals, or (2) a framework for evaluating trade-offs among competing ISR capability needs and assessing how ISR investments contribute towards achieving goals. Further, we reported that the department did not have complete information on ISR capabilities in use or being developed to help identify tradeoffs among potential future investments. We recommended that DOD develop an integrated architecture and complete information to use in understanding how changing investment levels in ISR would affect progress and achieving goals and, in comments on that report, DOD agreed with our recommendation and stated that plans of action should be finalized by 2008.

In 2010, USD(I) officials proposed development of a comprehensive architecture for DOD's entire ISR enterprise, to be called the Defense Intelligence Mission Area Enterprise Architecture. This architecture is intended to provide a standardized methodology for identifying and addressing efficiencies in the ISR portfolio and support objective investment decision making. However, this initiative is in the earliest phases of development, and its concept and implementation plans including resource requirements have not been fully developed. The absence of implementation goals and timelines will make it difficult to determine whether this initiative will make progress in achieving efficiencies.

In 2008, we also recommended that the Joint Staff collaborate with the USD(I) to develop a comprehensive source of information on all existing and developmental ISR capabilities throughout the ISR enterprise so that the military services and defense agencies can determine whether existing systems or those in development could fill their capability gaps. Based on this recommendation, in 2010, the Joint Staff, in collaboration with the USD(I) and the services, began an initiative to develop a comprehensive source of information on all existing and developmental ISR capabilities for use in conducting ISR-related assessments. According to Joint Staff officials, this decision support[22] tool is designed to use measurable data to enable assessment of the relative utility and operating costs of different ISR capabilities and has the potential to identify overlap and duplication and inform trade-off decisions. Currently this tool includes information on airborne ISR capabilities. The USD(I) is currently collaborating with the Joint Staff to enhance the decision support tool to address operational requirements across ISR domains. However, it is not clear whether funding will be available to implement plans to maintain and expand the experimental tool to include all ISR capabilities and, with funding uncertain, goals and a timeline for completion have not been established.

DOD HAS DEVELOPED AN ISR INTEGRATION ROADMAP BUT HAS ONLY PARTIALLY ADDRESSED MANAGEMENT ELEMENTS REQUIRED BY LEGISLATION OR IDENTIFIED BY CONGRESSIONAL COMMITTEES

The National Defense Authorization Act for Fiscal Year 2004[23] required DOD to develop an ISR Integration Roadmap to guide the development and integration of DOD ISR capabilities over a 15-year period, and to report to Congress on the content of the roadmap, including specific management elements that DOD should address. In response to both of these requirements, DOD issued an ISR Integration Roadmap. In addition to other matters, DOD was required to include: (1) fundamental goals, (2) an overview of ISR integration activities, and (3) an investment strategy.[24] The House of Representatives Committee on Armed Services provided further guidance in a 2008 committee report, after which DOD issued an updated roadmap in 2010. Our review of DOD's 2007 and 2010 ISR roadmaps found that DOD has made progress in addressing the issues that Congress directed to be included, but neither roadmap included all the specified elements or addressed the important issue of how to invest future resources among competing priorities. As illustrated in figure 4, DOD's 2010 ISR Integration Roadmap addressed two more required elements than did the 2007 roadmap. However, the 2010 roadmap does not represent an integrated investment strategy across the department or contain key elements of an integrated enterprise architecture, such as metrics to help evaluate trade-offs between alternatives and assess progress in addressing capability shortfalls. Further, unlike the 2007 roadmap that catalogued military and national ISR capabilities across the enterprise, the 2010 roadmap is organized by separate intelligence disciplines, such as signals intelligence and imagery intelligence, and is not integrated, making it more difficult to examine potential investments and trade-offs departmentwide.

Effort	2007 ISR Integration Roadmap	2010 ISR Integration Roadmap
2004 National Defense Authorization Act Requirements	○	●
Covers a 15-year period (FY 2004 through 2018).	●	●
Contains fundamental goals.	●	●
Provides an overview of ISR integration activities of the military departments and the DOD intelligence agencies.	◐	○
Includes an investment strategy for achieving— (i) an integration of DOD ISR capabilities that ensures sustainment of needed tactical and operational efforts; and (ii) efficient investment in new ISR capabilities.	○	○
Discusses how intelligence gathered and analyzed by DOD can enhance the role of the DOD in fulfilling its homeland security responsibilities.	○	◐
Discusses how counterintelligence activities of the Armed Forces and DOD intelligence agencies can be better integrated.	○	○
Recommends how annual funding authorizations and appropriations can be optimally structured to best support the development of a fully integrated DOD ISR architecture.	○	○
May 2008 Congressional Committee Report Guidance	○	○
Discusses the appropriate mix of national overhead systems and manned and unmanned airborne platforms to achieve strategic goals that is based on an analysis of future ISR demand.	N/A	○
Includes a comprehensive set of metrics to assess ISR effectiveness in meeting DOD's strategic goals.	N/A	○

● Addresses
◐ Partially addresses
○ Does not address
Source: GAO analysis of 2007 and 2010 ISR Integration Roadmap.
Note: Because DOD submitted the roadmap to satisfy the reporting requirement, the 2004 requirements for the roadmap and the report have been combined in this table.

Figure 4. Extent to Which 2007 and 2010 ISR Integration Roadmaps Address Management Elements Required by Legislation or Identified by Congressional Committees.

The 2010 ISR Integration Roadmap addresses four and partially addresses one of seven management elements set forth in the 2004 National Defense Authorization Act. Specifically, the 2010 ISR Integration Roadmap includes information on:

- **A 15-year time period**—The 2010 ISR Roadmap includes investment strategies for each type of intelligence activity and addresses planned capabilities through at least 2025.
- **A description of fundamental goals**—The 2010 ISR roadmap outlines broad national defense, ISR, and military goals along with missions supported by various intelligence disciplines, and contains fundamental goals such as (1) stewardship of funding, (2) serving fundamental requirements, and (3) leveraging technology effects.
- **A description of ISR Integration activities**—The 2010 ISR roadmap provides an overview of ISR integration activities across DOD such as the structure and membership of the ISR Task Force, the ISR Integration Council, and the Battlespace Awareness Functional Capabilities Board[25] among others.
- **A description of the role of intelligence in homeland security**— The 2010 ISR roadmap contains a section outlining how intelligence can enhance DOD's role in fulfilling its homeland security responsibilities.
- **Counterintelligence integration**—The 2010 ISR roadmap partially addresses counterintelligence integration as it generally describes DOD's counterintelligence mission, but it does not specifically address how it will be integrated among DOD agencies and the armed forces.

The 2010 ISR Integration Roadmap does not address two of the seven management elements in the 2004 National Defense Authorization Act that were also restated in the 2008 House of Representatives Committee on Armed Services report. Specifically, the 2010 Integration Roadmap does not do the following:

- **Describe an investment strategy**—The 2010 roadmap contains general strategies for individual intelligence disciplines, discusses current and future capabilities, identifies supported mission sets for each discipline, and describes long-term actions and challenges. For certain intelligence disciplines, the 2010 roadmap also generally illustrates future needs for certain capabilities. However, it does not contain a comprehensive investment strategy for the ISR enterprise. For example, it does not clearly represent what ISR capabilities are required to achieve strategic goals, and it does not allow DOD decision makers to assess current capabilities across different goals because it is structured according to individual intelligence disciplines. Additionally, the roadmap does not provide estimated costs associated with these capability needs and does not prioritize ISR capabilities.
- **Discuss improving the structure of funding and appropriations**—The 2010 roadmap does not discuss how annual funding authorizations and appropriations can be optimally structured to best support the development of a fully integrated DOD ISR architecture. DOD included a section in the roadmap entitled "Funding an Integrated ISR Architecture," which provides an overview of the Military Intelligence Program, the National Intelligence Program, and the Battlespace

Awareness Capability Portfolio, but does not include information on how annual appropriations can be best structured for ISR.

The 2010 ISR Integration Roadmap also does not address the additional guidance included in the 2008 House Committee on Armed Services report.[26] Specifically, the 2010 ISR Integration Roadmap does not address the appropriate mix of national overhead systems and manned and unmanned airborne platforms to achieve strategic goals and does not include an analysis of future ISR demand. Certain intelligence discipline sections generally describe the types of overhead capabilities needed in the future; however, these capabilities are not prioritized across the entire ISR enterprise.

DOD officials acknowledged that the 2010 ISR Integration Roadmap has some limitations that DOD is planning to address in a later version. For example, because the investment strategy section is organized by intelligence area it does not address capabilities that collect multiple types of intelligence data. The USD(I) also highlighted that recent agreements between the Director of National Intelligence (DNI) and the USD(I) have resulted in the creation of the Consolidated Intelligence Guidance, which is designed to synchronize activities and investments between the DNI and DOD. They stated that this guidance is specifically goal-based and is effective for managing the shorter-term Future Years Defense Program[27] budget. DOD officials also acknowledged that the organization of future iterations of the ISR roadmap by missions instead of intelligence discipline may better illustrate integration and interoperability of capabilities across the department. They stated that the roadmap is a living document and the intent is for future versions to create linkages between the existing DOD strategic guidance and the longer-term investment strategies. USD(I) officials stated that it is developing a useful set of metrics for the next iteration of the roadmap.

Requirements of the 2004 National Defense Authorization Act, additional guidance provided by the House Committee on Armed Services, and our prior work have all emphasized that the roadmap should include a clearly defined investment strategy. Without a unified investment approach, senior DOD leaders do not have a management tool for conducting a comprehensive assessment of what investments are required to achieve ISR strategic goals, and they cannot be well-positioned to prioritize ISR investments and make resource allocation and trade-off decisions when faced with competing needs. Furthermore, until DOD develops an integrated ISR investment strategy, the defense and intelligence communities may continue to use resources that are not necessarily based on strategic priorities, which could lead to gaps in some areas of intelligence operations and redundancies in others.

CONCLUSIONS

With demand for ISR growing and DOD planning to make additional investments in ISR capabilities, the challenges the department faces in integrating ISR capabilities, managing and conducting oversight of ISR funding, and addressing efficiency efforts will likely be exacerbated by expected budget pressures. Fragmented authority for ISR operations among multiple agencies with different, and sometimes competing, priorities hampers DOD's progress in planning for new capabilities and targeting investments to joint priorities. The USD(I) could be better positioned to facilitate integration and provide oversight of ISR activities if it had more visibility into current capabilities and clarity into the total amount that is being spent on ISR activities funded through multiple sources. More complete information would also be useful to the USD(I) in developing an integrated ISR roadmap, including an investment strategy.

DOD's recent emphasis on efficiencies has extended to its ISR enterprise, and it has initiated efforts to identify areas of overlap and duplication. However, limitations in the scope of its current efficiency efforts and undefined goals and timelines to implement its newer efforts reduce the likelihood that all possible efficiencies will be identified and action taken to achieve them. For example, more work remains for DOD to identify efficiencies across the entire ISR enterprise, such as exploring efficiencies in ISR collection activities. Efficiency efforts in the earliest phases of development and implementation could be tools to inform decisions about trade-offs between competing priorities and may be helpful in identifying opportunities for increased efficiencies and cost savings. If designed and implemented properly, these tools could result in cost savings across the ISR enterprise by reducing the likelihood of developing unnecessarily duplicative capabilities. However, without plans for completion and timelines to build momentum, DOD will not have the ability to monitor progress and take corrective actions, if necessary, to ensure that potential savings are realized.

DOD's 2010 ISR Integration Roadmap does not provide enough detailed information on integrated goals and priorities for the ISR enterprise to enable development of a long-term investment strategy. Without a detailed investment strategy, DOD and the military services may not have a common understanding of how activities should be prioritized to meet goals. Until DOD addresses challenges related to managing funding, integrating ISR capabilities, and minimizing inefficiencies in its ISR enterprise, the department risks investing in lower-priority and even duplicative capabilities while leaving critical capability gaps unfilled.

RECOMMENDATIONS FOR EXECUTIVE ACTION

To improve management of DOD's ISR enterprise and increase its ability to achieve efficiencies, we recommend that the Secretary of Defense direct the USD(I) to take the following three actions:

- Collect and aggregate complete financial data—including information on dual-use assets, urgent operational needs, capability funding from multiple sources, and military personnel funding—to inform resource and investment decisions.
- Establish goals and timelines to ensure progress and accountability for design and implementation of its defense intelligence enterprise architecture, including clarifying how the department plans to use the architecture and tools it is developing to achieve efficiencies.
- Expand the scope of current efficiency efforts to include ISR collection activities.

To identify efficiencies in ISR capability development, we recommend that the Secretary of Defense direct the Chairman of the Joint Chiefs of Staff and the USD(I) to collaborate in developing decision support tool(s), such as the Joint Staff's decision support tool, and to establish implementation goals and timelines for completion of such efforts.

MATTER FOR CONGRESSIONAL CONSIDERATION

To ensure that future versions of the ISR Integration Roadmap meet all of the elements of an integrated ISR roadmap identified in the National Defense Authorization Act for Fiscal Year 2004 as well as the 2008 House of Representatives Committee on Armed Services report, Congress should consider establishing additional accountability in legislation, such as conditioning a portion of ISR funding on completion of all congressionally directed management elements, including the development of an integrated ISR investment strategy.

AGENCY COMMENTS AND OUR EVALUATION

In commenting on a draft of this report, DOD concurred or partially concurred with all our recommendations and stated that there are ongoing activities to address our recommendations. DOD did not agree with the matter we raised for congressional consideration. DOD's comments are reprinted in their entirety in appendix II. In addition, DOD provided technical comments, which we have incorporated into the report as appropriate.

DOD partially concurred with our recommendation that the Secretary of Defense direct the USD(I) to collect and aggregate complete financial data to inform resource and investment decisions. In its written response, DOD stated that the USD(I) is working to collect, aggregate, and expand access to complete battlespace awareness portfolio financial data to include information on dual use assets, urgent operational needs, and multiple-source funding through a variety of means and to extend its visibility over DOD's ISR enterprise. DOD described its process for receiving complete information regarding dual use assets and urgent operational needs and discussed how it works to aggregate Military Intelligence Program data. DOD also stated that the USD(I) maintains visibility and access to programs of interest that are non–Military Intelligence Program–funded through access to DOD's Office of Cost Assessment and Program Evaluation's financial data warehouse. While increasing the USD(I)'s visibility into ISR programs is a positive step, we believe that formally aggregating complete intelligence-related financial data would give a better overall picture of DOD's current ISR spending and ensure that DOD considers its entire ISR enterprise when making future resource and investment decisions.

DOD concurred with our recommendation that the Secretary of Defense direct the USD(I) to establish goals and timelines to ensure progress and accountability for implementing its defense intelligence enterprise architecture. In its written comments, DOD described current efforts to develop tools—such as the Defense Intelligence Information Enterprise, the Distributed Common Ground System, and the Joint Intelligence Operations Center for Information Technology demonstration—that provide a common framework for some ISR activities and stated that goals and timelines for implementing these efforts will be displayed in the next ISR Integration Roadmap. However, DOD's comments did not address how the department plans to integrate these separate efforts into defense intelligence architecture that would facilitate analysis of gaps and redundancies and inform future investments. Our recommendation that DOD establish goals and timelines for implementation was intended to improve management accountability for the completion of an integrated defense intelligence architecture, including clarifying how the tools it mentioned will contribute to the architecture, as well as planning how the department will use the architecture and tools to achieve efficiencies. We have revised the recommendation language to clarify its intent.

DOD partially concurred with our recommendation that the Secretary of Defense direct the USD(I) to expand the scope of the current efficiency efforts to include ISR collection activities. In its written comments, DOD stated that the Secretary of Defense's current efficiency initiatives include an effort to identify, track, and determine the future disposition of multiple intelligence organizations that were established to provide ISR support to ongoing combat operations. We agree and acknowledge in the report that current efficiency initiatives are focused on organizations that conduct analysis. The department also noted that the USD(I) is collaborating with the ODNI and the Under Secretary of Defense for Acquisition, Technology and Logistics to further ensure ISR collection investments are fully integrated in the acquisition processes of the department and intelligence community. While these efforts are positive, we maintain that formally expanding the scope of current efforts to include identification of efficiencies in ISR collection activities would help ensure that these efforts receive continued management priority.

DOD also partially concurred with our recommendation that the Secretary of Defense direct the Chairman of the Joint Chiefs of Staff and the USD(I) to collaborate in developing decision support tool(s), such as the Joint Staff's emergent decision support tool, and to establish implementation goals and timelines for completion of such efforts. DOD responded that it is exploring different portfolio management tools and will consider goals and timelines when the efficacy of such tools is verified. We agree that assessing options is an important part of developing the most effective and efficient decision support tool. However, DOD did not explain in its comments how it would consider the efficacy of the tools it plans to assess, or when it expects to choose and begin implementation of such a tool. Establishing goals and timelines for assessing the efficacy of decision support tools and taking actions to implement the selected tool could help ensure that these efforts will be fully implemented in a timely manner.

DOD disagreed with our suggestion that Congress consider establishing additional accountability measures in legislation, such as conditioning funding, to encourage the department to address all the management elements Congress required in its 2004 legislation calling for an integrated ISR roadmap. In its written comments, DOD interpreted our matter as proposing the withholding of funds for ISR activities, and DOD stated that withholding funds for ISR would be counterproductive. However, we did not suggest withholding funding; rather we proposed that Congress consider using the conditioning of funding as a tool to provide an incentive for compliance with legislative requirements that have been in place since 2004—specifically, establishing fundamental ISR goals and an integrated ISR investment strategy. Since 2004, none of the ISR roadmap updates DOD has issued has fully addressed these congressionally required elements. We believe that given the substantial resources allocated to DOD's ISR enterprise, completion of an integrated ISR roadmap that includes an investment strategy could help DOD and congressional decision makers ensure that DOD is effectively using its ISR resources.

We are sending copies of this report to interested congressional committees, the Chairman of the Joint Chiefs of Staff, and the Secretary of Defense. This report will be available at no charge on GAO's Web site, http://www.gao.gov. If you or your staff have any questions about this report, please contact me at (202) 512-5431 or by e-mail at dagostinod@gao.gov. Contact information for our Offices of Congressional Relations and Public Affairs may be found on the last page of this report. GAO staff who have made major contributions to this report are listed in appendix III.

Davi M. D'Agostino
Director, Defense Capabilities and Management

List of Committees

The Honorable Carl Levin
Chairman
The Honorable John McCain
Ranking Member
Committee on Armed Services
United States Senate

The Honorable Thad Cochran
Ranking Member
Subcommittee on Defense
Committee on Appropriations
United States Senate

The Honorable Howard McKeon
Chairman
The Honorable Adam Smith
Ranking Member
Committee on Armed Services
House of Representatives

APPENDIX I: SCOPE AND METHODOLOGY

To describe the challenges, if any, that the department is facing in managing costs, developing strategic plans, and identifying unnecessary fragmentation, overlap, and duplication for the intelligence, surveillance, and reconnaissance (ISR) enterprise, we reviewed and analyzed documents related to the enterprise and discussed the enterprise with cognizant Department of Defense (DOD) officials.

To determine the full scope and cost of DOD's ISR enterprise, we assessed DOD's ISR funding and program elements reported in the Military Intelligence Program for Fiscal Years 2010, 2011, and 2012, conducted an analysis of DOD's ISR spending in the Future Years Defense Program, and discussed with DOD, military service, and intelligence agency officials their ISR funding and capabilities. Specifically, we interviewed cognizant Under Secretary of Defense for Intelligence (USD[I]) and military service officials to determine the content of DOD's ISR enterprise, the extent to which intelligence-related costs are tracked and visible, and the resourcing challenges inherent in a complex enterprise. To determine the extent to which DOD manages the scope and cost of the ISR enterprise, we compared information obtained in these interviews against criteria documents in DOD directives related to the Military Intelligence Program and the USD(I). We reache d out to DOD's combat support agencies— including the Defense Intelligence Agency, the National GeospatialIntelligence Agency, and the National Security Agency—as part of this effort and received high-level information regarding how they use their Military Intelligence Program funds. We also conducted a high-level discussion with the Office of the Director of National Intelligence related to processes used to identify duplication, overlap, and fragmentation within the National Intelligence Program.

To evaluate to what extent DOD has identified and minimized the potential for unnecessary duplication, we assessed the progress of DOD efforts to identify unnecessary fragmentation and overlap and reviewed strategic guidance, and directives for their relative emphasis and priority on unnecessary fragmentation, overlap, and duplication. We assessed to what extent DOD was addressing fragmentation and duplication in strategy documents by reviewing key strategies such as 2010 Quadrennial Defense Review and the Defense Intelligence Strategy. We also reviewed guidance related to DOD's recent efficiency initiatives including memorandums and directives. We evaluated DOD's guidance to determine whether it incorporated best practices on measures of accountability needed to ensure specific initiatives are fully implemented. We also asked DOD, military service, and intelligence officials to provide examples of unnecessary duplication and any actions taken to resolve them.

Finally, to assess the extent to which DOD's ISR Integration Roadmap addresses congressional requirements, two analysts independently evaluated the ISR Integration Roadmap against elements identified in the 2004 National Defense Authorization Act and the House Report from the Committee on Armed Services that accompanied the 2009 National Defense Authorization Act. We determined that an element was addressed if the 2010 ISR Integration Roadmap contained that element; however we did not assess the overall quality of the section(s) that addressed that element. We also compared the 2007 roadmap against these criteria to show any relative differences between the two roadmap versions. We conducted interviews with knowledgeable DOD, military service, and intelligence officials to obtain information on the process to prepare the 2010 Integration Roadmap and plans for future versions of the roadmap.

In addressing all of these objectives, we received briefings on DOD's ISR enterprise and its initiatives to reduce fragmentation, overlap, and duplication in the enterprise, and we analyzed key documents related to these initiatives. We interviewed and received presentations from each of the following commands and agencies about the ISR enterprise's scope, cost, strategic plans, and initiatives to reduce fragmentation, overlap, and duplication: the USD(I); the Joint Staff; the ISR Task Force; headquarters of the Army, Air Force, Navy, and Marine Corps; Defense Intelligence Agency; National Geospatial-Intelligence Agency; National Security Agency; and Office of the Director of National Intelligence.

We conducted this performance audit from August 2010 through June 2011, in accordance with generally accepted government auditing standards. Those standards require that we plan and perform the audit to obtain sufficient, appropriate evidence to provide a reasonable basis for our findings and conclusions based on our audit objectives. We believe that the evidence obtained provides a reasonable basis for our findings and conclusions based on our audit objectives.

APPENDIX II: COMMENTS FROM THE DEPARTMENT OF DEFENSE

OFFICE OF THE UNDER SECRETARY OF DEFENSE
5000 DEFENSE PENTAGON
WASHINGTON, DC 20301-5000

INTELLIGENCE

Ms. Davi M. D'Agostino
Director
Defense Capabilities and Management
U.S. Government Accountability Office
441 G Street, NW
Washington, DC 20548

MAY 1 1 2011

Dear Ms. D'Agostino:

Attached is the Department of Defense (DoD) response to the GAO Draft Report, GAO-11-465, "Intelligence, Surveillance, and Reconnaissance: Actions are Needed to Increase Integration and Efficiencies of DoD's ISR Enterprise," dated April 8, 2011 (GAO Code 351533). Here is our response:

- Recommendation 1: Partially Concur
- Recommendation 2: Concur
- Recommendation 3: Partially Concur
- Recommendation 4: Partially Concur
- Matter for Congressional Concern: Non-concur

The Department appreciates the opportunity to comment on the draft report. My point of contact for this effort is Mr. David M. Taylor, (703) 695-4260, david.taylor@osd.mil.

Sincerely,

Kevin P. Meiners
Deputy Under Secretary of Defense
(Portfolio, Programs and Resources)

Attachment:
As stated

GAO DRAFT REPORT DATED APRIL 8, 2011
GAO CODE: 351533

"INTELLIGENCE, SURVEILLANCE AND RECONNAISSANCE: ACTIONS ARE NEEDED TO INCREASE INTEGRATION AND EFFICIENCIES OF DOD'S ISR ENTERPRISE"

DEPARTMENT OF DEFENSE COMMENTS TO THE GAO RECOMMENDATIONS

RECOMMENDATION 1: The GAO recommends that the Secretary of Defense direct the Under Secretary of Defense for Intelligence to collect and aggregate complete financial data- including information on dual use assets, urgent operational needs, capability funding from multiple sources, and military personnel funding - to inform resource and investment decisions.

DoD Response: Partially Concur. The Office of the Under Secretary of Defense for Intelligence (OUSD(I)) is making every effort to extend its visibility over all financial data necessary to manage the broader Battlespace Awareness (BA) portfolio. We are working to collect, aggregate, and expand access to complete BA portfolio financial data to include information on dual use assets, urgent operational needs, and multiple-source funding through a variety of means.

All Military Intelligence Program (MIP) financial data is collected, maintained and managed by OUSD(I). Disconnects between Departmental guidance, including guidance from OUSD(I), and Service and Agency budget decisions are resolved through the program review process, allowing the Department to integrate ISR capabilities in accordance with the ISR Roadmap. Additionally, recent agreements between the Director of National Intelligence (DNI) and the USD(I) have resulted in the creation of the Consolidated Intelligence Guidance, which helps to synchronize activities and investments between the MIP and the National Intelligence Program (NIP). This guidance is specifically goal-based and is effective for managing the shorter term Future Years Defense Program budget.

OUSD(I) currently maintains visibility over dual-use programs using a variety of means, to include the Joint Capabilities Integration and Development System (JCIDS) and Functional Capability Board (FCB) processes. OUSD(I) also coordinates across the Intelligence Community (IC) with the Office of Director of National Intelligence (ODNI) through the Executive Committees (EXCOM) and the Deputy Executive Committees (DEXCOM) who provide leadership, governance and management on capability issues impacting the entire IC.

The Combatant Commands (COCOMs) have the responsibility to identify, validate and prioritize warfighter urgent operational needs within their area of responsibility. The Joint Staff has the responsibility to process, validate and resource combatant commander urgent needs after full consideration by the appropriate Functional Capability Board (FCB). The FCBs confirm each element of the urgent operational need submission and investigate potential solutions available through other combatant commands or service programs. Once the FCBs have fully considered the alternatives, the urgent operational needs are forwarded to the Joint Rapid Acquisition Cell (JRAC) who determines if further action is warranted. Once that determination has been made, the designated urgent operational need is sent to the appropriate service or agency for action. As USD(I) representatives are members of the BA FCB, there is normally sufficient visibility on urgent needs to manage integration activities within established processes.

The MIP budget process continues to fully account for the number of military personnel assigned to MIP activities. The decision to remove military personnel funding from MIP Congressional justification material was based on the realization that neither the MIP components nor the MIP executive (USD(I)) could influence the military personnel appropriation. Military personnel funding rates are dictated to the Services by a number of factors that are not related to any Defense intelligence plans, policies or operations.

Finally, USD(I) maintains visibility and access to programs of interest that are non-MIP funded through access to CAPE's financial data warehouse. We will continue to extend our visibility on financial matters across the BA portfolio through the mechanisms described above.

RECOMMENDATION 2: The GAO recommends that the Secretary of Defense direct the Under Secretary of Defense for Intelligence to establish implementation goals and timelines to ensure progress and accountability for implementation of its defense intelligence enterprise architecture.

DoD Response: Concur. The Defense Intelligence Information Enterprise (DI2E) is being designed to provide a common framework of tools for security, access authentication, analytical tools, and intelligence sharing. In Fiscal Year (FY) 2010, the Under Secretary of Defense for Intelligence (USD(I)) directed a Joint Intelligence Operations Center for Information Technology (JIOC-IT) demonstration, which was led by National Reconnaissance Office. The demonstration was designed to begin development of JIOC intelligence sharing capabilities consistent with DI2E Council guidelines. USD(I) is continuing this effort in FY 2011, with an increased emphasis on Allied data sharing. The Department's efforts are focused on enabling new methodologies for intelligence information sharing which will integrate Enterprise capabilities, provide interoperable tools needed for mission requirements, and implement information sharing efforts with war fighting and coalition partners. As an example, the fielding of the Distributed Common Ground/Surface System (DCGS) across DoD is designed to enhance the commonality of data transfer and sharing. Other enterprise-wide programs include the effort to obtain commonality across the IT suites in the various Combatant Command JIOCs. Goals and timelines for these efforts will be displayed in the next ISR Integration Roadmap.

RECOMMENDATION 3: The GAO recommends that the Secretary of Defense direct the Under Secretary of Defense for intelligence to expand the scope of the current efficiency efforts to include ISR collection activities.

DoD Response: Partially Concur. Evaluating ISR collection intelligence capabilities must include a balanced look at collection, TPED, and analysis. At present, the Secretary of Defense's efficiency initiatives include an effort to identify, track and determine the future disposition of multiple intelligence organizations that were established to provide ISR support to ongoing combat operations. USD(I) partners with the Office of the Director of National Intelligence (ODNI) and the Under Secretary of Defense for Acquisition, Technology, and Logistics (USD(AT&L)) to further ensure ISR collection investments are fully integrated in the acquisition processes of the Department and Intelligence Community. These collaborative processes help ensure ISR collection investments reflect DoD and IC priorities.

RECOMMENDATION 4: The GAO recommends that the Secretary of Defense, the Chairman of the Joints Chiefs of Staff, and the Under Secretary of Defense for Intelligence collaborate in developing decision support tool(s), such as the Joint Staff's decision support tool, and to establish implementation goals and timelines for completion of such efforts.

DoD Response: Partially Concur. DoD continues to explore current state-of-the-art collaborative portfolio management tools that capture not only Service requirements, but also capture the geographic Combatant Commander (COCOM) needs, and consider the measured or projected performance of programmed ISR systems. The Office of the Under Secretary of Defense for Intelligence is currently collaborating with the Joint Staff to enhance their developmental architectural tool to address operational requirements across domains and COCOM regional requirements. When the efficacy of this tool (and others like it) is verified, the Department will consider establishing goals and timelines for them.

Matter for Congressional Consideration: The Department does not recommend including this section in the final report. Withholding funds often has the effect of complicating further the processes for evaluating, procuring, and operating the best combination of ISR assets for our warfighters engaged in combat.

End Notes

[1] Pub. L. No 108-136, § 923(b)-(c), codified in part at 10 U.S.C. § 426 (2003).

[2] GAO, *Intelligence, Surveillance, and Reconnaissance: DOD Can Better Assess and Integrate ISR Capabilities and Oversee Development of Future ISR Requirements*, GAO-08-374 (Washington, D.C.: Mar. 24, 2008).

[3] Pub. L. No. 111-139 § 21, 124 Stat. 8, 29 (2010).

[4] For examples, see GAO, *Defense Acquisitions: DOD Could Achieve Greater Commonality and Efficiencies among Its Unmanned Aircraft Systems*, GAO-10-508T (Washington, D.C.: Mar. 23, 2010); *Intelligence, Surveillance, and Reconnaissance: Establishing Guidance, Timelines, and Accountability for Integrating Intelligence Data Would Improve Information Sharing*, GAO-10-265NI (Washington, D.C.: Jan. 22, 2010); GAO-08-374; and *Unmanned Aircraft Systems: Advanced Coordination and Increased Visibility Needed to Optimize Capabilities*, GAO-07-836 (Washington, D.C.: July 11, 2007).

[5] GAO-08-374.

[6] H.R. Rep. No. 110-652, at 423 (2008).

[7] Department of Defense Directive 7045.20, *Capability Portfolio Management* (Sept. 25, 2008).

[8] GAO-10-265NI.

[9] GAO, *Warfighter Support: DOD's Urgent Needs Processes Need a More Comprehensive Approach and Evaluation for Potential Consolidation*, GAO-11-273 (Washington, D.C.: Mar. 1, 2011).

[10] DOD Directive 5143.01, *Under Secretary of Defense for Intelligence (USD(I))* (Nov. 23, 2005).

[11] According to USD(I) officials, DOD also relies on National Intelligence Program capabilities, and a significant portion of DOD's intelligence agencies are funded from the National Intelligence Program. ODNI provided us with high-level classified budget numbers for DOD agencies funded through the National Intelligence Program.

[12] GAO-08-374.

[13] Department of Defense Directive 5143.01.

[14] GAO, *Standards for Internal Control in the Federal Government*, GAO/AIMD-00-21.3.1. (November 1999).

[15] GAO-11-273.

[16] DOD Financial Regulation, "Summary of Major Changes to DOD 7000.14-R, Volume 2b Chapter 16, Intelligence Programs/Activities," vol. 2b, ch. 16 (July 2010).

[17] DOD Directive 5100.01, *Functions of the DOD and Its Major Components* (Washington, D.C., December 2010).

[18] DOD Directive 7045.20, *Capability Portfolio Management* (Washington, D.C., September 2008).

[19] GAO, *Results-Oriented Cultures: Implementation Steps to Assist Mergers and Organizational Transformations*, GAO-03-669 (Washington, D.C.: July 2, 2003).

[20] GAO-08-374.

[21] GAO, *Combating Terrorism: Evaluation of Selected Characteristics in National Strategies Related to Terrorism*, GAO-04-408T (Washington, D.C.: Feb. 3, 2004).

[22] The decision support tool referred to in this section is the Joint Staff's ISR Capabilities Map and Next Dollar Sensitivity Tool.

[23] Pub. L. No. 108-136, § 923 (c)-(d), codified in part at 10 U.S.C. § 426 (2003).

[24] Fig. 4 includes a full list of these requirements.

[25] The Battlespace Awareness Functional Capabilities Board is one of the eight DOD Functional Capabilities Boards that review and analyze initial proposals for new military capabilities, and it is focused on ISR capabilities. These Functional Capabilities Boards support the Joint Requirements Oversight Council as it assists the Chairman of the Joint Chiefs of Staff in this role by reviewing and approving proposals for new military capabilities, among other responsibilities.

[26] H.R. Rep. No. 110-652, at 423 (2008).

[27] The Future Years Defense Program provides information on DOD's current and planned out year budget requests and visibility over DOD's projected spending.

In: Intelligence, Surveillance and Reconnaissance ...
Editor: Johanna A. Montgomery

ISBN: 978-1-61470-900-8
© 2011 Nova Science Publishers, Inc.

Chapter 3

COUNTERINSURGENCY (COIN) INTELLIGENCE, SURVEILLANCE, AND RECONNAISSANCE (ISR) OPERATIONS[*]

Department of Defense

This report is a product of the Defense Science Board (DSB). The DSB is a Federal Advisory Committee established to provide independent advice to the Secretary of Defense. Statements, opinions, conclusions, and recommendations in this report do not necessarily represent the official position of the Department of Defense.

The DSB Advisory Group on Defense Intelligence Task Force on Counter Insurgency (COIN) Intelligence, Surveillance and Reconnaissance (ISR) Operations completed its information gathering in January 2011.

This report is UNCLASSIFIED and releasable to the public.

OFFICE OF THE SECRETARY OF DEFENSE
3140 DEFENSE PENTAGON
WASHINGTON, DC 20341-3144
OVENSE SCIENCE HOARD

April 25, 2011

Memorandum for under Secretary of Defense for Acquisition.
Technology and Logistics under Secretary of Defense For Intelligence

SUBJECT: Final Report of the Defense Science Board (DSB) Advisory Group on Defense Intelligence on Counterinsurgency Intelligence, Surveillance, Reconnaissance Operations

---

[*] This is an edited, reformatted and augmented version of a Department of Defense, Defense Science Board Task Force on Defense Intelligence publication, dated February 2011.

I am pleased to forward the final report of the DSB Advisory Group on Defense Intelligence on Cbunrerinsurgency (COIN) Intelligence, Surveillance, Reconnaissance (ISR Operations.

The Advisory Group was tasked to identify the most effective support of COIN opetions by the Department of Defense. This report includes detailed observations and provides nine significant findings and associated recommendations. Underlying the study's key findings is the multi-phase challenge where counter-terrorism, contingency operations (force-onforce hostilities), and COIN may be occurring simultaneously, driving disparate and sometimes conflicting collection strategies on limited ISR resources. The study looked at ISR uniquely developed for Afghanistan to balance against ISR suited for other emerging COIN environments so the U.S. could prepare for the future.

I endorse all of the study's recommendations and strongly encourage you to implement them through your organizations.

Dr. Paul Kaminski
Chairman

OFFICE OF THE SECRETARY OF DEFENSE
3140 DEFENSE PENTAGON
WASHINGTON, DC 20301–3140
February 23, 2011

Memorandum for the Chairman, Defense Science Board

SUBJECT: Final Report of the Defense Science Board (DSB) Task Force on Defense Intelligence – Counterinsurgency (COIN) Intelligence, Surveillance, and Reconnaissance (ISR) Operations

Attached is the final report of the DSB Task Force on Defense Intelligence, Counterinsurgency (COIN) Intelligence, Surveillance, and Reconnaissance (ISR) Operations study. The Task Force was asked to identify how Department of Defense (DoD) intelligence can most effectively support COIN operations. The principal objective of the Terms of Reference was to influence investment decisions by recommending appropriate intelligence capabilities to assess insurgencies, understand a population in their environment, and support COIN operations. To arrive at the principal objective the Terms of Reference (TOR) requested the Task Force address five areas to include the developing role of DoD ISR in COIN operations, to include relevant customers and their respective requirements; allocation of DoD ISR resources to support COIN capabilities; changes to the ISR process to improve support to COIN; immediate improvements in network agility and information sharing across mission partners conducting COIN; and emerging technologies and methodologies likely to provide the highest payoff.

To respond to the TOR, the Task Force reviewed existing literature and met with more than 100 senior- and mid-level officials and representatives from across DoD, the Intelligence

Community (IC), industry, non-profit community, and academia involved in irregular warfare, COIN, ISR, and related activities. The Task Force examined the multi-phase COIN challenge, which includes the need to continue to support COIN operations in Afghanistan; prepare for emerging and urgent COIN ISR operations that will have to be met using current resources; and building a capability to deal with long-term COIN scenarios using new concepts of operations (CONOPS) and resources.

Based on its investigation the Task Force arrived at the following observations:

- DoD lacks a common understanding of COIN
- DoD has assumed responsibility for COIN ISR by default
- DoD ISR is narrowly interpreted to mean technical intelligence collection by airborne platforms
- ISR capabilities have not been applied effectively against COIN operations that deal with populations in part because a comprehensive set of intelligence requirements for COIN does not exist
- The U.S. Government is not investing adequately in the development of social and behavioral science information that is critically important to COIN
- ISR support for COIN is currently being overshadowed by counterterrorism and force protection requirements
- Increasing the focus of ISR for COIN on incipient insurgencies would provide more whole-of-government options and reduce the need for major commitment of military forces
- New S&T solutions must address the crisis in processing, exploitation, and dissemination (PED) and associated communications caused by the deluge of sensor data
- New and emerging technologies and techniques can be employed to improve our understanding of COIN environments

The attached report provides the rationale for the Task Force's findings and recommendations, responds to five specific TOR tasks, and notes substantial policy guidance on aspects of COIN and ISR as well as numerous and inconsistent definitions of key terms associated with the study.

We appreciate the contributions made by the Department of Defense, Intelligence Community, industry, and academia who took the time to provide us with their knowledge and expertise; the members of this study; the Executive Secretary; the DSB Secretariat and its military assistant.

Maj Gen Richard O'Lear, USAF (Ret)
Co-Chairman

EXECUTIVE SUMMARY: TASKING AND KEY FINDINGS

Why this Study Was Conducted

This report was conducted at the request of then Under Secretary of Defense for Intelligence (USD(I)), The Honorable James R. Clapper, and assigned by the Defense Science Board (DSB) to its Permanent Defense Intelligence Task Force. This request followed the publication of Major General Michael T. Flynn's "blueprint" paper on intelligence support to counterinsurgency (COIN) operations in Afghanistan. In his paper, MG Flynn provided a candid assessment of intelligence support:

> Ignorant of local economics and landowners, hazy about who the powerbrokers are and how they might be influenced, incurious about the correlations between various development projects and the levels of cooperation among villagers, and disengaged from people in the best position to find answers – whether aid workers or Afghan soldiers – U.S. intelligence officers and analysts can do little but shrug in response to high level decision-makers seeking the knowledge...to wage a successful counterinsurgency.[1]

MG Flynn's comments come at a time when Department of Defense (DoD) resource constraints and challenges are becoming more evident, even as the Department faces a wide range of prospective COIN operations in the future. As a result, the Department must take into account what it has learned in recent and current COIN operations, the need to continue supporting current operations as effectively as possible, and the challenges of preparing for the future. This report represents an effort to understand the balance that will be required to meet these challenges, and to plan accordingly.

This study comes at an important moment in the evolution of United States (U.S.) national security. A Defense Science Board 2004 Summer Study examined the need to put capabilities in place to prepare – on a Government-wide basis – for hostilities, as well as the need to diminish U.S. military involvement in those activities in an orderly and effective manner.[2] The report noted the need for capabilities in "stabilization and reconstruction; strategic communication; knowledge, understanding and *intelligence;* and identification, location, and tracking for asymmetric warfare."[3] The price of not having these capabilities in place or of not planning to use these capabilities was still unfolding as that study was written. The enormous cost of not fielding these capabilities is clear today. It's a price the U.S. is paying in lives and in national treasure. The 2004 report noted the wide set of requirements that must be met to address the full life-cycle of hostilities. This study takes into account the observations and recommendations of that effort, extending its recommendations into concepts to enhance the capabilities of the U.S. Government (USG) in general, and the Intelligence Community (IC) in particular, to put in place intelligence capabilities that support emerging requirements for COIN operations throughout the entire life-cycle of those operations, from planning, to exit.

Finally, the pertinence of this report is amplified by the words of Secretary of Defense Robert Gates, who noted in an address at the United States Military Academy at West Point that the U.S. Army and the rest of the U.S. Government need capabilities to "prevent festering problems from growing into full-blown crises which require costly — and controversial — large-scale American military intervention."[4]

As the nation builds a new national security structure that addresses both global challenges and fiscal realities, these capabilities will be difficult to obtain. This report makes specific recommendations regarding the ISR approaches and resources needed to gain these COIN capabilities.

Terms of Reference (TOR)

The USD(I)'s TOR for the study (Appendix A) identified five tasks:

1) What is the developing role of DoD intelligence, surveillance, and reconnaissance (ISR) in COIN operations; who are the customers and what are the requirements?
2) What is the recommended allocation and use of DoD ISR resources to sustain COIN capability along with other competing intelligence requirements, for example, counterterrorism?
3) What changes can be made to the ISR process to improve support to COIN?
4) What can be done in the immediate future to improve network agility and information sharing across the broad spectrum of mission partners conducting COIN and during the promotion of regional stability?
5) What emerging methodologies and technologies, combinations of sensors, and investments in information fusion and analysis are likely to provide the highest payoff?

Study Methodology

Over the last six months the Task Force conducted a comprehensive literature review on issues relevant to the TOR, and met with more than 100 senior and midlevel officials and representatives from across the DoD Components, the IC, industry, academia, and the non profit community. These experts in COIN, irregular warfare, and ISR included serving and retired military officers from fourstar generals to noncommissioned officers, field commanders, and senior civilian leaders and policymakers. The Task Force also engaged intelligence collection and analysis experts, physical scientists, engineers, social scientists, and a variety of leading think tank scholars. A complete listing of briefings received by the Task Force can be found in Appendix C.

Key Findings

Underlying this study's key findings is the multiphase COIN challenge: the need to continue supporting COIN operations in Afghanistan; simultaneously preparing for emerging and urgent COIN scenarios that will have to be met using existing resources; and building a capability to deal with longterm COIN scenarios using new Concept of Operations

(CONOPS) and resources. Key findings are presented in summary below, and in detail in Section 4, which also provides recommendations.

1. DoD Lacks a Common Understanding of COIN

The lack of a single authoritative definition of COIN is impeding a common understanding and unified approach to COIN operations within the DoD and across the USG. Accompanying this lack of definition is a multiplicity of COIN CONOPS.

2. DoD Assumed Responsibility for COIN ISR by Default

Despite a national strategy and civil military campaign plan that calls for a whole of government, population centric approach to COIN, the USG is not employing all elements of national power in the planning and conduct of COIN operations. DoD assumed responsibility for virtually all COIN intelligence requirements by default. Indeed, apart from being a signatory to the 2009 *U.S. Government Counterinsurgency Guide,* the Department of State has shown little evident interest in building or supporting the partnership described by the *Guide*.[5] This lack of partnership impedes progress toward a wider approach to COIN.

3. DoD and IC Officials Tend to Focus Narrowly on Airborne Technical Collection Capabilities and Systems Rather than on the Wider Capabilities Needed to Support COIN

This observation is supported by the fact that technical collection platforms command larger portions of the budget and produce more *immediate* effects rather than *longer term,* foundational information for population-centric operations. The Task Force notes that discussions with DoD senior officials regarding ISR for COIN turned frequently to the subject of technical collection systems and capabilities while excluding other collection sources (e.g. Open Source Intelligence (OSINT), Human Intelligence (HUMINT)) and processing, exploitation, and dissemination (PED) issues. The Defense Science Board's Summer Study of 2010 noted that in 2009 DoD represented 62 percent of the requirements for OSINT, but provided only 3 percent of OSINT funding.[6] The lack of attention to OSINT is buttressed by the report's finding that in 2009 DoD had only 14 percent of the IC's OSINT manpower, and funded that proportion largely through Defense budget supplementals.[7]

Overall, these problems tend to exclude valuable sources of social and behavioral science data, including human geography.

4. ISR Capabilities Have Not Been Applied Effectively Against COIN Operations that Deal with Populations in Part Because a Comprehensive Set of Intelligence Requirements for COIN Does Not Exist

The defense intelligence community has not translated those aspects of commander's intent dealing with COIN into intelligence requirements, though the *United States Government Integrated Civilian-Military Campaign Plan for Support to Afghanistan* describes in detail the need to focus on population security, governance, and economic development.[8] The reasons for this apparent reluctance to engage on this issue are varied, but one key reason is that intelligence agencies, at least those in the Washington, D.C. area, tend to be reactive, waiting for questions to be asked, rather than trying to anticipate them. This approach may be too conservative in a period of rapid social change, promoted by instant communications.

5. The USG Is Not Investing Adequately in the Development of Social and Behavioral Science Information that Is Critically Important for COIN

Many, if not most, specific COIN ISR requirements are population-centric and are not exclusively solvable with hardware or hard, physical science scientific and technical (S&T) solutions. One senior intelligence officer with years of field experience pointed out that 80 percent of useful operational data for COIN does not come from legacy intelligence disciplines. Good intelligence on COIN exists outside the traditional intelligence organizations. Anthropological, socio-cultural, historical, human geographical, educational, public health, and many other types of social and behavioral science data and information are needed to develop a deep understanding of populations. Such data, collected and analyzed using the scientific method, is vital to COIN success.

6. ISR Support for COIN Is Currently Overshadowed by Counterterrorism (CT) and Force Protection Requirements

In real terms, ISR support of COIN is not as high a priority for the Combatant Commands, Military Departments, and Defense Agencies as CT and force protection, thus adversely impacting the effectiveness of COIN operations. COIN is not necessarily an alternative to CT; some ISR requirements are common to both kinds of operations, but COIN, particularly population-centric COIN, requires some ISR of its own.

7. COIN ISR Has Not Been Addressed Early in the Conflict Spectrum and Has Not Sufficiently Included a Whole-of-Government Approach. The Lack of Focus on Incipient Insurgencies Limits Options and Increases Risk of Unrecoverable COIN Problems, Despite the Commitment of Major Military Forces

> Insurgency has been the most prevalent form of armed conflict since at least 1949. Despite that fact, following the Vietnam War and through the balance of the Cold War, the U.S. military establishment turned its back on insurgency, refusing to consider operations against insurgents as anything other than a "lesser included case" for forces structured for and prepared to fight two major theater wars.[9]

Historical studies of insurgencies over the years highlight the fact that insurgencies are more likely if a state cannot provide fundamental services and if the population believes they are at risk. In addition, other factors, such as the quality of leadership in a particular country and that country's political culture can be important factors in whether or not an insurgency develops. The Task Force does not propose that any specific combination of factors will result in an insurgency. Nonetheless, recent history can be instructive. Colombia, for example, has been gripped by a tenacious insurgency, even as the drug trade has imperiled that government's ability to govern effectively. Colombia's strong political leadership, however, has made effective use of U.S. security and development assistance, as well as the political and diplomatic support of U.S. leaders. As a result, the U.S. has not been compelled to commit substantial U.S. forces to combat an insurgency and defend the sovereign prerogatives of Colombia's government. In contrast, the years leading up to 9/11 witnessed little U.S. government involvement in Afghanistan. As a result, U.S. information sources in Afghanistan were limited, which constrained U.S. potential to help shape in Afghanistan a situation less dangerous to U.S. interests. The events of 9/11 left the U.S. with few options in Afghanistan; combat a regime that allowed terrorists to attack us, or live with a dangerous status quo. The Task Force therefore judges that early intervention prior to an insurgency taking hold would give the U.S. more options and reduce the likelihood of major combat intervention.[10]

In light of this record, it is the view of the Task Force that irregular warfare and insurgencies will continue to be an enduring challenge to regional stability and U.S. national security interests. Emerging and enduring COIN issues need attention now. Addressing potential insurgencies in their incipient phase (i.e., "left of bang") will provide policymakers and commanders more whole-of-government options and a better prospect for deterring or preventing the need for combat operations. Building a collection and analytic effort "left of bang" also provides the means for sustained, consistent, and more effective ISR support should an insurgency become active. This makes necessary a more focused approach to COIN intelligence support, including a National Intelligence Manager (NIM) for COIN, intelligence requirements directed specifically to COIN (including population-centric knowledge), and a strategic indications and warning (I&W) model to enable early implementation of whole-of-government options. Some I&W indicators are probably already available.

A. Effective Coin, and Intelligence for Coin, Must Reflect a Whole-of-Government Effort and Whole-of-Government Capabilities

As noted in the 2004 DSB Summer Study, the U.S. requires the means to transition into an out of hostilities. Nowhere is this need more salient than for COIN. Addressing the entire life-cycle of COIN requires knowledge management capabilities that serve a wide variety of U.S. Government departments and agencies (DoD, Department of State, the Intelligence Community, etc.) A NIM for COIN would be able to facilitate efficient and effective intelligence support to COIN enabling a knowledge management capability that supports whole-of-government efforts and which would encourage use of a broader range of information sources that go beyond legacy intelligence collection.

8. *The Deluge of Sensor Data Is Creating a Crisis in Processing, Exploitation, and Dissemination (PED) and Associated Communication, as Well as an Increasing Need for Advanced Analysis that Addresses Behavior of Groups and the Cultural Framework of Group Decisions*

The insatiable demand for information and emphasis on collection is producing a deluge of data, overwhelming the ability to provide useful, actionable intelligence in a timely manner. This crisis in PED is exacerbated by planned and programmed collection assets and demands new S&T solutions to improve the efficiency and effectiveness of ISR support for COIN.

Moreover, there is a need to develop and train people to do Advanced Analysis – and this must be done much earlier in the careers of the best analysts. This level of analysis is needed at the very front end of any future conflict, not several years down the road. Training for Advanced Analysis would start at the very beginning of an analyst's career and continue throughout his/her career. It includes language, deep cultural awareness, and select forms of environmental training which encourages and supports analysis on the health of a region.

Analysts need to make progress to understand the culture first hand and they need to return to critical assignments within their intelligence agency. More and more, the analysts will need to be placed in the field in order to be best postured for intelligence operations and conflicts as they arise.

9. *New and Emerging Technologies and Techniques Can Be Employed to Improve Understanding of COIN Environments*

Technologies are emerging to improve understanding of the physical attributes (mineral resources, climates, geographies, including cultural geography), as well as those pertinent to identifying pattern of life activities of groups and individuals. Technologies can relate these attributes to incipient and real insurgencies. New analytic technologies hold the promise of "scaling up" the ability to filter raw data, identify meaning patterns of activity, and present analysts with material useful to understanding COIN situations, thus allowing analysts to perform real analysis, rather than exhaust themselves culling raw data. Technology can also be employed to understand what is "normal" in a particular environment, helping to spot trends that represent anomalies that may portend long-term changes and the rise of instability.

1. INTRODUCTION, TASKING, AND STUDY STRUCTURE

This report conveys the findings and recommendations of the Permanent Defense Intelligence Task Force (Task Force or TF) of the Defense Science Board relative to ISR in support of COIN operations. This report is submitted in response to the Terms of Reference of March 8, 2010, provided by the Office of the Under Secretary of Defense for Intelligence (OUSD(I)). A copy of the TOR is provided in Appendix A to this report.

This study comes at an important moment in the evolution of U.S. national security. A study published by the Defense Science Board in 2004, examined the need to put capabilities in place to prepare – on a Governmentwide basis – for hostilities, as well as to diminish U.S. military involvement in those activities in an orderly and effective manner. [11] The 2004 report noted the need for capabilities in "stabilization and reconstruction; strategic communication; knowledge, understanding and *intelligence;* and identification, location, and tracking for asymmetric warfare."[12] The price of not having these capabilities in place, or planning to use these capabilities was still unfolding as that study was written. The enormous dimensions of that price are clear today. It's a price the U.S. is paying in lives and in national treasure. The 2004 report noted the wide set of requirements that must be met to address the full lifecycle of hostilities. This study takes into account the observations and recommendations of that report, extending its recommendations into concepts to enhance the capabilities of the USG in general, and the IC in particular, to put in place intelligence capabilities that support emerging requirements for COIN operations throughout the entire lifecycle of those operations, from planning, to exit.

The TOR directed the Task Force to provide findings that can be used to influence ISR investment decisions as they relate to COIN. Although the TOR emphasized science and technology given their potentially significant contribution to intelligence support to COIN, the TOR also directed the Task Force to "assess insurgencies" and "understand a population in their environment." The TOR also noted that "host nation civilian sentiment critically impacts COIN success, indicating anthropological and sociocultural factors must also be addressed." These factors, and the multidimensional, coalition nature of COIN operations, have implications for the scope of this Task Forces efforts, a point made clear by the discussions offered in Sections 3.1.2 (Who are the customers?) and 3.2.1 (The diversity of intelligence mission), and elsewhere in Section 3.

The TOR posed five specific questions for the Task Force to address:

1) What is the developing role of DoD ISR in COIN operations; who are the customers, and what are the requirements?
2) What is the recommended allocation and use of DoD ISR resources to sustain COIN capability along with other competing intelligence requirements, for example, counterterrorism?
3) What changes can be made to the ISR process to improve support to COIN?
4) What can be done in the immediate future to improve network agility and information sharing across the broad spectrum of mission partners conducting COIN and during the promotion of regional stability?
5) What emerging methodologies and technologies, combinations of sensors, and investments in information fusion and analysis are likely to provide the highest payoff?

With the concurrence of the OUSD(I), the Task Force (members are identified in Appendix B of this report) chose a broad interpretation of the TOR as reflected in the derived questions shown in red in Figure 1. As the TF examined the TOR's five specific tasks, it developed these derived questions which it believed were necessary adjuncts to the five basic tasks.

The five specific tasks in the TOR on first glance seemed straight forward. As the Task Force began to examine the first task ("What is the developing role of DoD ISR in COIN ops?"), the Task Force decided to use an "authoritative" definition for each term—ISR and COIN to establish a clear baseline for what to address in the study.

The Task Force found several inconsistent definitions for the term COIN included in a variety of authoritative sources, as well as differing CONOPS. These different definitions allow DoD organizations and IC members to choose the one(s) they like best, causing confusion and different interpretations among decision-makers and operators. These differences are significant when one tries to relate COIN to other military actions; e.g., counterterrorism, irregular warfare, and force protection.

"DoD ISR" also has a number of definitions. In its simplest form, "DoD ISR" is used by most DoD and IC members to mean technical collection from manned or unmanned airborne platforms like the MQ-9/Reaper, RQ 4/Global Hawk, or MC-12/Liberty. This view, when applied to COIN, tends to exclude other traditional sources of intelligence; e.g., OSINT and HUMINT. It also ignores and precludes the use of other extremely valuable sources of data and knowledge from the social sciences that have particular utility for COIN. These terms, and a description of how the Task Force used them, are addressed in greater detail in Section 2 of the report.

> **Terms of Reference – Tasks & Derived Tasks**
>
> 1. What is the developing role of DoD ISR in COIN ops; who are the customers and what are the requirements?
>   A. How should we define COIN and ISR?
>   B. What's the right balance among COIN vs. CT vs. Force Protection vs. population-centric activities for ISR resources?
>   C. What's the proper balance between COIN and major contingency ops (Force structure, training, etc.)?
>   D. What's the role of DoD in COIN vs. other US agencies?
>   E. Role of social science in the DSB's examination of "technology fixes"—How much emphasis on eliminating grievances prior to COIN/insurgency?
>   F. Phase of conflict for COIN ops (pre-hostilities, conflict, post-conflict)—Should US put more energy into pre-hostilities phase? Is so, how, and what ISR would be needed?
>   G. Balance between Afghanistan and Pakistan (AFPAK) ops (current fight) and future COIN ops—How much of a "standard" COIN template can we build?
>   H. Does a solid list of COIN intelligence requirements exist?
> 2. What is the recommended allocation and use of DoD ISR resources to sustain COIN capability along with other competing intelligence requirements, for example counterterrorism?
> 3. What changes can be made in the ISR process to improve support to COIN?
>   A. Do we emphasize collection too much? What PED improvements are necessary?
>   B. What kinds of DoD intelligence analysts do we need?
> 4. What can be done in the immediate future to improve network agility and information sharing across the broad spectrum of mission partners conducting COIN and during the promotion of regional stability?
> 5. What emerging technologies and methodologies, combinations of sensors, and investments in information fusion and analysis are likely to provide the highest payoff?

Figure 1. TOR and "Derived" Tasks.

The second part of the first task ("...who are the customers and what are the requirements?") also raises some very significant issues. A number of different U.S. policy documents state the need for a whole-of-government approach to national security challenges.[13] For example, a number of U.S. policy documents give the Department of State (DoS) and U.S. Agency for International Development (USAID) prominent COIN responsibilities. In the preface to the 2009 *U.S. Government Counterinsurgency Guide*, signed by the Secretaries of State and Defense, and the Administrator of the USAID, the Counselor of the Department of State notes:

> Irregular warfare is far more varied than conventional conflict: hence the importance of an intellectual framework that is coherent enough to provide guidance, and flexible enough to adapt to circumstances. Counterinsurgency places great demands on the ability of bureaucracies to work together, with allies, and increasingly, with non-governmental organizations (NGOs). That it is co-signed by the leaders of the Departments of State and Defense and the U.S. Agency for International Development says a great deal about the partnership between these and other departments that has been, and will be, required if we are to succeed in the future. Although much of our ability to knit together lines of effort arises from the field, there is an important role for policy-relevant thought about first order questions. This Guide provides that.[14]

The *Guide's* preface also notes:

> American counterinsurgency practice rests on a number of assumptions: that the decisive effort is rarely military (although security is the essential prerequisite for success); that our efforts must be directed to the creation of local and national governmental structures that will serve their populations, and, over time, replace the efforts of foreign partners; that superior knowledge, and in particular, understanding of

the 'human terrain' is essential; and that we must have the patience to persevere in what will necessarily prove long struggles.[15]

Despite these words, the absence of the necessary DoS and other resources and capabilities means that the burden of conducting most COIN operations fell to the DoD by default. Hence, the DoD acquired a series of new (or at least non-traditional) ISR requirements for COIN operations that may or may not match well with their capabilities and Tactics, Techniques, and Procedures (TTP). As one looks at specific COIN ISR requirements, one can conclude that many, if not most, are "population-centric" and are not readily solvable with hardware or even hard, physical science S&T solutions.

The Task Force discovered that although ISR for COIN in Afghanistan gets considerable lip service, most senior civilian and military leaders take a fairly constrained view, concluding that more technical collectors (e.g., Reapers or Predators) will answer the requirements. Non-traditional sources of military ISR get very little support in terms of funding, manpower, or tasking priorities. In Afghanistan, the priority for DoD ISR for COIN is overshadowed by ISR requirements for CT and force protection.

The Task Force discerned two imperatives for the near-term and future ISR requirements for COIN. The conflict in Afghanistan is and should be the top current priority. The TF makes a number of near-term recommendations to improve ISR support for COIN/CT operations in Afghanistan. However, as the U.S. phases down combat operations and moves toward a 2014 withdrawal of most forces from Afghanistan, the TF concluded that in the post-Afghanistan environment, COIN will be an enduring issue for the U.S. This second priority, "emerging COIN challenges," should be planned for now so that a gradual shift in emphasis can occur as operations in Afghanistan draw down. The Task Force notes, however, that several potential COIN scenarios may require U.S. engagement with resources substantially the same as those in use today. As witnessed in the recent Middle East unrest, these surprise scenarios may erupt even as the U.S. undertakes the shift shown in Figure 2.

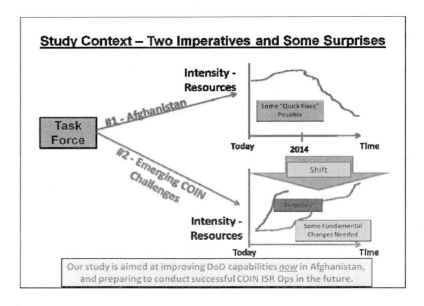

Figure 2. Study Context - Two Imperatives.

The TF makes a number of recommendations with respect to these "emerging COIN challenges," even as the U.S. may have to deal with more urgent COIN scenarios. The Task Force believes now is the time to consider how to address COIN intelligence requirements for the future. As the *U.S. Government Counterinsurgency Guide's* preface notes: "Whether the United States should engage in any particular counterinsurgency is a matter of political choice, but that it will engage in such conflicts during the decades to come is a near certainty.[16]

ISR for COIN may differ from country to country, but there are some generic basic ISR requirements (that underlie the Task Force's findings and recommendations) that can be identified and then modified to suit a specific country depending on current strategic requirements. The Task Force identified, as illustrated in Figure 3, a representative list of countries that currently pose a potential COIN challenge. Some of these countries may represent an emerging COIN challenge, while others may become more urgent. It should be emphasized that this list is provided for illustrative purposes and does not necessarily represent any assessment by the DoD or the IC regarding emerging COIN situations, nor is the list in priority order. Setting the actual priorities would be a very dynamic process based on current national security objectives.

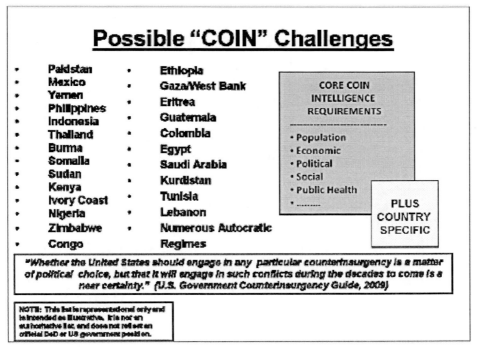

Figure 3. Possible Coin Challenges.

The Task Force observed that economic crises, climate change, demographic pressures, resource scarcity, or poor governance could cause these states (or others) to fail or become so weak that they become targets for aggressors/insurgents. The Task Force believes that a government's loss of its ability to exercise sovereign prerogatives in important regions, including border areas, allowing an insurgency to gain "critical mass," may represent an important COIN predictor. Instability can assume regional dimensions – rapidly. Information, global information infrastructure, and social media can amplify the speed, intensity, and momentum of events that challenge regime stability. The threat of the proliferation of weapons of mass effects in the hands of more nations and non-state actors further complicates the matter. Such areas could become sanctuaries from which to launch attacks on the U.S. homeland, recruit personnel, and finance, train, and supply operations.

Therefore, in addition to S&T, the TF chose to examine the contributions that social sciences (including anthropology and sociology) can make to ensuring effective ISR support to COIN, as well as the investments that might be made in human resources/professional development. The Task Force's considerations were influenced as well by discussions that illustrated differences among the current COIN operations (Afghanistan and Iraq), and past and prospective COIN operations such as in Vietnam, the Horn of Africa, Lebanon, or Mexico.

The Task Force concluded that if U.S. policy is to deter and prevent COIN situations from becoming major conflicts more emphasis should be placed "left of bang" (before the need to make a major commitment of combat troops) and while the insurgency is still in its incipient phase. As the 2011 *National Military Strategy of the United States of America* notes: "Preventing wars is as important as winning them, and far less costly." [17] There are many reasons to consider this shift to "left of bang." Figure 4 summarizes the key advantages and disadvantages of making this shift.

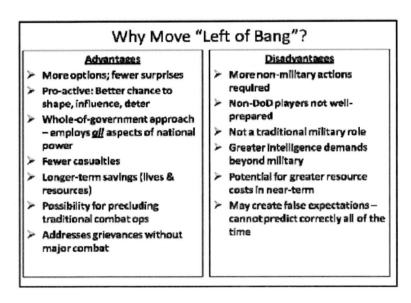

Figure 4. Advantages and Disadvantages of Moving "Left of Bang".

Should the U.S. move to a "left of bang" approach to COIN, useful indicators to help predict insurgency scenarios and deal with them early are needed, thus making indications and warnings (I&W) indicators an important component of future COIN planning and operations (see Figure 5). It is important to note that it is possible to have simultaneous operations (e.g., COIN, CT, conventional, etc.) depending on the definition(s) chosen.

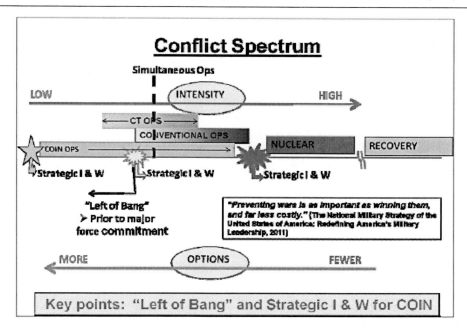

Figure 5. Coin and the Conflict Spectrum.

During the Cold War, the U.S. was able to develop a strategic I&W model that was well-understood. It produced clearly defined intelligence requirements intended to prevent a surprise nuclear attack. It drove ISR physical technologies, collection methods, and analysis; it yielded key "indicators" (principally military in nature); and it required "activity norms" to discover significant changes.

It is the Task Force's belief that a similar strategic I&W model can be designed for COIN. This model would need new and different ISR requirements; a clear understanding of the environment critical to determining causes/origins of problem(s); and the addition of social sciences to the physical sciences. Key indicators will most likely be non-military such as political, economic, social, and loss of government sovereign prerogatives in key regions. Such an approach would require a whole-of-government plan to determine requirements, collection, analytical, and dissemination priorities.

While a population-centric approach to Afghanistan appears well-suited to the village-based nature of Afghan society, a different approach may be required to counter insurgencies that draw their strength from drug cartels or other motivating forces. Nonetheless, recent COIN thinking has been influenced greatly by the population-centric view of COIN, one that emphasizes social, political, and cultural context as much as detailed information about the adversary. As MG Flynn notes, *"...tendency to overemphasize detailed information about the enemy at the expense of the political, economic, and cultural environment..."*[18]

This view of current COIN doctrine appears to exert more or less influence on military leaders, depending on their orientation and experience. While this Task Force does not express an opinion on COIN doctrine and concepts of operations, it views the social sciences as important to understanding target populations, the role of insurgencies within and connected to these populations, and the need to separate the interests of target populations from those of insurgencies. The Task Force also notes that post-World War II scientific research included work in the development of organizational design and dynamics and systems analysis as ways to approach results driven military operations and the efficient allocation of resources to achieve results.

In general, the Task Force views U.S. counterinsurgency as an effort to deny success to insurgent movements who would use the territory they control to endanger the safety of the United States and its allies. As a result, the scope of the Task Force's consideration included the wide range of potential COIN scenarios and operations; a wide variety of science, technology, and other resources; and a view that science includes the use of the scientific method of hypothesis generation, data collection, and analysis associated with the social sciences. Any "left of bang" approach to COIN will require the use of social sciences in ISR, in addition to the application of the physical sciences.

2. Defining COIN and ISR

The Task Force reviewed current policy, doctrine, strategy, and plans that establish the vision, objectives, guidelines, and responsibilities within the USG and the DoD for COIN; other aspects of irregular warfare including CT, unconventional warfare (UW), foreign internal defense (FID), and stability operations (SO); as well as ISR. The purpose of the review was to establish a clear baseline for this study.

In reviewing these authoritative sources, the Task Force found that there is substantial policy guidance on key aspects of COIN and ISR as well as numerous, and inconsistent definitions of the key terms associated with this study. Examples of these discrepancies are displayed in Tables 1 and 2.

Table 1. Definitions of COIN

Counterinsurgency (COIN)	
Definition	Source
1 - The blend of comprehensive civilian and military efforts designed to simultaneously contain insurgency and address its root causes. Unlike conventional warfare, non-military means are often the most effective elements, with military forces playing an enabling role.	U.S. Government Interagency COIN Guide (Jan 2009)
2 - Those military, paramilitary, political, economic, psychological, and civic actions taken by a government to defeat insurgency.	Joint Publication (JP) 1-02 Department of Defense Dictionary of Military and Associated Terms (April 2001, amended 2010)
3 - Comprehensive civilian and military efforts taken to defeat an insurgency and to address any core grievances.	JP 3-24 COIN Operations (Oct 2009)
4 - A counterinsurgency campaign is a mix of offensive, defensive, and stability operations conducted along multiple lines of operations.	Army Field Manual (FM) 3-24 Counterinsurgency (Dec 2006)

Counterinsurgency (COIN)	
Definition	Source
5 - COIN operations include supporting a Host Nation's military, paramilitary, political, economic, psychological, and civic actions taken to defeat an insurgency. Avoiding the creation of new insurgents and forcing existing insurgents to end their participation is vital to defeating an insurgency. COIN operations often include security assistance programs such as foreign military sales programs, the foreign military financing program, and international military training and education programs. Seven key COIN Lines of Effort: 1) Establish civil security 2) Establish civil control 3) Support HN security forces 4) Support to governance 5) Restore essential services 6) Support to economic and infrastructure development 7) Conduct information engagement	FMI 3- 24.2 Tactics in COIN (March 2009)
6 - Support to COIN is defined as support provided to a government in the military, paramilitary, political, economic, psychological, and civic action it undertakes to defeat insurgency (JP 1-02). Implicit in this definition is a legitimate partner nation (PN) government in power with some capacity to direct and conduct COIN operations. Support to COIN can include indirect support, direct support (not involving combat) and direct support (involving combat).	Air Force Doctrine Document (AFDD) 2-3 Irregular Warfare (August 2007)
7 - The set of political, economic, social, military, law enforcement, civil and psychological activities with the aim to defeat insurgency and address any core grievances.	Bi-SC Joint Operations Guidelines (JOG) 10/01 (NATO) (May 2010)
8 - Attributes of COIN: • Political primacy (and a clearly-defined political objective) • It is a struggle for the population, not against the population • The relevance of legitimacy • Intelligence drives operations • Unity of effort (the requirement of a coordinated government structure) • Neutralize the insurgency and isolate the insurgents from their support • Prepare for a protracted campaign • Security under the rule of law is essential • Hand over responsibility to the local forces as soon as practicable • Learn and adapt quickly	Allied Joint Doctrine (AJP) 3.4.4 Joint Doctrine for COIN (NATO pub on COIN) (Nov 2008)

Table 2. Definitions of ISR

Intelligence, Surveillance, and Reconnaissance (ISR)	
Definition	Source
1 - An activity that synchronizes and integrates the planning and operation of sensors, assets, and processing, exploitation, and dissemination systems in direct support of current and future operations. This is an integrated intelligence and operations function.	JP 1-02 Dictionary of Military and Associated Terms (April 2001, amended 2010)
2 - Intelligence, surveillance, and reconnaissance is an activity that synchronizes and integrates the planning and operation of sensors, assets, and processing, exploitation, and dissemination of systems in direct support of current and future operations. This is an integrated intelligence and operations function. For Army forces, this combined arms operation focuses on priority intelligence requirements while answering the commander's critical information requirements. (JP 2-01 contains ISR doctrine.) Through ISR, commanders and staffs continuously plan, task, and employ collection assets and forces. These collect, process, and disseminate timely and accurate information, combat information, and intelligence to satisfy the commander's critical information requirements (CCIR) and other intelligence requirements. When necessary, ISR assets may focus on special requirements, such as information required for personnel recovery operations. It supports full spectrum operations through four tasks: ISR synchronization, ISR integration, Surveillance, Reconnaissance.	FM 3-0 Operations (Feb 2008)
3 - The purpose of intelligence, surveillance, and reconnaissance (ISR) operations during a COIN is to develop the intelligence needed to address the issues driving the insurgency. Several factors are particularly important for ISR operations in COIN environments. These include the following: a focus on the local populace; collection occurring at all echelons; localized nature of insurgencies.	FM 3-24 Counterinsurgency (Dec 2006)
4 - The goal of ISR operations is to provide accurate, relevant, and timely intelligence to decision makers. The Air Force best achieves this goal through effective employment of ISR capabilities, and by capitalizing on the interoperability existing among our ISR systems, as well as nontraditional sources, to create synergy through integration.	AFDD 2-9 ISR (Jul 2007)
5 - Surveillance and reconnaissance refer to the means by which the information is observed. Surveillance is "systematic" observation to collect whatever data is available, while reconnaissance is a specific mission performed to obtain specific data.	Military Transformation: Intelligence Surveillance, and Reconnaissance (Jan 2003)

As indicated previously, different definitions of terms and associated interpretations of their meaning allow the DoD components, including the intelligence components of the military departments and combatant commands and the combat support agencies that are part of the IC, to choose the one(s) they prefer. This, in turn, produces a lack of clarity and causes confusion about what is meant by both COIN and ISR.

Some defense officials, for example, neither differentiate COIN from other irregular warfare operations such as CT nor distinguish it from traditional kinetic military operations. While irregular warfare can be conducted independently or in combination with traditional warfare (see Figure 5), COIN is part of a spectrum of irregular warfare activities and operations including CT, UW, FID, and SO. However, real distinctions exist among traditional warfare and irregular warfare and the failure to understand the differences between COIN, CT, force protection, and conventional strike operations has adverse consequences for the execution of U.S. national security policy and strategy. This failure has a deleterious effect on the DoD and IC's understanding of the intelligence requirements for effective support of U.S., multinational, and coalition COIN operations.

The Task Force discovered a similar lack of clarity and confusion within and between DoD components and the IC about the term "ISR." The aggregation of ISR is itself somewhat confusing since it equates the importance of intelligence, surveillance, and reconnaissance. In fact, intelligence is the objective of ISR, and surveillance and reconnaissance are carried out to contribute to that objective.

Moreover (and as noted previously), the Task Force found that some equate "Defense ISR" with technical collection in general and manned and unmanned aircraft in particular. Such misinterpretation unnecessarily constrains the view of policymakers, planners, and warfighters to a relatively narrow set of technical collection platforms rather than the broad array of assets resourced by the Military Intelligence Program (MIP), much less the overall capabilities and capacity of the nation's intelligence enterprise.

ISR for COIN (and ISR in general) includes all intelligence disciplines, all sources of information, and all aspects of the process of collecting data and turning it into operationally useful intelligence upon which to establish context, create knowledge, and inform decisions and actions. It encompasses planning and direction of intelligence, mission and collection management, tasking, human and technical collection, processing, exploitation, production, and dissemination. Moreover, with respect to OSINT it includes non-traditional sources of political, socio-cultural, behavioral, economic, and other social science information found in the public and private sectors.

For the purposes of this study, the Task Force used the definitions found in Joint Publication (JP)1-02, *Department of Defense Dictionary of Military and Associated Terms*:[19]

- Irregular Warfare (IW): "A violent struggle among state and non-state actors for legitimacy and influence over the relevant population(s). Irregular warfare favors indirect and asymmetric approaches, though it may employ the full range of military and other capacities, in order to erode an adversary☐s power, influence, and will." (246)
- Insurgency: "The organized use of subversion or violence by a group or movement that seeks to overthrow or force change of a governing authority. Insurgency can also refer to the group itself." (233)

- Counterinsurgency (COIN): "Comprehensive civilian and military efforts taken to defeat an insurgency and to address any core grievances." (111)
- Counterterrorism (CT): "Actions taken directly against terrorist networks and indirectly to influence and render global and regional environments inhospitable to terrorist networks." (113)
- Intelligence: "The product resulting from the collection, processing, integration, evaluation, analysis, and interpretation of available information concerning foreign nations, hostile or potentially hostile forces or elements, or areas of actual or potential operations. The term is also applied to the activity which results in the product and to the organizations engaged in such activity." (234)
- Surveillance: "The systematic observation of aerospace, surface, or subsurface areas, places, persons, or things by visual, aural, electronic, photographic, or other means." (456)
- Reconnaissance: "A mission undertaken to obtain, by visual observation or other detection methods, information about the activities and resources of an enemy or adversary, or to secure data concerning the meteorological, hydrographic, or geographic characteristics of a particular area." (393)
- ISR: "An activity that synchronizes and integrates the planning and operation of sensors, assets, and processing, exploitation, and dissemination systems in direct support of current and future operations. This is an integrated intelligence and operations function." (237)

In summary, influencing foreign governments and populations is a complex and inherently political activity. The military role in irregular warfare campaigns in general, and COIN in particular requires the ability to plan, conduct, and sustain integrated operations of interagency and multinational civilian and military organizations to support a foreign government or population threatened by irregular adversaries. In other words, it requires the whole-of-government approach described by the Secretaries of State and Defense in the *U.S. Government Counterinsurgency Guide*. While U.S. forces are superbly trained in the traditional aspects of violent combat, these irregular warfare and COIN campaigns may fail if waged by military means alone. Given that it is USG policy to deter and counter insurgencies, then the defense intelligence community should place more emphasis on "left of bang" – before the need for a large commitment of U.S. combat troops – while an insurgency is still in an incipient stage of development, and that the whole-of-government approach should be given the capabilities necessary to succeed. ISR should be crafted and resourced to support this approach.

3. TOR TASKS

3.1. TOR Task 1: What Is the Developing Role of DoD ISR in COIN Operations; Who Are the Customers and What Are the Requirements?

A key objective of the Task Force was to examine the developing role of defense intelligence in COIN operations, and to identify the customers and requirements for COIN.

The Task Force recognizes that the global security environment is complex, uncertain, and dangerous. Threats to the United States, its allies, and regional stability may arise from weak or failing states as well as failed states and ungoverned areas. Poor governance, resource scarcity, economic crises, and even climate change could exacerbate such instability. Non-state adversaries will, of course, seek to exploit such circumstances for their own ends. Throughout history this has always been the case. Indeed, the majority of conflicts involved a state fighting a non-state actor.[20] As recent and ongoing conflicts in Lebanon, Iraq, and Afghanistan demonstrate, adversaries may choose to employ both traditional and irregular modes of warfare concurrently to achieve their political objectives.

The DoD in general and the defense intelligence community in particular, must recognize that irregular warfare is strategically important in an era of hybrid or multi-modal armed conflict. Consequently, the Task Force notes that in accordance with DoD Directive 3000.07, *Irregular Warfare*, it is DoD policy to maintain capabilities and capacity so that the Department is as effective in irregular warfare as it is in traditional warfare to ensure that, when directed, it can:

1) Identify and prevent or defeat irregular threats from state and non-state actors across operational areas and environments.
2) Extend U.S. reach into denied areas and uncertain environments by operating with and through indigenous foreign forces.
3) Train, advise, and assist foreign security forces and partners at the ministerial, service, and tactical levels to ensure security in their sovereign territory or to contribute forces to operations elsewhere.
4) Through direct or indirect means, and on a large scale when required, support a foreign government or population threatened by irregular adversaries.
5) Create a safe, secure environment in fragile states and, if required, provide essential governmental services, emergency infrastructure restoration, and humanitarian relief.[21]

The USD(I) is assigned responsibility to:

a) Maintain standards and guide the development of capabilities and capacity for persistent intelligence, surveillance, and reconnaissance and assessment of operational areas and environments that may serve as safe havens for irregular threats.
b) Advance intelligence and information partnerships with interagency and international partners, as appropriate, to identify and prevent or defeat irregular threats from state and non-state actors across operational areas and environments.
c) In accordance with strategic guidance documents, improve all-source collection to identify irregular threats from state and non-state actors. Ensure timely information dissemination from the strategic to the tactical level, recognizing that irregular warfare places particular reliance on releasable products to facilitate working with foreign security partners.

d) Manage the development of appropriate analytical intelligence models, tools, and data to provide intelligence support to U.S. Armed Forces for irregular warfare.
e) Incorporate into intelligence products information derived from social and behavioral science sources in the public and private sectors.
f) Project activity patterns on a regional and global scale for analyzing both friendly and adversary human networks through modeling and simulation capabilities.
g) In conjunction with the CCDRs, prioritize capabilities to identify, locate, track, and target adversary networks, cells, and individuals in order to neutralize their influence and operational capacity.
h) Promote intelligence and counterintelligence career paths that attract and retain the quantity and quality of personnel with irregular warfare-relevant skills, in coordination with the Secretaries of the Military Departments and the Under Secretary of Defense for Personnel and Readiness (USD(P&R)).[22]

There is a substantial gap between the policy guidance and its implementation. This report examines those reasons, including the exigencies of ongoing combat operations.

3.1.1. Developing Role of DoD ISR in Coin Operations

Since the end of the Cold War, the focus of the defense intelligence community has changed to address new threats to U.S. national interests. In addition to the large formations of relatively static targets comprising the armed forces and supporting infrastructure of an adversarial state, the defense intelligence community must now focus on small, dispersed targets that characterize such non-state actors as terrorist and insurgent networks. It may also need to support whole-of-government COIN strategies, as well as support the efforts of allies with which the U.S. may desire to work with in meeting COIN challenges around the world. Section 3.4.1 notes that networks of allies and NGOs are often incompatible with U.S. systems, thus hindering operations that require resources beyond those of the U.S. government.

These threats and needs do not have a common doctrine or CONOPS. They have neither big signatures to observe nor enduring signals to intercept. They conceal themselves within the local population and utilize global communications, finance, and telecommunications infrastructures to help command, control, and execute their operations. These threats are hidden, masked, and fleeting. Moreover, counteracting these threats and denying them the ability to achieve their political-military objectives requires new and different types and combinations of intelligence/information.

Addressing these new threats thus requires intelligence/information not only from traditional intelligence sources and methods, but also from all echelons of warfighters as well as non-traditional sources. There is no dominant or single intelligence discipline or source of information to solve the challenges posed by COIN operations. Indeed, all-source and multi-INT intelligence is essential for achieving the persistent, predictive, activity-based ISR required to successfully counter an insurgency as shown in Table 3.

Table 3. Selected ISR Sources for Irregular Warfare

Selected ISR Sources for IW	
COMINT	GMTI
ELINT	Thermal Analysis
FISINT	Cyber Activity
EO IMINT (e.g., PAN, MSI, FMV)	HUMINT Interrogation
RADAR IMINT	Source Operations
RF MASINT	Debriefings
EO MASINT	Biometrics
RADAR MASINT	Human Geography/ Terrain Analysis
Geophysical MASINT	Document Exploitation (DOCEX)
Post event forensics	Debriefings
Human/Cultural Geography	Social Group/Network Dynamics

Unlike traditional ISR, where the focus typically is on the location of an anticipated activity, ISR for irregular warfare must focus on discovering the unknown activity of an adversary, characterizing it, and exploiting it. For support of COIN operations it also requires a clear and sustained focus on population-centric activities such as governance, development, and local population – sometimes before the start of hostilities. This demands a thorough understanding of historical, socio-cultural, economic, educational, and environmental aspects of the area of operations in addition to political and military factors and trends. This in turn requires more basic or fundamental intelligence as well as associated social, behavioral, and political sciences information from sources in the public and private sectors. Table 4 compares and contrasts other aspects of ISR for traditional versus irregular warfare.

As noted above, there are major gaps in ISR capabilities and capacities for COIN operations, particularly in population-focused collection and analysis. Moreover, there is an absence of analytical capability that adheres to methodologies of modern social science and psychological research techniques and assessment tools. The absence of this expertise in the field denies analysts, planners, and operators an important "what if" tool for assessing the consequences of plans.

To that end, the Task Force focused on how ISR can support those aspects of COIN, as defined in the broadest sense. The Task Force appreciates the pitfalls of considering the application of DoD ISR capabilities that go beyond traditional military operations, but there is an implicit need to apply some ISR capabilities against aspects of COIN that are primarily civilian in nature. If winning over the local populace is the goal, then the U.S. must employ ISR capabilities in a population-centric manner without, however, precluding ISR's inherent value in dealing with insurgents through kinetic means.

In particular, a key developing role of Defense ISR in COIN and other irregular warfare-related network operations is to provide activity-based intelligence (ABI). ABI is cross-discipline and multi-INT and is applicable both to physical and non-physical activities and transactions, including socio-cultural beliefs and behaviors, financial transactions, open-source information, and cyber activities. It lends itself to understanding "patterns of life," larger social networks, and unusual or suspicious activity.

Table 4. Traditional Warfare vs. Irregular Warfare Surveillance

Traditional Warfare vs. Irregular Warfare Surveillance		
	Traditional Warfare Concepts	Irregular Warfare Paradigm
War Time Horizon	Relatively Short Decisive Battles	Long War
Persistent ISR	Unblinking Eye	Smart collection management based on the frequency of change
Persistent Surveillance	Single Sensor 24/7, IMINT PED	Activity Surveillance, multi-INT PED, Exploitation and collection no longer temporally synchronized
Geo-registration	Discovery to geo-register	Geo-register to discover
Collection Focus	Target driven	Activities and transactions driven
Intent of Collection	Find remained pieces to a puzzle	Understand mysteries; Unravel networks
Collection Period	Minutes / hours	Weeks / months
PED Philosophy	IMINT	Multi-INT
Exploitation Process	1st, 2nd, 3rd phase exploitation	Time phased, layered approach, Real-time and forensics
PED Products	IPB / BDA / Over-watch	PED may not yield a finished intelligence product
Targets	Military Order of Battle	People and networks
Target Signatures	Soviet style military signatures	Non-conventional signatures such as organizational structure, communications, movement
Target Identifier	BE Number	Proper Name
Data Tagging	Stovepiped within INT	Metadata tagged to link sensor to activity to geo-reference to action
Sensor Utilization	Not integrated	Fully integrated
Doctrine and TTPs	Well Established	New concepts, learning while doing
Training	Single INT specialization	Multi-INT Ops-Intel specialization
Information Sharing	Need to know	Need to share / multi-INT synergy

The blending of ABI with wide area surveillance, human geography, and other capabilities appears to be a particularly promising path for DoD ISR to support COIN operations. Such a blend will help support:

- Detection, geolocation, and characterization of transactions/activities;
- Identification and geolocation of the entities conducting transactions/activities;
- Identification and geolocation of networks among actors/entities;

- Development of patterns of life supporting I&W, predictive analysis, and counter denial and deception; and
- Understanding the broader interactions between/among networks.

3.1.2. Who Are the Customers?

The Task Force believes that the commanders and warfighters of U.S. military forces planning and conducting COIN operations are no longer the only customers of the DoD ISR enterprise. In order to effectively plan, conduct, and sustain the integrated operations of interagency and multinational civilian and military organizations in support of a foreign government or population threatened by irregular adversaries, there must be an understanding of the broader array of defense intelligence customers, and some customers outside of the DoD (consistent with the approach described in the *U.S. Government Counterinsurgency Guide)*. Customers include other U.S. Government departments and agencies, foreign security partners, and selected international and nongovernmental organizations. In Afghanistan today, for example, the set of customers for defense intelligence includes the Department of State, USAID, Provisional Reconstruction Teams (PRTs), and a plethora of NGOs in addition to the coalition forces

3.1.3. What Are the Requirements?

Based on assimilated data and received briefings, the Task Force believes that ISR capabilities in Afghanistan are primarily employed in support of force protection and CT missions. As a result, many aspects of the COIN campaign, broadly defined, are relatively under-served by ISR, including intelligence that supports achieving the transformative effects called for by the Commander of the International Security Assistance Force (ISAF) and the United States Ambassador to Afghanistan, as well as to support to stability operations and foreign internal defense.

To say that ISR under-served these aspects of COIN is not meant as a criticism of how ISR is operating today. In many respects, ISR is enormously successful in supporting the operations of U.S. forces to defeat terrorists and insurgents.

Why have ISR capabilities not been applied consistently against those aspects of COIN operations that deal with populations? One member of the Task Force, who interviewed intelligence managers, collection managers, and intelligence analysts at three of the regional commands in late 2010, concluded that:

> The *United States Government Integrated Civilian-Military Campaign Plan for Support to Afghanistan* had not been widely read, dissected, and mapped into specific intelligence requirements or translated into integrated concepts of operation. Intelligence shops had not yet received a demand signal from commanders in the field for this type of data and analysis. Competing needs for force protection and the find, fix, and finish mission made reallocation of intelligence resources against the broader COIN missions problematic.

ISR in COIN has always been a tough job, and it becomes nearly impossible to do well if support to kinetic missions is not balanced with support to efforts focused on population security, economic development, and governance.

There are many intelligence requirements on the books pertinent to supporting the broad missions of COIN, but few examples of how intelligence collection and analysis are actually targeted to answer these questions. There are fewer that describe the direct and indirect signatures that should be collected and analyzed, and none at all that propose improvements in ISR operations. In a similar vein, ISR requirements "left of bang" and for whole-of-government efforts have yet to be well described.

One set of requirements that could be used as a point of departure for guiding future ISR operations are the detailed tasks outlined in the *United States Government Integrated Civilian- Military Campaign Plan for Support to Afghanistan* (also cited as the *McChrystal/Eikenberry campaign plan*). There are 116 such tasks (called Main Efforts) that are associated with the Transformative Effects called for in the plan. Each of these tasks could be mapped into specific observables, both direct and indirect, that would become part of an ISR collection and analysis plan. To illustrate how this might be done, the Task Force considered the key issue of population security.

Achieving security of the population is the first step in a COIN campaign. In Afghanistan, as in any region subject to an insurgency, the people must feel free from violence and coercion by insurgents, criminals, and terrorists, and must come to trust the security forces of the government to protect them. The challenges to achieving this level of security in Afghanistan are substantial:

- There are insufficient forces present (Afghan National Security Forces (ANSF) and ISAF) to secure population centers.
- Afghan National Police (ANP) development has lagged due to corruption and abuse, poor quality and ethnic balance of recruits, high casualty rates, attrition, inadequate logistics, poor leadership, insufficient ANSF cooperation, and under-resourcing and mentoring.
- International military action resulting in civilian casualties exacerbated popular insecurity and increased alienation.

To remedy these shortfalls and create a secure environment for the population, the *McChrystal/Eikenberry campaign plan* called for twelve tasks to be executed:

Community Level Tasks:

- Establish basing and conduct operations for security presence in critical areas.
- Reduce civilian casualties and other acts that create opposition among the population.
- Reform and mentor ANP units to protect communities and establish rule of law.
- Ensure equal access to ANP recruitment for all population groups through political outreach.
- Mobilize support and trust for ANSF efforts.

Provincial Level Tasks:

- Build and mentor COIN-capable Afghan National Army (ANA) to defeat internal threats and support the ANP as necessary.
- Improve ANSF interoperability, coordination, cooperation, and mutual support, particularly ANA in support of the ANP in contested areas.
- Place Afghans in charge of operations working towards transfer of lead security responsibility.

National Level Tasks:

- Develop Ministry of Defense (MOD), ANA and Ministry of the Interior (MOI) capacity for accountability, interoperability, and oversight.
- Develop strategies and incentives to mitigate high levels of ANSF attrition.

Tasks at all Levels:

- Support reduction of ANSF corruption and abuse.
- Improve border security efforts to stem cross border flow of insurgents and insurgent logistics.[23]

Each of these tasks implies designing a set of ISR tasks. For example, the first two tasks at the Community Level call for establishing basing and a security presence in critical areas and reducing civilian casualties (presumably from both insurgents and coalition forces). ISR support would require such basic data as physical assessments of terrain, lines of sight, and access to key infrastructure. Equally important would be the evaluation of normal population movement patterns and activities, characterization of changes in patterns, and an understanding of how activities vary in the course of a day or week.

Reducing population casualties would entail determining the proximity of insurgent activities to civilian homes and businesses. However, it might also mean developing an ISR strategy to proactively detect threats against key local leaders and representatives of local government, warning criteria for transmitting threats to Afghans who are targeted, the capability to track local leaders during threat periods, and procedures for search and rescue of locals. Such an effort would need to be worked out with local Afghan police.

ISR operational planning will need to take into account protection of sources and methods, sharing policies, and operational limitations in the local environment. While each of these issues will require a dedicated effort to resolve, the most important point in this example is that ISR use should be balanced between "find, fix, and finish" (F3) missions and direct support to monitor the security of populations and key individuals.

3.2. TOR Task 2: What Is the Recommended Allocation and Use of DoD ISR Resources to Sustain Coin Capability Along with Other Competing Intelligence Requirements, for Example CT?

3.2.1. The Diversity of Intelligence Mission Needs

As long as the U.S. has on-going combat operations and the need to interdict terrorist operations against U.S. forces and the homeland, then CT is the highest priority. Yet the case for balancing the intelligence needs of a COIN or population-centric plan with those focused on counterterrorism is laid out clearly in the *ISAF Commander's Counterinsurgency Guidance*. The *Guidance* focuses on explaining why conventional military operations cannot defeat the insurgency in Afghanistan. GEN McChrystal wrote that the math doesn't add up:

> From a conventional standpoint, the killing of two insurgents in a group of ten leaves eight remaining: 10-2=8. From the insurgent standpoint, those two killed were likely related to many others who will want vengeance. If civilian casualties occurred, that number will be much higher. Therefore, the death of two creates more willing recruits: 10 minus 2 equals 20 (or more) rather than 8.[24]

For this basic reason, GEN McChrystal called for military and civilian officials to take a different, more population-centric path. With this approach, coalition troops must become, and be seen as providing a positive force in the community, shielding the people from harm, and fostering stability. This means putting less emphasis not only on using force but also on force protection measures (such as body armor and heavily armored vehicles), which distance the security forces from the population. It also entails placing a much higher degree of intelligence support on the protection of critical local leaders and key individuals to ensure they can survive and execute the political and economic goals associated with countering the insurgents.

In addition to these tactical reasons, putting more emphasis on COIN operations is strategically important as it creates the potential for creating "left of bang" detection and effects which may preclude or minimize the necessity of future kinetic operations and create more options for senior leaders to curb progression toward conflict.

More generally, the diversity of intelligence needs is a consequence of COIN's presence within the spectrum of irregular warfare operations the DoD must be prepared to conduct. CT, COIN, and Counter-Improvised Explosive Device (C-IED) efforts are all counter-network operations. The mission objectives of each are distinct and their associated information needs are different, yet overlapping. Planned and executed properly, the different types of counter-network operations will produce synergistic benefits. Conversely, they will create problems if planned and conducted without regard for the relationships among COIN, CT, and C-IED operations.

The complexity of COIN and other counter-network operations requires a strategic rather than *ad hoc* approach to ISR mission management. The intelligence requirements to support a population-centric COIN strategy are different from those to counter terrorist networks. In particular, the scale and granularity of information required to assess patterns of behavior at local, tribal, and societal levels and comprehend that activity are different. An array of collection assets and sensor phenomenology as well as associated tasking, processing, exploitation, and dissemination capabilities are being employed to obtain and understand pertinent data and information. These capabilities are typically not being orchestrated in a way to ensure that critical questions about the COIN campaign can be answered. Unfortunately, the COIN campaign appears to be a secondary, or perhaps tertiary, priority for ISR, behind force protection and CT. COIN undertaken "left of bang" however, offers the potential to diminish the need for subsequent force protection and even CT operations. As the 2011 *National Military Strategy* notes: "While such [CT] operations disrupt in the short-term, they cannot be decisive and do not constitute a viable long-term strategy for combating extremism."[25]

The Task Force's investigation of ISR operations today found a high degree of emphasis on missions that involve the rapid defeat of terrorist networks through the effective application of F3 tactics. The Task Force did not find a clear articulation of the desired balance between those missions and the missions that are specified in the *McChrystal/Eikenberry campaign plan*.[26]

The defense intelligence culture is evolving slowly to meet the demands of supporting multi-modal, hybrid operations (and whole-of-government operations). That culture is primarily focused on "targeteering" and "weaponeering" to enable U.S. military forces to destroy enemy combatants and their war-making capacity. In addition, DoD tradecraft and culture separate targeteers and general analysts. There is insufficient attention to the need to provide intelligence support of complex operations and counteract hybrid, multi-modal conflict. As the COIN problem becomes more strategic and prevalent, the expertise of operators needs to be more closely coupled with the general analyst and with analysts in fields ranging from target analysis and mission planning to the social sciences.

Finally, the need to address COIN counterintelligence requirements requires more emphasis. Hard lessons in Iraq and Afghanistan, not to mention other environments (from Algeria to Lebanon) underscore the sophisticated intelligence capabilities of insurgent movements. These capabilities provide insurgents the means to infiltrate government entities "left of bang," to anticipate the military operations of the governments they fight, and to deploy technologies (including signals intelligence and imagery) in support of their own objectives. U.S. forces in Afghanistan have witnessed first-hand the ability of insurgents to conduct human intelligence operations. Press reports suggest that Hezbollah forces in Lebanon received Iranian Unmanned Aerial Vehicles (UAVs) and may have received Iranian support in their operation. Given these developments, U.S. COIN operations must include the ability to counter insurgency intelligence capabilities and maintain a sustained information advantage throughout all phases of COIN operations.

3.2.2. Mission-Based Needs Should Drive Effects-Based ISR

Conventional operations and CT generally require a more simple approach to intelligence than COIN. With kinetic-centric operations, it is important to identify the target, develop precise coordinates and use an appropriate weapon to minimize collateral damage. With COIN, the intelligence problem is more complex and drives a more subtle strategic plan that seeks an overall effect where the population impact of an action is important: how will the population react to the target's elimination, will they react differently to the method (e.g., more sensitive to drone missile strikes than sniper fire), will the operation negatively impact a local political balance, how will it affect future HUMINT information gathering relationships? COIN ISR does not have an identifiable end-point in terms of collection. With CT, ISR assets are re-allocated once the target is identified and engaged upon. With COIN, ISR continues over an indefinite period of time to understand the behavior of an individual, group, or population and assess how behavior changes as the COIN campaign unfolds.[27] This patterns-of-life development is an intelligence-intensive effort. Furthermore, the range of intelligence needed to be effective is drastically broader for COIN, including intelligence dependent on cultural factors that cannot be provided by overhead sensors alone.

As the commander's emphasis shifts from conventional operations to CT and to COIN, ISR needs to shift from target collection management to effects-based management. With COIN, ISR becomes more complex and the analyst is required to understand and merge more and more diverse data sources to fully understand the impacts and consequence of a COIN operation.

Further, intelligence analysis is driven toward a population-centric approach where the centers of gravity, as perceived by the population, must be identified and understood in order to assess the true impact of an emergent event to derive meaningful information to inform decision-makers. To accomplish this, Collection Management (and, ultimately Mission Management) needs to shift toward meeting need-based requirements where users describe a need to the intelligence enterprise that it is tied directly to security, governance, or economic components of a COIN campaign plan and where Collection Managers then plan a coordinated ISR strategy for achieving a desired effect, that is, the needed knowledge to execute a component of the COIN plan. This shift forces a more dynamic relationship between the user, enterprise, and collection platform, and drives a coordinated effort across intelligence agencies that goes beyond simple targeting missions that can typically be described as the F3 mission of CT. Figure 6 below illustrates this difference and how that leads to a different set of questions that must be answered by the intelligence collector and analyst. The process flow on the left is used more commonly and the flow on the right is what the Task Force views as needed particularly in a complex COIN context.

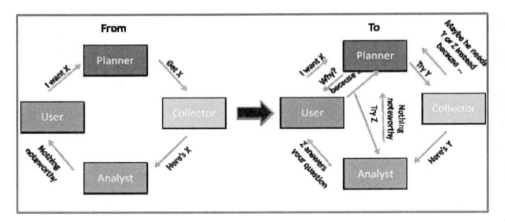

Figure 6. Desired Change in ISR Tasking Process.

Figure 6 captures the key changes needed but is simplistic. A more desired end state is illustrated in Figure 7.

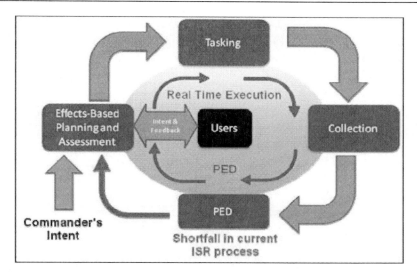

Figure 7. Effects-Based ISR Tasking Process.

By focusing efforts toward achieving an effect, multi-platform collection strategies will be refined, the intent of the user will be satisfied, and inappropriate ISR requests caused by lack of user knowledge on ISR capabilities is nullified. Effects-based ISR enables analysts to be more innovative and creative in developing collection strategies and fusing multi-INT data streams. To free up the analyst to problem-solve and strategically plan, automated methods must be developed (or improved) to focus the analyst more quickly on questionable activity and automated tools built to accomplish routine bookkeeping tasks.

A feedback mechanism is critical to successful effects-based ISR to assure user intent is met. Ideally, this feedback mechanism involves a real-time communications link between the user, analyst, and collector to facilitate immediate re-attack of a target deck while the platform is still in the area of interest. This real-time collaboration also allows the folding in of emergent opportunities of higher priority to the user.

3.2.3. A Formal Approach to Need-Based Analysis

It is important to allocate ISR resources based on a rigorous portfolio management process that balances desired operational needs today and those anticipated in the future. COIN ISR requirements should be seen in the context of the full spectrum of irregular warfare ISR requirements. In addition, COIN ISR requirements should be seen in the context of the ISR requirements for hybrid, multi-modal security operations. The Task Force believes that there is substantial overlap in the ISR resources required along this spectrum. However, the budget process has failed to recognize COIN operations as distinct from CT, C-IED and other irregular warfare requirements. This caused the ISR requirements process to skew against, and in some cases, overlook important COIN-related ISR capabilities, resulting in an underinvestment of Phase 0 and Phase 1 COIN operation ISR requirements as they relate to incipient insurgencies and population-centric security operations. Applying a formal portfolio management approach would ensure a more rigorous and transparent process by which ISR resource allocations can be made in support of COIN and all other inter-related modes of security operations.

Such a process can be applied at a number of echelons from, for example, a specific ISR mission plan, to the PED process, to the overall ISR mission architecture, or to strategy level for major ISR acquisition decisions. In each case, the key is to start with the objectives and determine the best option rather than the more tempting practice of starting with the familiar option. As noted in a previous DSB report, the use of formal decision-support approaches (including systems analysis and operations research) can aid in the development of an ISR portfolio, as well as in the selection of specific resources to achieve specific purposes. 28

Following such an approach will help ensure that the complexity of COIN ISR requirements is fully appreciated, and that these requirements are given proper attention in the resource allocation process. Such an approach can help balance COIN and other requirements, and allow ISR resources to be acquired and managed in the context of the wider requirements of a more complex, whole-of-government approach.

3.3. TOR Task 3: What Changes Can Be Made in the ISR Process to Improve Support to COIN?

As noted previously, there exists an increasing emphasis on the use of a population-centric approach to defeating insurgencies and improving the likelihood that the governments the U.S. supports will gain the respect and allegiance of the populations they intend to govern. However, the current ISR process does not reflect this approach, focusing instead on the need to achieve kinetic effects.

This current, traditional approach will continue to be an important part of the nation's approach to COIN. At the same time, ISR approaches and resources must also address the need to support population-centric strategies to COIN. The Task Force's recommendations include the need to better balance ISR resources between both missions, where priority is given to troops in combat and then shifts back to the population-centric aspects of COIN when combat ends. If more resources are applied to COIN "left of bang," fewer resources might be needed later for both approaches.

Consequently, the Task Force's response to this TOR question is framed in two ways:

- Discussions that relate to physical phenomenology associated with traditional counterinsurgency operations as practiced today in Afghanistan; and
- Discussions that relate to the application of social sciences, largely in the context of whole of government, population centric approaches to COIN.

3.3.1. ISR Support to Traditional Coin Activities

There appears to be no effective overarching, inter-agency COIN strategy, commitment, or coordination mechanism, despite the mandate by government leaders to adopt a whole-of-government approach. COIN operations appear to be assigned to DoD because of its greater capacity to meet the COIN challenge than other government agencies. Other USG entities (e.g., DoS, USAID, Treasury, Commerce) do not have the resources to carry out this mission today; nor do they have the perception that COIN is among their primary responsibilities. The Task Force raises these points to describe the environment in which the IC finds itself and the nature of the customer demands placed on it.

One of the implications of this situation is that there exists a lack of defense intelligence emphasis on operations planning and support for Phase 0 shaping and deterrence activities (see the earlier discussion on the phases of insurgencies in Section 3.2.3). The defense intelligence community is understandably focused on support of ongoing combat operations. Intelligence resources are allocated to support current operational priorities rather than Phase 0 shaping and deterrence activities in other areas of the world. Operational planning that drives intellectual effort and capability requirements for future contingencies was deemphasized because of the demands of current operations and a planning process that does not focus on the prevention of insurgencies.

The relatively low priorities assigned to covering the early phases of insurgencies (when insurgents are establishing their domination of a local population or establishing themselves at the expense of a government's sovereign prerogatives) have had a very real impact on the effectiveness of intelligence to warn of insurgent threats. For example, if an analyst has an innovative idea on how ISR might be applied to identify the early stages of an insurgency where "not much is happening," the analyst must first link the concept to an existing Commander's CONOP; otherwise nothing will get done. In the field, ISR assets are so scarce that they are allocated to locations where things are known, rather than places where things are relatively unknown. Intelligence analysts discovered through painful experience that the lack of activity in an area does not mean there is nothing of interest about which to be concerned. In 2004-2005, for example, United States Central Command (CENTCOM) intelligence analysts were providing all-source analytical support to the Combined Joint Task Force (CJTF)-76. Two brigades were deployed in the east of Afghanistan (one north and one south). The Taliban attacked every night in the east, so all of the limited ISR assets were allocated to track the enemy there. This meant that the interior of the country went largely uncovered, and as a result, during this period analysts missed how the insurgents were rebuilding themselves there.

To help remedy this problem, regional commands should set aside some portion of assets to focus on strategic changes that might be underway in regions where insurgencies are starting to take hold, even if there are few direct observations indicating that this is happening. The Task Force learned that those components of the IC responsible for COIN are constantly struggling to have some ISR resources available to track trends that are evolving over long periods of time as well as for discovering emerging threats (as opposed to only supporting tactical operations and force protection). Mission managers need to dedicate at least some resources to this strategic function and design a campaign plan that explains how these ISR assets would be used to inform the strategic components of the COIN fight, even if most of the resources are aligned with the tactical fight.

Even if the problem of allocating collection assets to strategic issues is solved, the overarching problem of understanding collection requirements will remain, as a requirements template for COIN ISR does not appear to exist. The Task Force found that within the IC there was no formalized set of ISR requirements for COIN (specifically in Afghanistan) nor was there an attempt to disaggregate and assign them, identify the gaps, develop metrics, allocate resources, and address progress. It appears that the *USG Integrated Civilian-Military Campaign Plan for Support to Afghanistan* was not formally addressed by the IC as an ISR requirements document, and ISR resources were not allocated necessarily to support it. More generally, the IC appears to have no structured requirements acceptance and management process for assessing, negotiating, acting upon, and overseeing a specific customer's intelligence needs when they are expressed in terms customers understand, rather than in terms familiar to the IC; that is, they are articulated in customer-speak rather than IC-speak. Some customers do not know how to communicate formally with the IC to ensure their requirements are addressed. As a result, COIN intelligence requirements are not materially impacting ISR collections. As evidence, the Task Force notes that the defense intelligence community has not translated the commander's intent as stated in the *USG Integrated Civilian-Military Campaign Plan for Support to Afghanistan* into intelligence requirements to support COIN operations. Although this plan was promulgated to articulate the strategy and tasks required to achieve U.S. and allied COIN objectives, there is no associated set of intelligence requirements derived to support execution of the plan. Nor is there a standing template of intelligence requirements to support COIN operations in general.

Looking at the problem from the IC's perspective, there are no mechanisms for systematically recording and following up on the satisfaction of intelligence requirements as they pertain to the different components of a COIN campaign. For example, the requirements database called COLISEUM does not provide the context behind requests for information. As a result, most requirements are levied outside the COLISEUM process through one-on-one discussions and emails.

To remedy this situation, the Task Force recommends that the DNI and the USD(I) undertake a comprehensive inventory of intelligence requirements as they pertain to COIN, including who originated the requirements, how they are recorded and distributed to the IC, the priority, and an assessment of how well the IC is servicing those requirements. Such an inventory should serve as the first step in developing a comprehensive, systematic process for guiding IC collection and analysis to support customer needs with respect to COIN.

The information needs of COIN and other complex operations require a mix of collection capabilities from many intelligence disciplines. Current methods for planning and financing future conflicts are largely driven by planning for Major Combat Operations (MCOs). This leads to an imbalance of future investment weighted toward large collection systems. This includes wide area persistent surveillance capabilities, full motion video (FMV), signals intelligence (SIGINT), ground moving target indication (GMTI), laser detection and ranging, computer network exploitation, financial intelligence (FININT), document exploitation, HUMINT, and biometrics. DoD fielded and programmed a vast array of technical collection capabilities that can be employed effectively to meet the traditional COIN challenge.

HUMINT and Special Operations Forces (SOF) that are assigned in a particular country or region over an extended period of time are particularly valuable assets for collecting information to support COIN operations. Case officers and Special Forces personnel who are immersed in the language and culture of a particular society are critical sources for collecting information to keep a finger on the pulse of a population and support COIN operations. For example, the *Marine Corps Expeditionary Intelligence Road Map* (now in draft) highlights the need for archiving and modeling social dynamics within particular cultures; effectively bringing together the work of hundreds of analysts for use by the United States Marine Corps (USMC). This work must be encouraged and allowed to grow. But often this is not happening. One senior intelligence officer with years of field experience pointed out that mid level managers at major intelligence agencies do not encourage language training or tours in the field, and in some cases discourage these altogether. The Task Force outlined throughout this report some recommendations, which if implemented in a sustained manner, will help improve the IC's ability to understand and report on local cultures.

In recent years the DoD's ISR collection investment necessarily focused on meeting the requirements of the current conflict, resulting in the procurement of a suite of sensors and platforms that are optimized for collection in desert and mountainous terrains. Moreover, these sensors are largely designed (and employed) to support F3 operations that are necessary for conducting CT and combat operations. This emphasis leaves DoD potentially short in the ability to collect in other types of terrain. (e.g. jungle) as well as other phases of the COIN mission (e.g., where insurgents may be starting to "turn" a population group). In addition, the mass of data being collected by the platforms and sensors currently in use is forcing the need to build a more effective PED capability, one that provides swifter forensics to examine and analyze antecedent activities, allows for all-source analysis, and makes better use of bandwidth and communication capabilities. Substantial efforts of DoD's ISR Task Force are underway to address this problem, but new PED systems and TTPs must be employed to handle the flood of new collection data. This will necessitate massive changes in culture to permit more automation, the discarding of less useful data, and the acceptance of new formats of ISR reporting.

Within the current operational environment, there are few effective, temporally acceptable methodologies for the integration (or fusion) of current levels of data streaming from the many space-based, airborne, mobile, in situ, and terrestrial remote sensors, let alone real time integration. This impedes DoD's ability to leverage multiple, networked sensor/platform combinations in a timely fashion to achieve dominant situational awareness. This fusion problem will only be exacerbated by the flood of data from new collection systems about to be fielded.

Efforts are underway to correct the massive problems of data access. The Information Sharing Integrated Product Team (IPT), established under the auspices of the USD(I), for the purpose of synchronizing information sharing initiatives in support of ISAF requirements and United States forces in Afghanistan, made substantial progress. However, the ISR Task Force should visit each of the main dissemination nodes (such as the Distributed Common Ground Station (DCGS)) to determine the extent to which analysts there have the necessary tools to execute their basic COIN mission and make necessary "quick fix" investments to remedy shortfalls.

In addition, the portfolio analysis approach described in the previous section would also help establish a better, short-term portfolio and balance of ISR resources for current COIN operations. Over time, expanded simulation, gaming, and field testing should be employed to support assessments of how ISR collection and analysis can be improved as it applies to a COIN campaign. For example, collection geometries of target areas are different for each region where insurgencies exist or could take root. For instance, Afghanistan is predominately rural, with high elevations, widely dispersed long and narrow settlements, and few vehicles; while Iraq has one large densely-populated urban area, where vehicles are attractive targets for tracking.

To facilitate this simulation effort, DoD might consider modifying or constructing a test range in mountainous terrain designed to assess COIN issues. Such a range might include widely-dispersed "villages" to facilitate and evaluate new collection and sampling strategies, as well as to test alternative security CONOPS and policies.

Finally, there is no apparent formal IC process for assessing IC performance against a customer's all-source requirements (i.e., metrics) – specifically for COIN – and measuring the opportunity cost for implementing such new requirements.[29] Further, metrics that evaluate progress of the insurgency, as seen from the viewpoint of the insurgent leadership, are a critical and often overlooked intelligence requirement.[30] This "red" perspective analysis must draw upon a deep understanding of the values and goals of insurgent leadership. A review of potential metrics for intelligence support to COIN should be undertaken by USD(I) (and perhaps the DNI) as part of an overall audit of intelligence requirements.

3.3.2. ISR in Support of Whole-of-Government, Population-Centric Coin Initiatives

Almost all definitions of COIN operations call for the involvement and constructive participation of the whole-of-government, with civilian agencies in the lead and the military in a supporting role – an approach outlined by the 2009 *U.S. Government Counterinsurgency Guide*. The active and constructive participation and leadership of allies, NGOs, a target nation's legitimate government, and the affected population, as well as the military, working together based on a coherent strategy is the most likely path to achieving U.S. COIN objectives. DoD leaders should make the case for such a strategy and work with leaders of other agencies to create the capacity for a whole-of-government approach. ISR resource planning should take into account the needs of a whole-of-government approach, and the need to support DoD and non-DoD components.

In a similar vein, ISR resource planning should accommodate emerging population-centric concepts as well. DoD has taken some steps in this direction. Studies on patterns-of-life and the use of human terrain intelligence yielded operational benefits in recent COIN campaigns. A Defense Science Board 2006 Summer Study noted:

> Human terrain preparation will enable U.S. forces to better understand how individuals, groups, societies and nations behave, and then use this information to (1) improve the performance of U.S. forces and (2) understand and shape behaviors of others in pre-, intra-, and post-conflict situations.[31]

The DSB's 2006 report, MG Flynn's observations concerning Afghanistan, and GEN McChrystal's efforts to bolster the use of these concepts underscore the need for more aggressive adoption throughout the DoD. The 2006 DSB report noted that Human Terrain Preparation should receive priority attention as well as a "continuous learning environment for training and professional military education."[32] In spite of these recurring observations about the criticality of this kind of intelligence most DoD ISR assts remain ill-suited to this kind of cultural, linguistically-based sociological, anthropological collection and reporting. In some quarters, there exists resistance to the recognition that population-centric approaches are useful, and that the social sciences necessary to enable these approaches can effectively contribute to COIN. In this regard, the following discussion addresses some of the needs and challenges facing DoD's ISR enterprise if it uses social sciences to more effectively address some of these unfulfilled requirements.

To be clear, research and analysis in the social sciences is far different from the legacy F3 missions normally associated with ISR. However, if DoD ISR is not prepared to support this research and analysis, how will it get done? And, if there is a need for getting out in front of insurgencies before they take root, should there not be a process in place to identify regional problems before they become full blown and require the massive cost of a military intervention?

Seen in this light, investments in ISR analytical capabilities that employ the social sciences seem reasonable. However, the DoD has a long way to go before it has a meaningful analytic cadre that can produce these assessments. An informal survey at one agency revealed that analysts operated largely by induction, studying and gaining familiarity with a country/region, and specific instances of an event and its analogues. Very little, if any deductive analyses using standard research techniques from social science, anthropological, or psychological disciplines were employed.

If DoD places a new emphasis on understanding socio-psychological and anthropological phenomena among societies affected or targeted by insurgencies, analysts will have to operate with a better balance of regional knowledge and theoretical/methodological competence. The regional expertise will continue to be essential, but will have to grow more specific and deeper as a basis for understanding the customs, culture, values, and semiotics of a society to see the insurgents and insurgency—as well as coalition forces and actions— through the populations' eyes. The masterful and rigorous use of theory (e.g., of social adaptation, of governance and democratization, economic development, and group dynamics) will be necessary to help analysts understand and predict events beyond what is familiar or covered in their experience.

If the IC wants to augment its expertise in social science and anthropological research techniques for use in COIN campaigns, it must rely on colleges and universities to train future analysts in how to ethically gather and process data from populations that are subject to insurgencies. However, academia is ill-equipped to do this and is likely to be pre- disposed to look at this mission with ambivalence.

Academic ambivalence in military matters has deep roots. The American Anthropological Association (AAA) and other elements of the social sciences disciplines tend to avoid efforts in which their research is used to enable coercive activities, such as military operations. As a result, social scientists tend to avoid situations in which their work may be structured explicitly to support those operations. The AAA appears aware, however, of the potential utility of the work of social scientists in understanding environments important to U.S. national security. This study recognizes the importance of social scientists' research and the utility of that research to help planners understand the environments in which they operate. The nature of the debate taking place among social scientists was highlighted by the work of the Commission on the Engagement of Anthropology with the U.S. Security and Intelligence Communities. The Commission looked at the work of the Army's Human Terrain System (HTS) and concluded that:

> While we stress that constructive engagement between anthropology and the military is possible, (the Commission) suggests that the AAA emphasize the incompatibility of HTS with disciplinary ethics and practice for job seekers and that it further recognize the problem of allowing HTS to define the meaning of □anthropology□ within DoD.[33]

Additional engagement between social science practitioners and the IC will be necessary if COIN is to gain further benefit from the use of these disciplines.

In addition, a University Department Head noted to the Task Force that most colleges and universities are no longer interested in supporting social science, anthropological, economic, or even political science research on those regions in which insurgencies take root. Today, academic interests are on the consequences of globalization, on applying models based on rational choice (decisions that are based on economic interests), and on the relationship between state and non-state actors. Area studies departments have largely been closed down, in part because funding dried up and in part because models of human behavior that are currently in favor treat cultural, religious, or regional affiliations as largely irrelevant.[34] The lack of academic disciplines with a regional-focus is a major reason why MG Flynn issued a call for the intelligence equivalent of DoD's Afghan Hands Program.[35]

Enlisting the aid of nationally recognized experts in psychological assessment of individual differences, the DoD and the IC could assess their analytic corps on these dimensions for the purpose of selecting and assigning analysts to the COIN missions. By a similar token, educational psychologists and training professionals might aid in designing curricula and training modules to help analysts develop and enhance these capabilities. They could also design curricula for training intelligence analysts in cultural assessment using the latest scientific findings on cultural dynamics and comparative cultures.

Colleges and universities have yet to sense a "demand signal" from the DoD (or the USG generally) for a major investment in area studies, whether on Afghanistan, Somalia, Indonesia, Mali, the Philippines or even those parts of India that are home to the Naxalite insurgents. At best, academia has created "virtual" area programs that represent a hodgepodge of courses from existing departments (Economics, Social Science, Political Science, and the like), coupled to language training. This is not nearly enough. The absence of academic support for research and analysis on regional problems that could lead to future insurgencies poses a credible vulnerability to U.S. national security posture.

Nonetheless, there exist pockets of excellence throughout DoD (e.g., the Defense Language Institute, USMC University) that provide very high quality and relevant training and education in the areas of language skill and cultural awareness for military personnel that are preparing for deployment or focusing on immediate defense priorities. That said, DoD and its primary feeder, academia, lack the capacity to meet the demand for people with advanced language skills and cultural awareness for the current conflict. The shortcomings are even greater for the many languages and areas of the world where the next COIN situation might occur.

The Task Force recognizes that the U.S. Army has made great efforts to incorporate social science and behavioral science into COIN planning via the HTS. The HTS was developed in response to gaps in commanders' and staffs' understanding of the local population and culture, and its impact on operational decisions; and poor transfer of socio-cultural knowledge to follow-on units. The HTS approach is to place the expertise and experience of social scientists and regional experts, coupled with reach-back, open-source research, directly in support of deployed units engaging in full-spectrum operations. This program is the first instance in which social science research, analysis, and advising has been done systematically, on a large scale, and at the operational level. Human Terrain Teams advise brigades on economic development, political systems, and tribal structures; train brigades as requested; and conduct research on topics of interest to the brigade staff. However, further development and application of ISR capabilities rooted in the social sciences will require a better understanding of the concerns of practitioners in these fields, ways to address their concerns, and more rigorous analysis of data gathered in the field.

As good as these initiatives are, the IC still has a long way to go to prepare its analysts to answer the questions pertaining to COIN that are asked of them. The Task Force found that intelligence components in the field often adhere to preferences in analytic tradecraft that can get in the way of addressing population-focused COIN issues. Some of these tradecraft preferences include:

- Placing more stock in quantitative methodological rigor over qualitative local knowledge;
- A tendency to misinterpret culturally-coded signals within the broader intelligence chatter;
- A preference for input metrics rather than results oriented output metrics; and
- Implicitly accepting Western concepts of state building, which prompts a focus on top down institutional structures rather than a bottom up approach of societal indicators.

Each of these preferences is familiar in one degree or another to the seasoned intelligence officer and in many ways is perfectly reasonable given, for example, the experience that analysts bring to the job and the understandable desire to rely on specific, quantifiable data in order to "get it right." But these preferences can lead to very real shortfalls in preparing assessments that address the population-centric issues of COIN. Understanding population behavior and determining who has power and who does not often has an historical basis that requires a greater depth of knowledge of a village, district, or province than can be acquired through the "snapshots" of village life gleaned from traditional intelligence sources. Something more is needed.

As useful as the HTS was in supporting operations directed against the insurgents, it was less useful in those missions focused on security requirements of local villagers, governance issues, and social control, particularly in Afghanistan's village-centric environment. What seems to be missing is a structured approach to documenting and analyzing trends in the behavior of population groups at the local level and understanding how villagers organize to govern themselves—in effect using social control assessments to explain how each political actor influences the behavior of population groups to support both attack planning and civil initiatives; and to measure and affect a government's capacity to govern legitimately at the local level. This problem is particularly evident in Afghanistan.

This shortfall was illuminated by one scholar who conducted extensive field research in Afghanistan, identifying and diagnosing the inherent tensions between Community Development Councils (CDCs) and customary organizations at the village level (village elders, mullahs, and government representatives). CDCs, which are promoted at the national level by the Ministry of Rural Rehabilitation and Development, facilitate the flow of resources at the local level. However, they also can have the effect of creating parallel structures of governmental control that may not be accepted by the local population. This researcher concluded that decentralized state building, not under the control of a national ministry, would actually improve the prospect for state development and would provide a more effective path for countering insurgents.

Despite best efforts, critical gaps remain in the USG's knowledge about why people join insurgencies and why they choose to leave. This critical question of "why" requires the USG to develop a deeper understanding of cultural dynamics that can only come through field research done on a systematic basis with social science techniques and procedures.

The DoD needs to understand how to gather information on local attitudes and beliefs. Polling firms know how to do this. The DoD should understand how they go about gathering information, how they understand and assess the environment, and their process for sharing that data. The DoD can reach out to private sector firms as well as social science researchers in academia (a good model for doing this is, for example, the Rich Contextual Understanding Project sponsored by Office of the Under Secretary of Defense for Acquisition, Technology and Logistics (AT&L)).

A foundation on which to build does exist. The Foreign Area Officer (FAO) program represents a resource that merits additional investment. FAOs can bring to COIN operations in all phases, deep understanding of the populations and geographic elements subject to insurgent and COIN operations. FAOs, however, are seen to suffer from a lack of career prospects, given their deep specialization. Effective COIN planning and ISR would benefit significantly from a strengthened FAO cadre, one that rewards sustained specialization in regions and countries in which U.S. interests are at stake.

All of this will take time, but some important steps can and should be taken in the near term. To that end, the Task Force proposes a measured approach that would help lay the framework for moving toward a whole-of-government solution:

- The USD(I), in collaboration with the DNI, should develop a strategic plan for developing links and processes to both the academic community and the USG civilian agencies, specifically to rally resources for population-centric counterinsurgency efforts intended to forestall active insurgencies. This strategic plan would have as its top priority the following goals:
    o DoD and the government generally should increase investment in social science disciplines (anthropology, ethnography, human geography, sociology, social-psychology, political science, and economics) to inform a whole-of-government approach to understanding local cultures and customs and to support future COIN campaigns.
    o Similar investments should be made in both basic and applied field research, following the guidelines of the specific academic discipline.
    o In the near term, improve cultural intelligence by adopting best practices across DoD intelligence components. The USD(I) should take a detailed look at the *Marine Corps Expeditionary Intelligence Road Map* (and other, similar initiatives) to determine which elements of cultural training, social science modeling, and database archiving could be adopted by the larger IC.
    o DoD should establish a long term commitment to grow area studies expertise by funding programs and endowing area studies chairs at academic institutions nationwide. This recommendation will be even more effective if it is accompanied by a supporting infrastructure that provides field researchers with the tools and techniques to assess local governance and economic conditions and to interact effectively with local populations.

3.4. TOR Task 4: What Can Be Done in the Immediate Future to Improve Network Agility and Information Sharing Across the Broad Spectrum of Mission Partners Conducting COIN and During the Promotion of Regional Stability?

3.4.1. The Current Situation

A multiplicity of ISR platforms supports U.S. intelligence collection activities around the globe today. The numbers and variety of sensors and platforms are steadily increasing, especially in Afghanistan. Moreover, DoD has fielded and programmed acquisition of a vast array of technical collection platforms and capabilities that can be employed effectively to address collection support for irregular warfare. Because of the immediacy and criticality of the current conflicts, DoD has not balanced technical collection capabilities with the PED required to more broadly make sense of the data and employ it effectively to support the operational level planning and execution across all phases of COIN operations.

The DoD is also seeing a dramatic growth in the variety, velocity, and volume of data collected by defense ISR platforms. However, the rapid increase of collected data will not be operationally useful without the ability to store, process, exploit, and disseminate this data. The programmed expansion of broad area, full motion video and other advanced sensors will further exacerbate this problem. Communications bandwidth remains an operational constraint both for pushing intelligence out to the tactical edge and for reach back from the theater of operations. Current collection generates data that greatly exceeds the ability to organize, store, and process it. Moreover, this PED gap will grow quickly as new platforms and sensors come into use.

This deficiency results in serious missed opportunities for the nation. First, these processing shortfalls limit the Department's ability to use that data to answer a commander's existing Priority Intelligence Requirements (PIRs) and other important requirements, especially for historical and trend analysis, and for any questions that would benefit from automated (or even semi-automated) fusion of massive, noisy, data. Second, these massive data are collected around the world using a wide range of observational phenomenon. It is entirely possible that the data that ends up "on the floor" could be used to improve the U.S.'s ability to generate foundation data around the globe.

Another major impediment in the current processing shortfall is the shortage of cleared personnel proficient in the languages and cultures of interest. The shortfall becomes more pronounced when considering high risk regions that are not currently the center of attention. In consequence, the defense intelligence community does not have the foreign language and culture depth and breadth necessary to plan and support COIN operations. Foreign language proficiency is essential to gain perspective and comprehend the thinking and values of foreign political cultures. The shortage of foreign language skills adversely affects, among other things, the exploitation of HUMINT, SIGINT, and document exploitation. The DoD is only beginning to make investments in enterprise level planning and execution of the intelligence information infrastructure so that oversight is provided and Services are held to standards. The recently created Defense Intelligence Information Enterprise (DI2E) is a step in the right direction. In addition, Service-specific data sharing networks must become interoperable with other networks and data must be discoverable.

Finally, data on COIN collected by intelligence systems are not accessible sufficiently by the civilian and coalition components that need it. At the policy level, security rules and classification of information prevent sharing. At the technical level, the networks of allies and NGOs are often incompatible with U.S. systems, thereby limiting connectivity even when policy challenges are overcome. The USD(I) Information Sharing IPT has outlined some 400 specific findings that should be translated into action in areas that cover dissemination and discovery, using metadata to facilitate information sharing, achieving common security standards, supporting a Battlefield Information, Collection, and Exploitation System (BICES), augmenting support to foreign disclosure procedures, and improving knowledge management resources. One specific positive example of information sharing that is being put into place under USD(I) auspices is UnityNet. UnityNet seeks to encourage a self-sustaining, open sharing environment that provides open source data sharing for NGOs, coalition partners, and intelligence analysts alike. UnityNet is an environment where unclassified information can be pushed and shared without the constraints of classified networks. It also affords a mechanism to reach out to populations subject to insurgencies and provide them access to the global community via the Internet, thereby adding a measure of stability to afflicted regions.

The need for information sharing is challenged by recent experience with information releases through WikiLeaks. Nonetheless, better security measures (including the use of stronger cybersecurity techniques and counterintelligence practices) can enable wider information sharing without exposing sensitive information to unauthorized dissemination and exposure; complex COIN operations simply cannot succeed without rich information sharing.

3.4.2. Improvements in the Immediate Future

It is important to recognize the intensity of the resource limitations under which the DoD is operating, the growing severity of these limitations, and the enormous costs to sustain current operations in Iraq, Afghanistan, and elsewhere. The Task Force is aware of the demands of operational commanders for additional support in terms of more and more collection platforms and sensor systems. Given these intense pressures, it is difficult to imagine undertaking fundamentally new initiatives in the immediate future. However, improvements modest in their cost can be undertaken immediately. These improvements include more use of systems analysis, operations research, and planning efforts to improve the efficiencies of TTPs and limited ISR resources, and better inter-Service coordination to achieve efficiencies in interoperability of Service-specific systems. The Task Force strongly endorses the work of the ISR Task Force in improving the PED situation in the light of the coming enormous growth in collection data, and in responding as best they can to the demands of operational commanders. Training of ISR personnel – particularly interactive training wherein trainers can learn efficiencies from students who have relevant practical experience – can also be used to improve performance with current or fewer resources.

ISR commanders should reassess the balance between "need to know" and "need to share" in their own commands to ensure that the right intelligence is placed in the hands of *all* the people who need it, and arbitrary security restrictions are waived locally when required for successful completion of the mission.

The Task Force recognizes that dealing with insurgencies will also require access to a wide range of information that typically is not derived from traditional intelligence sources. These sources of information would include, for example, social science data developed from field research, data collected by civilian reconstruction teams that are deployed as part of a COIN effort, or data published in open source or by third parties (medical personnel, religious leaders, local business leaders, law enforcement, etc.). Mechanisms to collect, store, process, and share these data will be needed to enable COIN missions.

Finally, to whatever degree is possible in the near-term, ISR officers should take the time and expand their efforts to become more knowledgeable in the human terrain and cultural features of their areas of responsibility in order to be more responsive to operational commanders. This knowledge will enable them to provide those supported commanders a richer understanding of the situation - an understanding that includes the context in which decision must be made as well as the numbers of things in the area.

3.5. TOR Task 5: What Emerging Technologies and Methodologies, Combinations of Sensors, and Investments in Information Fusion and Analysis Are Likely to Provide the Highest Payoff?

Section 1 of this report provides an illustrative list of countries that represent a wide spectrum of different potential COIN environments. When considering the ISR capabilities needed for population centric operations (to include CT, COIN, FID, SO, and UW), planners must take into account this wide range of different environments. Nevertheless, there are a number of ISR related technologies, methodologies and bodies of scientific knowledge that prove useful in support of different TTPs, at different operational phases, over different geographies, and in very different kinds of population centric operations. The opportunities to advance these capabilities by expanding scientific and technical frontiers would ultimately yield benefits just as widely.

3.5.1. Computational Social Sciences/Social Network Analysis

All population centric operations require not only the ability to positively identify individuals within the population, but also to understand social structure in terms of the social relationships among the population. In the process of protecting the population from nefarious actors, various counter network operations must be undertaken. In order to conduct these efficiently, and without unnecessary collateral damage, social network analysis driven by the computational social sciences is critical. Advancing the frontiers of social science and technology through additional investment would have high leverage.

While these social networks can be derived in many ways, and through many different methodologies, increasingly the Internet and social media are critical sources of social network analysis data in societies that are not only literate, but also connected to the Internet. Monitoring the blogosphere and other social media across many different cultures and languages is emerging as a critical dimension of the computational social sciences and social network analysis. Investment in such activities is warranted in order to be prepared to deal with population centric operations. It is important to note, however, that the usefulness of this data is linked to the ability to employ the social sciences for its analysis, to spot meaningful trends, and to derive valid hypothesis pertinent to COIN challenges.

3.5.2. Behavior Modeling and Simulation

There is a major shortfall in the availability and maturity of modeling and simulation capabilities that support the planning, rehearsal, execution, and evaluation of population-centric operations. This shortfall crosses every dimension of the modeling and simulation value chain. The biggest gaps exist in the analysis tools that would support plan development for Phase 0 operations. These tools include valid models that emphasize the economic, diplomatic, and social interventions that could prevent a nascent insurgency from maturing. Social simulations such as multi-agent simulations show promise in this area but require further investment. Required investments should include foundation data on populations, human networks, geography, and other economic and social characteristics.[36] Human-in-the-loop simulations are beginning to be fielded to support very basic cultural training in support of the current conflict. However, these simulations do not generalize to other environments and require further investment to make them useful for the next potential conflict.

The key characteristic of COIN is its population-centric orientation. One tool to better understand and anticipate the actions of a population is behavioral modeling and simulation. The key challenges to this are:

1) "*Modeling strategy - matching the problem to the real world*: Difficulties in this area are created either by inattention to the real world being modeled or by unrealistic expectation about how much of the world can be modeled and how close a match between the model and world is feasible.

2) *Verification, validation, and accreditation*: These important functions often are made more difficult by expectations that verification, validation, and accreditation (VV&A) – as it has been defined for the validation of models of physical systems – can be usefully applied.

3) *Modeling tactics – designing the internal structure of the model*: Problems are sometimes generated by unwarranted assumptions about the nature of the social, organizational, cultural, and individual behavior domains, and sometimes by a failure to deliberately and thoughtfully match the scope of the model to the scope of the phenomena to be modeled.

4) *Differences between modeling physical phenomena and human behavior – dealing with uncertainty and adaption*: Problems arise from unrealistic expectation of how much uncertainty reduction is plausible in modeling human and organization behavior, as well as from poor choices in handling the changing nature of human structures and processes.

5) *Combining components and federating models*: Problems arise from the way in which linkages within and across levels of analysis change the nature of system operation. They occur when creating multilevel models and when linking together more specialized models of behavior into a federation of models."[37]

The Department would benefit from more basic and applied research in automated tools and techniques that reason with massive amounts of data including unstructured text. Such work would support the creation of a "social radar" sensor whose output could be fused with more traditional sensor outputs to more efficiently and effectively improve population focused situational awareness. There are a number of efforts currently underway that show promise in this area. Two examples, the Defense Advanced Research Projects Agency (DARPA) Integrated Crisis Early Warning System (ICEWS) and the Office of Naval Research's (ONR) Human Social Culture Behavioral Modeling Program (HSCB) represent attempts to exploit unstructured data.[38] Although these efforts and others do not yet meet immediate operational needs, they represent the promise this data may hold in addressing the COIN challenge, both in the near future and in the long term.

Finally, technology can also be employed to understand what is normal in a particular environment, thus helping spot trends that represent anomalies that may portend long-term changes and the rise of instability.

3.5.3. Natural Resource Monitoring

Increasingly, population-centric operations will be needed in nascent resource conflicts, whether based on water crises, agricultural stress, environmental stress, or rents to be achieved from precious mineral resources. Understanding agricultural and hydrological dynamics via remote sensing, terrestrial monitoring and predictive modeling could be essential to understanding incipient or stabilizing social dynamics. A crop failure or a water crisis could precipitate insurgency, or undermine hard won stabilization efforts. Environmental distress that could undermine traditional industry (dependent on fishing, and the like) could do the same. To foresee such crises allows commanders and decision-makers to allocate resources that might prevent a wide-spread population crisis and resultant insurgency.

Such crises, of course, are often driven by rapidly growing populations which outgrow the natural carrying capacity of the land they occupy. Population bulges are being observed in many unstable geographies as a key factor in driving instability. Monitoring population demographics as an organic part of the natural resource framework is key in anticipating difficult security situations before they happen.

Also, understanding mineral deposits within a region is critical. They must be understood in terms of the global mineral/mining industry's understanding, as they establish the market and market price for such resources. They must also be understood in terms of the local power-broker's understanding, as they could be used to instigate security crises that provide them tactical advantage over such resources. Rare earth minerals could be geopolitical flashpoints in regions of the world where vulnerable populations are used as pawns. Monitoring such minerals, and even the impact of their mining, on the larger natural resources/population dynamics framework is critical to ward off unnecessary population-centric operations.

3.5.4. Overhead Video Surveillance

Overhead video surveillance is one capability that is widely applicable across the entire spectrum of population-centric operations. However, it is clear that technological challenges related to persistence, spatio-temporally coincident multi-phenomenological collection, and real-time PED (including communication) limit the effectiveness of overhead video surveillance with regard to particular classes of population-centric requirements.

Not all overhead FMV is the same, certainly in terms of its applicability to population-centric operations. Different combinations of sensors, platforms, communications, and PED can provide different fields of view, different resolutions (both natively and at the point of exploitation), different geo-locational accuracies, different phenomenological cross-sections (Electro-Optical (EO), Infrared (IR), Synthetic Aperture Radar (SAR)/GMTI, Spectral, SIGINT, etc.), different levels of persistence, and different degrees of timeliness. Earlier forms of FMV offered a narrow field of view, moderate resolution, poor geo-locational accuracy, phenomenologically simple (EO only) data, with little persistence, but with real-time data downlink. This constellation of capability required that multiple FMV assets be coordinated, either to maintain persistence as each platform completed its feasible on-station dwell time, or to track multiple targets dispersing from a given surveillance location. Whether dealing with targeted kill/capture operations, or monitoring human dynamics within a population, commanders are demanding longer persistence, wider field of view, better resolution, better geo-locational accuracy, and multiple phenomenologies, all with real-time downlink.

Capabilities such as DARPA's Argus are certainly moving in this direction. However, Argus is a platform-agnostic sensor package, which has observational characteristics that are bound to the achievement of airborne persistence at a certain altitude. Persistence, then, requires advancement in airborne platforms that offer the kind of size, weight and power (SWaP) characteristics needed to achieve long dwell. Persistence of such a capability (or even of more than one such capability in a given airspace) also then requires high bandwidth communications solutions that fall outside of the traditional RF domain, as battlefield spectrum is increasingly saturated. Persistence over such a wide area field of view requires computer-assisted tracking of both vehicles and dismounts, as otherwise the exploitation of this data will be human-intensive, and will not scale.

Consensus appears to exist for the achievement of such a persistent, wide field of view, high-resolution, geospatially-accurate, multi-phenomenology, real-time downlinked overhead surveillance capability with a computer-aided tracking solution. This capability would be of use across operational phases and across different kinds of population-centric operations. Yet, it would require not only substantial technological leaps, but also the commoditization of such technology, if the defense and intelligence communities are to effectively (and cost-effectively) field the needed number of combat air patrols (CAPs) of such a capability.

3.5.5. *Improvements to Characterizing Terrain*

When conducting population-centric operations, mission planning, rehearsal, and execution all depend upon the availability of human-scale terrain data – particularly when operations are arrayed over urban and complex terrain. Both LiDAR and SAR technologies have been harnessed in order to generate large volumes of terrain data of such scales, though many scientific and technical limitations prevent such terrain data from becoming ubiquitous. Older photogrammetric techniques are still viable when stereo imagery is available, but achieving human-scale terrain models of useful post spacing or better is still a technical challenge with commercial satellite imagery.

Such terrain data is of great value in augmenting full motion video processing, which often requires high-resolution base imagery and terrain data in order to be properly registered. It is also critical to effectively geo-locating SIGINT at a human scale.

Technologies for extracting 3D features from such high resolution terrain data have been developed under DARPA and Advanced Concept Technology Demonstration (ACTD) efforts, but there are still considerable technological hurdles to be overcome before a LiDAR or SAR collect can be transformed in near-real time into an actionable mission-planning, rehearsal, and execution dataset. The management of such data (for instance the LiDAR .las point cloud with gridded terrain surfaces, 3D feature data, and behavioral data must be imputed to these features, e.g., door movements) is a technological frontier itself, which will require considerable work.

In the end, the realization of a force structure capable of succeeding at the full spectrum of population-centric operations will require the existence of high resolution 3D terrain data over the extent of this population, and any adjacent havens for nefarious actors.

The value conveyed by traditional ISR phenomenologies is highly dependent upon the availability of foundational data of the requisite scale, over which the ISR data can be arrayed. In the case of COIN ISR, this foundational data includes human-scale data of the physical and built terrain. In general, the ability of ISR assets to successfully support COIN depends on the availability of such foundational data, which is often collected not by the IC, but by the topographic engineering community.

3.5.6. Processing, Exploitation, and Dissemination (PED)

Too often, PED is used as a monolithic catchall category to address everything beyond a sensor and platform. This often serves to obscure the actual technology, policy, and tradecraft challenges that face the effective use of a particular sensor for a particular mission. Often, the term PED is narrowly applied to the realms of imagery intelligence (IMINT) (including FMV) and SIGINT, providing inadequate focus to the challenges posed by a truly cross-organization, multi-mission, multi-INT requirement.

Different aspects of PED and some persistent technical challenges in the realm of PED are addressed below.

3.5.6.1. PED – Cloud Computing

Within the DoD and IC, there exists a lack of cloud computing capability (e.g., processing and storage) available on the key warfighting networks (e.g., SIPRNet, JWICS) for the deployment of ISR PED both at the tactical edge and within backoffice datacenter environments. Cloud computing offers the potential to gain resource efficiencies in a number of services (storage, processing, analytic applications). Secure cloud architectures are emerging that may merit deployment by the DoD and IC.

3.5.6.2. PED – Spatio-Temporal

The critical process of data fusion fundamentally requires a consistent spatiotemporal framework for organizing and indexing the data flowing from each intelligence and operational data source. While it is now widely recognized that SIGINT is made much more powerful when geolocated and exploited with the coincident geospatial intelligence (GEOINT) (e.g., IMINT, FMV, Mapping, Charting, and Geodesy (MC&G), human geography, etc.), it unfortunately has not been recognized that data from all INTs and operational sources would be much more valuable (particularly in support of population centric operations) when managed and fused within a common spatiotemporal context. All data and analytic products should be discoverable, browsable, and accessible both spatially and temporally. This would provide a PED that offers critical context to operators and analysts attempting to make sense of new incoming streams of data. Only then can PED infrastructures help operators and analysts to understand the "story."

3.5.6.3. PED – Cross-Domain and Classification

There is an unhealthy redundancy with which data is hosted across the national security community. Data is being overclassified by placing it on networks of a higher classification than the data. Combat commanders are invested with the authority and discretion to adjust the classification of data as needed in support of operational exigencies, however the complexity and rigidity of their information systems make it difficult to get electronic copies of these data from one domain to the other. The Unified Cross Domain Management Office (UCDMO) was established to mainstream Intelligence Community Directive (ICD) 503 PL4 and PL5 cross domain solutions that could reduce unnecessary redundancy and generate more efficient data release/declassification.[39] However, the UCDMO has had less impact on the cross domain capability of everyday networks then is needed, and further effort and priority should be applied in this area.

3.5.7. Human Terrain Data Collection and Management

There are still enormous challenges in the realm of human terrain data management. Standardized and well-accepted data schemas have yet to be developed for use in various deployed capabilities, particularly schemas that are temporally-enabled, allowing operators and analysts to track change over time, and even to understand historical dynamics that are relevant to present data human dynamics. Perhaps most importantly, human terrain data is largely not managed geospatially. Spatio-temporal management of human terrain data is key to effective commander decision-support. Mission planning, rehearsal and execution of population-centric operations fundamentally requires that the human terrain be arrayed across the high resolution 3D physical and built terrain. Without this, military commanders and other USG leaders cannot expect to successfully engage in an Intelligence Preparation of the Battlefield (IPB)-like process that could support population-centric operations.

Other social science frameworks, such as behavioral theories from anthropology and sentiment observation strategies (from polling and survey disciplines) also have important implications for the development of human terrain data management solutions. In the end, however, all such social science frameworks must support spatio-temporal encoding and analysis if it is to realize its potential to commanders, operators, and decision-makers.

3.5.8. Terrestrial Sensorwebs

In population-centric operations of all kinds, it is important to closely monitor what is going on over large tracts of land. However, in some cases, the achievement of persistence over a particular environment may not be feasible. Even if feasible, there is additional observational power that can be drawn from the deployment of distributed sensorwebs of mobile, *in situ*, and remote terrestrial sensors arrayed across a landscape.[40]

While defense/intelligence research and development (R&D) investment resulted in standards-based frameworks, such as the Open Geospatial Consortium's Sensor Web Enablement (OGC SWE) web services architecture, relatively little investment has been made in ensuring that all Tasking, Collection, Processing, Exploitation, and Dissemination (TCPED) have implemented OGC SWE interoperability specifications, in addition to legacy Application Program Interfaces (APIs). The achievement of OGC interoperability in general, and OGC SWE interoperability in particular, would have enormous mission benefits, ensuring that each space-based, airborne, mobile, *in situ,* and terrestrial remote sensor could be accessed as web-accessible services which can flexibly be re-deployed and reorchestrated in support of new mission challenges. As population-centric operations must adapt as the people adapt their behavior, it is important to have all kinds of ISR assets available for use outside of their particular TCPED stovepipes. Interoperability of each sensor at the network level is important, but interoperability of each sensor as a web-accessible service that complies with international, industry-driven, government-sponsored technical standards such as OGC SWE is even more vital.

3.5.9. Biometrics

In all phases of dealing with insurgencies, positive identification is necessary to effectively separate insurgents from the regular population. Historically, such positive identification was achieved by provisioning identification documents which were easily forged until the inclusion of rudimentary biometrics such as a finger print and/or photograph. As various forms of biometric technology emerged, positive identification has come to depend upon multiple forms of biometric authentication such as fingerprints, retina scans, and DNA samples. Great strides have been made in the realm of biometric measurement, storage and recall. However, distributing multiform biometric authentication technologies to the point of service of the most basic administrative processes has yet to take hold, undermining positive identification at critical junctures. In some cases, biometric enrollment has been used, but identification cards have not been provisioned based on this biometric enrollment. Moreover, there is often a lack of a larger identification infrastructure which might tie identity to all an individual's transactions. Only when each individual entity can be resolved, and all transactions are tied back to each unique entity, can the necessary positive identification be available for the conduct of population-centric operations.

3.5.10. Natural Language Processing

In literate societies, and particularly in connected societies, analysts and operators will often be faced with large volumes of textual data that they must tackle in the course of their operations. The more connected they are, the more likely this data will come in digital form. While natural language processing technologies for thematic clustering and entity extraction have become quite mature for English, they are less mature in many of the languages used in areas of the world that are likely candidates for population centric operations.

3.5.11. Operations Research

As COIN intelligence requirements are defined, enormous challenges emerge as to their realization. How can ISR resources be optimized against such a dynamic challenge?

Operations Research (OR) is the application of advanced analytical methods to help make better decisions.[41] OR has contributed to military and ISR issues since its inception. As early as 1942, the first president of the Institute for Operations Research and Management Sciences (INFORMS), Phillip Morse, organized the Anti-submarine Warfare Operations Research Group (ASWORG) for the US Navy who were faced with the problem of Nazi German Uboat attacks on transatlantic shipping. "That Morse's group was an important factor in winning the war is fairly obvious to everyone who knows anything about the inside of the war," wrote historian John Burchard.[42]

While the current challenges are certainly unique, one must draw upon the lessons learned on how to apply OR to ISR challenges. Previous deliberations of the Intelligence Task Force of the Defense Science Board on just this subject found that "Operations Research represents a powerful tool to help improve the quality of investment decision making by illuminating key issues, assumptions, and sources of information" yet "Operations Research is applied inconsistently throughout the Defense and ISR communities and each lacks standard OR processes and practices, and consistent organizational models or commitments."[43] This is still the case.

3.5.12. Cross Domain Technologies

Though it is often stated that information sharing is more of a policy, cultural or leadership issue, and less of a technical issue, the DoD and Intelligence Community is still very anemic in its use of ICD 503 PL5 cross domain security technologies that would allow data to flow more readily across security domains (of course, based on security markings). Mission environments are still dominated by colliding networks, each of which has slightly different security caveats that prevent information sharing, or make it prohibitively difficult. In recent years, substantial technical leaps have been made in cross domain technologies, removing the traditional bandwidth bottlenecks. Interesting implementations of such technologies have enabled email from multiple security domains to arrive in a single highside inbox, even with the ability to seamlessly reply. The widespread application of such cross domain technologies would vastly improve information sharing, and has the potential for vast cost savings in the area of network expenditures.

4. FINDINGS AND RECOMMENDATIONS

Section 3 conveys detailed observations and findings concerning a wide range of issues. This section provides the Task Force's most significant summary findings, as well as pertinent recommendations.

1. DoD Lacks a Common Understanding of COIN

The lack of a single authoritative definition of COIN is impeding a common understanding and unified approach to COIN operations within the DoD and across the USG. Accompanying this lack of definition is a multiplicity of COIN CONOPS.

Recommendation

The Under Secretary of Defense for Policy (USD(P)), in coordination with the Chairman, Joint Chiefs of Staff (CJCS), should promulgate a joint definition of COIN and use it to create a common understanding across the DoD Components and the USG. As a starting point,

USD(P) should consider the 2009 *U.S. Government Counterinsurgency Guide*, signed by the Secretaries of State and Defense, and the Administrator of the USAID.

2. DoD Has Assumed Responsibility for COIN ISR by Default

Despite a national strategy and civil military campaign plan that calls for a whole of government, population centric approach to COIN, the USG is not employing all elements of national power in the planning and conduct of COIN operations. DoD has assumed responsibility for virtually all COIN intelligence requirements by default. Indeed, apart from being a signatory to the 2009 *U.S. Government Counterinsurgency Guide,* the Department of State has shown little evident interest in building or supporting the partnership described by the *Guide*. This lack of partnership impedes progress toward wider approach to COIN.

Recommendation

The Secretary of Defense and the Chairman, Joint Chiefs of Staff should advocate the need for a comprehensive, whole of government approach to COIN with the National Security Council (NSC). The Secretary of Defense should look to the 2009 *U.S. Government Guide to Counterinsurgency* as a starting point for this approach.

The (USD(I)) should work with the Director of National Intelligence (DNI) to provide policy, guidance, and resources that enhance national and departmental IC support for COIN.

3. DoD and IC Officials Tend to Focus Narrowly on Airborne Technical Collection Capabilities and Systems Rather than on the Wider Capabilities Needed to Support COIN

This observation is supported by the fact that technical collection platforms command larger portions of the budget and produce more *immediate* effects rather than *longer term*, foundational information for population-centric operations. The Task Force notes that discussions with DoD senior officials regarding ISR for COIN turned frequently to the subject of technical collection systems and capabilities while excluding other collection sources (e.g. OSINT, HUMINT) and PED issues. The Defense Science Board's Summer Study of 2010 noted that in 2009 DoD represented 62 percent of the requirements for OSINT, but provided only 3 percent of OSINT funding.[44] The lack of attention to OSINT is buttressed by the report's finding that in 2009 DoD had only 14 percent of the IC's OSINT manpower, and funded that proportion largely through Defense budget supplementals.[45] Overall, these problems tend to exclude valuable sources of social and behavioral science data, including human geography.

Recommendation

The USD(I), in coordination with the Directors of the Defense Intelligence Agency (DIA), National Security Agency (NSA), National Geospatial Intelligence Agency (NGA), and National Reconnaissance Office (NRO), and the Service intelligence chiefs, should ensure policymakers, planners, warfighters and other users understand the breadth and depth of defense ISR requirements, shortfalls, and capabilities necessary to support COIN operations more effectively. This recommendation could be best implemented by a single authority, for example the proposed National Intelligence Manager (NIM) for Irregular Warfare/COIN.

4. ISR Capabilities Have Not Been Applied Effectively Against COIN Operations that Deal with Populations in Part Because a Comprehensive Set of Intelligence Requirements for COIN Does Not Exist

The defense intelligence community has not translated those aspects of commander's intent dealing with COIN into intelligence requirements, though the *United States Government Integrated Civilian-Military Campaign Plan for Support to Afghanistan* describes in detail the need to focus on population security, governance, and economic development. The reasons for this apparent reluctance to engage on this issue are varied, but one key reason is that intelligence agencies, at least those in the Washington D.C. area, tend to be reactive, waiting for questions to be asked, rather than trying to anticipate them. This approach may be too conservative in a period of rapid social change, promoted by instant communications.

Recommendation
The defense intelligence community should develop a set of high-level intelligence requirements for COIN that encompass the need to support current and near-term operations, as well as population-centric and whole-of-government approaches to COIN. In doing so, the defense intelligence community should look to the 2009 *U.S. Government Counterinsurgency Guide*, as a starting point for doctrine that can be used to drive high-level requirements. This recommendation could be best implemented by a single authority, for example the proposed NIM for Irregular Warfare/COIN.

In addition, senior intelligence managers should have the necessary experience to anticipate the needs of their customers. So as part of this recommendation, the Task Force suggests that senior intelligence officers (SES, O-6) serve forward for a period of time as, for example, a Deputy J2 or a Fusion Cell Director. Even if for only shorter deployments (i.e., 3 to 4 months at a time) this would be worth doing. These officers, having had this experience, would be able to drive intelligence analysis and support back in Washington, DC to anticipate problems and find creative solutions. The DoD should be prepared to do this on a consistent basis over prolonged periods of time (years if necessary).

5. The USG is Not Investing Adequately in the Development of Social and Behavioral Science Information that is Critically Important for COIN

Many, if not most, specific COIN ISR requirements are population centric and are not exclusively solvable with hardware or hard, physical science S&T solutions. One senior intelligence officer with years of field experience pointed out that 80 percent of useful operational data for COIN does not come from legacy intelligence disciplines. Good intelligence on COIN exists outside the traditional intelligence organizations.

Anthropological, sociocultural, historical, human geographical, educational, public health, and many other types of social and behavioral science data and information are needed to develop a deep understanding of populations. Such data, collected and analyzed using the scientific method, is vital to COIN success.

Recommendation

The DoD and IC should undertake discussions with authoritative representatives of the social sciences (e.g., the American Anthropological Association) to develop concepts by which the social sciences can be employed to gain sufficient understanding of the environments in which COIN operations might take place. DoD and the IC should develop and implement a program to support academic institutions nationwide in building research capabilities regarding countries and regions in which COIN operations might take place. DoD should build a stronger Foreign Area Officer program and more favorable career prospects for officers who engage in sustained country and region specific specialization. The USD(I), USD(P), USD(AT&L), and the DNI should jointly develop this capability.

6. ISR Support for COIN is Currently Overshadowed by CT and Force Protection Requirements

In real terms, ISR support of COIN is not as high a priority for the Combatant Commands, Military Departments, and Defense Agencies as CT and force protection, adversely impacting the effectiveness of COIN operations. COIN is not necessarily an alternative to CT; some ISR requirements are common to both kinds of operations, but COIN, particularly population-centric COIN, requires some ISR of its own.

Recommendation

The USD(I) should ensure the Military Intelligence Program (MIP) and National Intelligence Program (NIP) intelligence resources are allocated to enhance support of COIN.

The USD(I), in coordination with the USD(AT&L), USD Comptroller (C), Assistant Secretary of Defense for Special Operations / Low-Intensity Conflict and Interdependent Capabilities (SOLIC&IC), and the DNI should ensure that the Military Departments, Defense Agencies, and the U.S Special Operations Command (USSOCOM) are acquiring the ISR capabilities identified in this study to support COIN.

7. COIN ISR Has Not Been Addressed Early in the Conflict Spectrum and Has Not Sufficiently Included a Whole-of-Government Approach. The Lack of Focus on Incipient Insurgencies Limits Options and Increases Risk of Unrecoverable COIN Problems, Despite the Commitment of Major Military Forces

Insurgency has been the most prevalent form of armed conflict since at least 1949. Despite that fact, following the Vietnam War and through the balance of the Cold War, the U.S. military establishment turned its back on insurgency, refusing to consider operations against insurgents as anything other than a "lesser-included case" for forces structured for and prepared to fight two major theater wars.[46]

Historical studies of insurgencies over the years highlight the fact that insurgencies are more likely if a state cannot provide fundamental services and if the population believes they are at risk. In addition, other factors, such as the quality of leadership in a particular country and that country's political culture can be important factors in whether or not an insurgency develops. The Task Force does not propose that any specific combination of factors will result in an insurgency. Nonetheless, recent history can be instructive. Colombia, for example, has been gripped by a tenacious insurgency, and the drug trade has imperiled that government's ability to govern effectively. Colombia's strong political leadership, however, has made effective use of U.S. security and development assistance, as well as the political and diplomatic support of U.S. leaders. As a result, the U.S. has not been compelled to commit substantial U.S. forces to combat an insurgency and defend the sovereign prerogatives of Colombia's government. In contrast, the years leading up to 9/11 witnessed little U.S. government involvement in Afghanistan. As a result, U.S. information sources in Afghanistan were limited, which constrained U.S. potential to help shape in Afghanistan a situation less dangerous to U.S. interests. The events of 9/11 left the U.S. with few options in Afghanistan; combat a regime that allowed the terrorists to attack, or live with a dangerous *status quo*. The Task Force therefore judges that early intervention prior to an insurgency taking hold would give the U.S. more options and reduce the likelihood of major combat intervention.[47]

In light of this record it is the view of the Task Force that irregular warfare and insurgencies will be an enduring challenge to regional stability and U.S. national security interests. Emerging and enduring COIN issues need attention now. Addressing potential insurgencies in their incipient phase (i.e., "left of bang") will provide policymakers and commanders more whole-of-government options and a better prospect for deterring or preventing the need for combat operations. Building a collection and analytic effort "left of bang" also provides the means for sustained, consistent, and more effective ISR support should an insurgency become active. This makes necessary a more focused approach to COIN intelligence support, including a NIM for COIN, intelligence requirements directed specifically to COIN (including population-centric knowledge), and a strategic indications and warning (I&W) model to enable early implementation of whole-of-government options. Some I&W indicators are probably already available.

Recommendation

The USD(I) should work with the DNI to create a NIM for Irregular Warfare (including COIN)

USD(I), in coordination with the DNI, develop a comprehensive Indications and Warning system for COIN

A. Effective Coin, and Intelligence for COIN, Must Reflect a Whole-of-Government Effort and Whole-of-Government Capabilities

As noted in the 2004 DSB Summer Study, the U.S. requires the means to transition into an out of hostilities. Nowhere is this need more salient than for COIN. Addressing the entire lifecycle of COIN requires knowledge management capabilities that serve a wide variety of U.S. Government departments and agencies (DoD, Department of State, the Intelligence Community, etc.) A NIM for COIN would be able to facilitate efficient and effective intelligence support to COIN enabling a knowledge management capability that supports wholeofgovernment efforts and which would encourage use of a broader range of information sources that go beyond legacy intelligence collection.

Recommendation

There exists little appetite for new government departments and agencies, despite the need to build and employ capabilities for COIN the U.S. does not yet possess. However, building a whole-of-government intelligence capability for COIN (and other COIN capabilities) can be facilitated by creating a virtual community of COIN experts from throughout the government, and possibly beyond the government to the academic world. Information technology exists today to build virtual communities of experts. Such technology can be used to build a community of COIN experts that could constitute, a Government-wide, critical mass of planning and intelligence experts. Building such a virtual community would also provide a wider group of experts to identify I&W pertaining to COIN scenarios more swiftly than is possible today. Some of these technologies have already been employed by the ODNI. The use of these technologies would be a swift way to assemble the critical mass of experts needed in a manner consistent with the government's emphasis on using enterprise information technology to make more effective and rational government components. The NIM for COIN could start this virtual community, given access to sufficient enterprise information technologies and infrastructure. In doing so, however, the NIM should include the widest possible community of potential experts throughout the IC, and at all levels. As a further step the NIM could advocate the stand-up of an Institute of Intelligence for Behavioral Analysis that focuses on performing advanced analysis of group and social networks in regions susceptible to insurgencies.

The Task Force recognizes the importance and merit of organizational and process solutions that would integrate all departments of government to support COIN campaigns as recommended in the 2004 DSB Summer Study. The Task Force applauds this goal, and in light of the painful experiences in Iraq and Afghanistan, sees the need as more urgent than ever. The Task Force also recognize however, it is beyond the its charter which focuses on improvements to ISR for COIN.[48]

8. The Deluge of Sensor Data Is Creating a Crisis in Processing, Exploitation, and Dissemination (PED) and Associated Communication, as Well as an Increasing Need for Advanced Analysis that Addresses Behavior of Groups and the Cultural Framework of Group Decisions

The insatiable demand for information and emphasis on collection is producing a deluge of data, overwhelming the ability to provide useful, actionable intelligence in a timely manner. This crisis in PED is being exacerbated by planned and programmed collection assets and demands new S&T solutions to improve the efficiency and effectiveness of ISR support for COIN.

Moreover, there is a need to develop and train people to do Advanced Analysis – and this must be done much earlier in the careers of the best analysts. This level of analysis is needed at the very front end of any future conflict, not several years down the road. Training for Advanced Analysis would start at the very beginning of an analyst's career and continue throughout his/her career. It includes language, deep cultural awareness, and select forms of environmental training which encourages and supports analysis on the health of a region. Analysts need to make progress to understand the culture first hand and they need to return to critical assignments within their intelligence agency. More and more, the analysts will need to be placed in the field in order to be best postured for intelligence operations and conflicts as they arise.

Recommendation

The USD(I), in coordination with USD(AT&L), Military Departments, Defense Agencies, and DNI should create a focused PED initiative to make more effective its use of the increasing velocity, volume, and variety of data.

At the very start of any new collection program, the USD(I) and the DNI should ensure that PED requirements are fully understood and funded as part of the overall program initiative. A number of technologies, ranging from better use of communication bandwidth to cloud computing, are available to support this recommendation.

Moreover, the USD(I) and the DNI should implement a plan to develop and train the best people to do Advanced Analysis. Training for Advanced Analysis would start at the very beginning of an analyst's career and continue throughout the career. It should encompass language, deep cultural awareness, and select forms of environmental training which encourages and supports analysis on the health of a region. Analysts in this program would go forward to understand a culture first hand and then return to critical assignments within their intelligence agency, posturing the IC for intelligence operations and conflicts as they arise.

9. New and Emerging Technologies and Techniques Can Be Employed to Improve Understanding of COIN Environments

Technologies are emerging, for example, to improve understanding of the physical attributes (mineral resources, climates, geographies, including cultural geography) as well as those pertinent to identifying pattern of life activities of groups and individuals, and relate these attributes to incipient and real insurgencies. New analytic technologies hold the promise of "scaling up" the ability to filter raw data, identify meaning patterns of activity, and present analysts with material useful to understanding COIN situations, thus allowing analysts to perform real analysis, rather than exhaust themselves culling raw data. Technology can also be employed to understand what is "normal" in a particular environment, helping to spot trends that represent anomalies that may portend long-term changes and the rise of instability.

Recommendation

The USD(I), through the ISR Task Force, should undertake acquisition of these technologies and integrate these technologies into whole-of-government approaches to COIN. The USD(I) should focus on the acquisition of those technologies for which development has already occurred or has already advanced significantly. The USD(I) should also employ new technologies for data fusion, natural language processing, and information sharing to build a more holistic approach to understanding and analyzing COIN environments.

5. Cost Considerations

The adjustments associated with the findings and recommendations described in Section 4 represent a significant change in the manner in which intelligence support to COIN operations is considered. These adjustments give additional emphasis to building the infrastructure associated with regional and country specific research and the social sciences. Such costs, while not negligible, would be hardly material in comparison to the costs associated with technical collection systems.

Nonetheless, this report does not represent a rigorous effort to derive the costs of implementing these recommendations, nor does it attempt to enter the "trade space" in which investment in these capabilities would be offset by savings associated with cuts to current capabilities. Although there exists broad recognition that COIN represents a whole of government and population centric challenge, specific intelligence requirements associated with meeting this challenge have yet to be developed. The notional list of countries provided in Section 1 represents a possible starting point for crafting a transition in intelligence requirements from today's approach to COIN to the emerging population centric approach advocated by MG Flynn and others. At the core of that transition lays the change in requirements that would make possible a more precise estimate of costs.

However, cost savings are almost certain. Population centric approaches (that rely on population centric intelligence) would significantly reduce the likelihood of costly, major combat operations. Building a national infrastructure of country and region specific experts, reinvigorating the Foreign Area Officer program, and establishing COIN intelligence programs within the major intelligence agencies would represent a fraction of the cost of a major military intervention to counter a future insurgency. The costs associated with improving portions of PED are also relatively modest. Cloud computing and virtualization technologies are now available commercially, and the IC is already experimenting with these technologies, as well as with commercial data center technologies. Indeed, a Federal effort underway now to consolidate data centers may prove instructive toward consolidating and rationalizing the use of information technology for information sharing and collaboration.

APPENDIX A. TERMS OF REFERENCE

OFFICE OF THE UNDER SECRETARY OF DEFENSE
5000 DEFENSE PENTAGON
WASHINGTON, DC 20301-5000

08 MAR 2010

INTELLIGENCE

MEMORANDUM FOR CHAIRMAN, INTELLIGENCE TASK FORCE, DEFENSE SCIENCE BOARD

SUBJECT: Terms of Reference – Counter Insurgency (COIN) Intelligence, Surveillance and Reconnaissance (ISR) Operations

You are requested to perform a Defense Science Board Intelligence Task Force study to identify how Department of Defense (DoD) intelligence can most effectively support COIN operations and what emerging science and technology would have the greatest intelligence potential in this type of warfare. The principal objective is to influence investment decisions by recommending appropriate intelligence capabilities to assess insurgencies, understand a population in their environment, and support COIN operations.

COIN involves a protracted campaign where both enemy and friendly forces continuously seek advantage by adapting systems, tactics, techniques and procedures. COIN uses all instruments of national power to sustain an established indigenous government and improve or defend its credibility against adversaries. Long-term success requires the local populace to accept the established government and become self-sufficient in managing affairs that enable security, justice and economic growth.

Recent history has shown COIN operations will be conducted by a coalition of nations with support of the internationally recognized government. This disparate set of cultures and intelligence collection capabilities makes information sharing with interagency, host nation, and coalition partners a challenge. Host nation civilian sentiment critically impacts COIN success, indicating anthropological and socio-cultural factors must be also be addressed. DoD ISR capabilities must adapt to this demanding environment. Per Major General Flynn, we must "…build a process from the sensor all the way to the political decision makers…" to ensure our senior leaders have the right decision making information.

This "COIN Intel Ops Study" should address the following:

(1) What is the developing role of DoD ISR in COIN ops; who are the customers and what are the requirements?
(2) What is the recommended allocation and use of DoD ISR resources to sustain COIN capability along with other competing intelligence requirements, for example counterterrorism?
(3) What changes can be made in the ISR process to improve support to COIN?

(4) What can be done in the immediate future to improve network agility and information sharing across the broad spectrum of mission partners conducting COIN and during the promotion of regional stability?
(5) What emerging technologies and methodologies, combinations of sensors, and investments in information fusion and analysis are likely to provide the highest payoff?

The study is sponsored by the Under Secretary of Defense for Intelligence (USD(I)). USD(I) is authorized to act upon the advice and recommendations of the Board. Col J. Scott Winstead, OUSD(I) 703-607-0410, will serve as the Executive Secretary.

The Task Force will operate in accordance with the provisions of P.L. 92-463, the "Federal Advisory Committee Act," and DoD Directive 5105.4, the "DoD Federal Advisory Committee Management Program." It is not anticipated that this Task Force will need to go into any "particular matters" within the meaning of Section 208 of Title 18, United States Code, nor will it cause any member to be placed in the position of action as a procurement official.

Kevin P. Meiners
Acting Deputy Under Secretary of Defense
(Portfolio, Programs & Resources)

APPENDIX B. TASK FORCE MEMBERSHIP

CO-CHAIRMEN

Dr. Robert Lucky	*Private Consultant*
Maj. Gen. Richard O'Lear, USAF (Ret.)	*Private Consultant*

MEMBERS

Mr. Tom Behling	*Centra Technologies, Inc*
Mr. Marc Berkowitz	*Lockheed Martin*
Mr. Jack Keane	*JHU/APL*
Mr. Keith Masback	*U.S. Geospatial Intelligence Foundation*
Dr. Dan Maxwell	*KaDSCI, LLC*
Mr. Keith May	*Glimmerglass Networks*
Mr. Ken McGruther	*Private Consultant*
Mr. Howard Schue	*Technology Strategies & Alliances*
Dr. Les Servi	*MITRE Corporation*

Dr. Chris Tucker	*Private Consultant*
Mr. Samuel S. Visner	*CSC*

SENIOR REVIEWERS

Dr. Ruth David	*ANSER*
Dr. Bill Schneider	*Private Consultant*

EXECUTIVE SECRETARY

Col. John 'JScott' Winstead, USAF	*OUSD(I)/PP&R, ISR Programs*

DSB SECRETARIAT

Mr. Brian Hughes	*Defense Science Board*
Maj. Mike Warner, USAF	*Defense Science Board*

SUPPORT STAFF

Mr. Jimmy Hyatt	*OUSD(I)/PP&R, ISR Programs (Scitor)*
Ms. Tammy-jean Beatty	*SAIC*
Ms. Amely Moore	*SAIC*

APPENDIX C. BRIEFINGS RECEIVED

Briefer	Organization
Mr. Collin Agee	*National Geospatial-Intelligence Agency (NGA)*
Mr. Don Alexander	*Lockheed Martin*
The Honorable Charlie Allen	
Col Fritz Barth, USMC	*National Security Agency (NSA)*
Mr. Chris Baumgart	*The Johns Hopkins University/Applied Physics Lab (JHU/APL)*
Mr. Winston Beauchamp	*National Geospatial-Intelligence Agency (NGA)*
Mr. Bert Berliey	*National Geospatial-Intelligence Agency (NGA)*
Dr. Jennifer Brick-Murtazashvili	*Graduate School of Public and International Affairs, University of Pittsburgh*
Mr. Larry Burgess	*Deputy Under Secretary of Defense, HUMINT, Counterintelligence, & Security, USD(I)*
LTG Ronald Burgess	*Director, Defense Intelligence Agency (DIA)*
Dr. Kathleen Carley	*Carnegie Mellon University*
Mr. Mark Clark	*Director, Intelligence Analysis, Collection and Operations Chief of Naval Operations*
Mr. Robert Clemens	*Air Force Research Lab (AFRL)*
Mr. Rich Comfort	*National Ground Intelligence Center (NGIC)*

Briefer	Organization
Mr. Joe Czika	Security Strategies and Applications International, LLC
Ms. Davi D'Agostino	U.S. Government Accountability Office (GAO)
Mr. Al Di Leonardo	SKOPE
Mr. Thomas Ferguson	Under Secretary of Defense for Intelligence (Acting)
MG Michael Flynn, USA	Awaiting Assignment at ODNI
Dr. Kerry Fosher	USMC Center for Advanced Operational Culture Learning
Mr. Alex Gliksman	Security Strategies and Applications International, LLC
Mr. Jeff Green	OSD General Counsel
Mr. Jimmy Greene	National Geospatial-Intelligence Agency (NGA)
CAPT James Hamblet, USN	Joint Staff Pakistan Afghanistan Coordination Cell
COL Sharon Hamilton	Director Human Terrain Systems TRADOC G2
COL Derek Harvey, USA (Ret.)	Director of the Afghanistan-Pakistan Center of Excellence at U.S. Central Command
Mr. Rich Haver	
Mr. Chuck Havener	Security Strategies and Applications International, LLC
Gen. Mike Hayden, USAF (Ret.)	
MAJ Trevor Hough, USA	Director, SKOPE
Prof. Karl Jackson	Director, Asian Studies and Director, Southeast Asia Studies at Johns Hopkins
Dr. Dan Kaufman	Defense Advanced Research Projects Agency (DARPA)
Mr. Denis Kaufman	Defense Intelligence Agency (DIA)
Mr. Tim Kelly	Office of the Under Secretary of Defense for Policy (OUSD(P))
Lt. Gen. Craig Koziol, USAF	Director, ISR Task Force
Mr. Howard Larrabee	National Security Agency (NSA)
Dr. Bobby Laurine	National Geospatial-Intelligence Agency (NGA)
Director Letitia Long	Director, National Geospatial-Intelligence Agency (NGA)
Mr. Edward Loxtercamp	ISR Task Force
Mr. Jim Martin	Assistant Deputy Under Secretary of Defense for Portfolio, Programs and Resources(ADUSD(PP&R))
Dr. Mark Maybury	MITRE
GEN Stanley McChrystal, USA	
Mr. Tom McCormick	National Geospatial-Intelligence Agency (NGA)
Mr. Kevin P. Meiners	Deputy Under Secretary of Defense (acting) for Portfolio, Programs & Resources, Office of the Under Secretary of Defense (Intelligence)
Mr. Paul Meinshausen	National Ground Intelligence Center (NGIC)
Mr. Orrin Mills	National Geospatial-Intelligence Agency (NGA)
LTC John Nagl, USA (Ret.)	Center for a New American Security
Mr. Randolph Nunes	National Ground Intelligence Center (NGIC)
Mr. Sean O'Brien	DARPA

Appendix C. (Continued)

Briefer	Organization
Mr. John Orem	*Director, ISR Programs Division OSD(CA&PE)*
Mr. John Oswald	*National Geospatial-Intelligence Agency (NGA)*
Maj. Gen. Jim Poss, USAF	*Assistant Deputy Chief of Staff, USAF Intelligence, Surveillance, and Reconnaissance*
Dr. Richard Rees	*CENTRA Technology, Inc.*
Lt. Col. Frank Ruggeri, USAF	*ISR Task Force*
Dr. Pete Rustan	*National Reconnaissance Office (NRO)*
Mr. John Scali	*National Geospatial-Intelligence Agency (NGA)*
Ms. Jean Shepherd	*National Geospatial-Intelligence Agency (NGA)*
Ms. Lisa Spuria	*National Geospatial-Intelligence Agency (NGA)*
Dr. Larry Stotts	*Defense Advanced Research Projects Agency (DARPA)*
Mr. Neil Tipton	*ISR Task Force*
The Honorable Mike Vickers	*Assistant Secretary of Defense for Special Operations/Low Intensity Conflict, and Interdependent Capabilities*
Mr. Patrick Warfle	*National Geospatial-Intelligence Agency (NGA)*
Mr. Paul Weise	*National Geospatial-Intelligence Agency (NGA)*
Dr. Linton Wells	*National Defense University (NDU)*
Dr. Michael Wertheimer	*National Security Agency (NSA)*
Ms. Michele Weslander Quaid	*ISR Task Force*
Mr. Kevin West	*Defense Intel Info Enterprise (DIIE)*
Mr. Shaun Wheeler	*National Ground Intelligence Center (NGIC)*
Mr. Jeffrey White	*National Security Agency (NSA)*
Ms. Lynn Wright	*Defense Intelligence Agency (DIA)*
Mr. Ryan Yoho	*ISR Task Force*
LTG Richard Zahner, USA	*U.S. Army Deputy Chief of Staff, G-2*

APPENDIX D. SOME USEFUL CANDIDATE METRICS[49]

Metrics for understanding progress in a COIN campaign can be divided into four categories, based on the four key elements in any counterinsurgency: the population, the supported (host nation) government, the security forces (military and police), and the enemy. A selection of possible metrics includes the following:

Population-Related Indicators

- Voluntary reporting. The number of unsolicited tip-offs from the population, in relation to insurgent activity, can indicate popular confidence in the security forces

and willingness to support the government. This indicator must be verified by assessing the percentage of tip-offs that prove to be accurate.
- IEDs reported versus IEDs found. Reporting of IEDs is an important subset of the voluntary reporting metric, because accurate reporting indicates that the population is willing to act voluntarily to protect the security forces. Improvised Explosive Devices (IEDs) account for roughly 50% of ISAF casualties in Afghanistan. Yet approximately 80% of IEDs discovered are spotted through a basic visual check, often by an Afghan. Variations in the percentage of IEDs accurately reported by Afghans may therefore correlate with local support for ISAF and the government.
- Price of exotic vegetables. Afghanistan is an agricultural economy, and crop diversity varies markedly across the country. Given the free-market economics of agricultural production in Afghanistan, risk and cost factors – the opportunity cost of growing a crop, the risk of transporting it across insecure roads, the risk of selling it at market and of transporting money home again – tend to be automatically priced in to the cost of fruits and vegetables. Thus fluctuations in overall market prices may be a surrogate metric for general popular confidence and security. In particular, exotic vegetables – those grown outside a particular district and that have to be transported further at greater risk in order to be sold in that district – can be a useful tell-tale marker.
- Transportation prices. Again, Afghanistan's trucking companies tend to price risk and cost – the risk of insurgent attack, IED risk, kidnapping or robbery risk, and the costs of bribes, kickbacks and other forms of corruption – into the cost of transportation on the country's roads. Thus, variations over time in the cost of transporting a standard load on a given route can indicate the level of public perception of security, and the level of corruption and criminality, along that route. Like all other indicators, variations over time are more significant than the absolute cost.
- Progress of NGO construction projects. Numerous NGOs are engaged in construction projects across Afghanistan, using local materials and labor. Unlike government projects (which the insurgents may attack on principle), NGO projects tend to go well when they have access to low-cost materials and an adequate labor supply, and they tend to suffer when costs rise due to insecurity. Thus, NGOs running multiple projects at different points across the country may have a fairly clear idea of security conditions and confidence levels, based on the degree of progress in their projects.
- Influence of Taliban versus government courts. Taliban mobile courts operate across much of the south and east of the country, providing dispute resolution, mediation and Sharia-based rule of law services to the local population, making judgments that are enforced by local Taliban vigilante cells that operate much like insurgent "police". Rule of law and local-level governance has developed into a major insurgent focus over the past two years. Public willingness to seek, accept and abide by judgments from Taliban courts may indicate popular support for the insurgents, or it may simply reflect a default choice in the absence of an alternative – for example, in districts where there are no local government courts (most of the south) or where traditional tribal courts have been displaced. The range of movement and number of

cases heard by Taliban courts, compared against the number of cases brought in local government courts, may indicate whether the population sees the government or the insurgents as fairer, swifter or more able to solve their problems.
- Participation rate in programs. More generally, both the government and the insurgents run a range of community programs, economic programs and political activities that seek popular participation. The rate of participation in programs varies between villages and, within the same village, over time. While it is generally difficult to gauge participation in enemy programs with great precision, participation in Afghan government or coalition programs is easier to track and may indicate the degree to which the local community perceives the Afghan government as a legitimate actor with the ability to address its problems.
- Taxation collection. A classical counterinsurgency metric is taxation collection, specifically the compliance rate with government taxation programs versus the rate of payment of insurgent taxes. In Afghanistan, while the insurgents have a robust, predictable taxation system across most of the country, the government does not and collects hardly any taxes at the local level. By contrast, corrupt officials and police collect illegal tolls and taxes at checkpoints. Thus there is a three-way comparison: between insurgent taxation (where a high degree of local compliance indicates a high degree of insurgent control), government taxation (where the emergence of any fair and predictable system would represent an improvement in government effectiveness) and illegal extortion (which indicates the level of corruption of key local officials and may correlate to popular rage and discontent).
- Afghan-on-Afghan violence. Unlike statistics that track violence against the coalition, Afghan-on-Afghan violence (whether caused by insurgent action, the actions of government officials and security forces, or criminality) is a good indicator of public security. In areas where there is a high level of Afghan-on-Afghan violence the population is very unlikely to feel safe enough to put their weapons down and join in peaceful negotiation or support for the government. Likewise, a spike in Afghan-on-Afghan violence in a particular area probably correlates to a drop in public confidence.
- Rate of new business formation and loan repayment. The number of new local businesses being formed each month, along with the rate of loan repayment to local moneylenders, can be an indicator of public confidence and economic growth. In Afghanistan the rate of small-business formation is typically low, while the rate of repayment is usually fairly high. Both indicators, however, fluctuate in line with availability of capital and confidence in the future of Afghanistan. They also tend to vary markedly between urban and rural areas, and the contrasting numbers may serve as a measure of how public perceptions differ in the cities and larger towns, compared to smaller villages. The urban/rural divide is a longstanding social cleavage in Afghanistan, one that the Taliban has exploited in the past, and is worth tracking closely.
- Urban construction new-start rate. Especially in urban areas, the rate of new starts on construction projects (especially residential housing and markets) can be an important surrogate indicator for popular confidence in the future. People who lack a sense of security and an expectation that the future will be better than the past tend to

be less willing to invest in major construction projects. Like other indicators, fluctuations in the new-start rate over time may be more telling than the absolute number of new starts in any given area at any one time.
- Percentage of local people with secure title to their house and land. Land reform is a longstanding issue in many parts of Afghanistan. Land ownership was a major flashpoint in the Soviet-Afghan war, and back into the nineteenth century. In many areas there are complicated land disputes that are exploited by corrupt powerbrokers. The Taliban have sometimes acted as mediators and sought to resolve these disputes justly in order to further their influence, while at other times they have deliberately exacerbated and exploited land disputes to gain the allegiance of local people on one side of the dispute. A key part of public confidence and perception of stability is having secure title to land and other property. Therefore the percentage of people in a given district who have secure title to their property can be an indication of stability, whereas a large number of unresolved or power-locked land or title disputes can indicate potential for instability and insurgent exploitation.

Host Nation Government Indicators

- Assassination and kidnapping rate. The assassination and kidnapping rate of local officials, tribal elders, district notables and ordinary people in a district can be an indicator of instability. For example, a province where local sub-district governors, police officials or other government representatives are frequently assassinated, or where there is a high turnover in local people in positions of authority, may be experiencing a concerted insurgent push to displace or destroy a local elite. In general terms, a high rate of this type also indicates a high degree of instability, even in the absence of overt insurgent activity. Conversely however, a low assassination or kidnapping rate does not necessarily indicate that a district is pro-government – a district with a low assassination rate, that also produces low levels of voluntary reporting and has a low violence level, may simply be an enemy district that is stable under insurgent control.
- Civilian accessibility. While military accessibility (discussed above) is not a good indicator of insurgent activity, civilian accessibility is a better measure. If local officials are unable to travel or work in a given area, or must do so with an escort, or are frequently kidnapped or assassinated, or the local population avoids an area, this tends to indicate insurgent or criminal presence. Even in the absence of insurgent violence directed at coalition forces or Afghan security forces, "no-go areas" for civilian government officials tend to indicate a high degree of insurgent control.
- Where local officials sleep. A large proportion of Afghan government officials currently do not sleep in the districts for which they are responsible – district governors may sleep in the provincial capital, while some provincial governors sleep in Kabul or in their home districts in other provinces. In some cases, when a local official does not sleep in his assigned district, this may indicate a lack of security and high threat, in which case the district is likely to be heavily insurgent-contested or even insurgent-controlled. In other cases, the official may sleep with his own kin group in a different district out of personal preference, indicating that he may be

acting as an "absentee governor" or may have been appointed as an outsider to control the district, rather than representing it. In either case the official in question is less likely to be seen as legitimate and effective by the local population. Thus changes in this indicator may indicate changes in local perceptions of the government.

- Officials' business interests. It is often useful to map officials' business interests and those of their relatives and tribal kinship groups (ownership of companies, bids for coalition or Afghan contracts, control of local production resources) against incidents of violence and unrest in districts for which they are responsible. Determining these interests can be difficult (though the local population usually knows them) but can be revealing – incidents of violence against USAID construction projects, for example, may be insurgent inspired, or may simply reflect the efforts of an official, who owns a rival company, to undermine a project with a view to eventually taking it over. An official whose tribe or family is a party to a land or water dispute, or who has business interests in a particular piece of land, may also be an illegitimate broker in the eyes of the local population, who may turn to the Taliban for relief. Likewise, officials who engage energetically in counternarcotics operations but simultaneously own substantial poppy fields in other parts of the country may simply be eliminating their rivals' crops to further their own interests. A district based "register of officials assets", regularly updated, can therefore be a very useful tool for interpreting incidents of violence.

- Percentage of officials purchasing their positions. Many local government officials in parts of Afghanistan gain their official positions through an informal (and illegal) system of patronage and nepotism, where they purchase their positions for a substantial sum, paid to a higher level official, often a relative. This system creates incentives for corruption, since these officials must now recoup their investment through extorting money from the population, and may have to pass kickbacks to their patron. They have essentially purchased a "license to exploit", and over time government positions come to be seen as opportunities to fleece the population, rather than to serve Afghanistan. Obviously, this creates enormous opportunities for the insurgents to exploit. In a given district, therefore, a high percentage of officials owing their positions to the illegal purchase system tends to correlate with a high degree of corruption, and may correlate with higher than normal willingness by the population to collaborate with the insurgents.

- Budget execution. The rate of budget execution (how much of their allocated budget line ministries, provincial and central government officials, and local councils are actually able to spend) is a potential indicator for government effectiveness. Districts where allocated funds are being spent in a timely manner are more likely to be receiving an adequate level of government services, local officials are likely to be more capable managers, the absorptive capacity of the local economy is likely to be higher, and corruption may be lower. Conversely, districts that do not execute their budget effectively may be suffering from poor quality officials, lack of economic capacity, and a lesser degree of essential services. Coalition units may also be at fault – the tendency to dump CERP funds on underperforming districts through block grants can generate the appearance of a short term "quick fix," but can also have an addictive effect that causes local officials to sit on their own funds while letting the

foreigners spend, and may create habits of dependency that ultimately undermine the effectiveness of the local economy.
- Capital Flight. During the period of intense uncertainty in late 2009, as Afghans anxiously awaited the U.S. decision on which strategy to select and whether or not to reinforce the effort, we saw millions of dollars leaving the country on a weekly basis, as Afghans shifted their assets outside the country in expectation of instability and possible civil war. When this type of behavior spikes, as it did in late 2009, this may indicate a significant lack of confidence in the future and public uncertainty. Changes in the rate of capital movement outside the country may track closely with changes in public confidence, and hence in the credibility and legitimacy of Afghan government and international community efforts in the eyes of local elites.
- Rate of anti-insurgent lashkar formation. Districts that are opposed to the insurgents but also distrustful of the government tend to have a high rate of formation of lashkars (tribal or district militias) that seek to protect the community against all comers. Thus, the formation of anti-insurgent militias in a given area may indicate that the population distrusts both the government and the insurgents, and is a possible indicator of "swing voter" behavior or autarkic "a plague on all your houses" attitudes on the part of local community leaders.
- Public safety function. The side that performs the public safety function – protecting the population from crime and violence – tends to be seen as the more legitimate and effective. Given the high level of police corruption and abuse in some parts of Afghanistan, many of our interlocutors scoff at the idea of going to the police for protection. By contrast, the Taliban have been carefully building a reputation for swift, harsh, but fair punishment of criminals, and for protecting local people from abuse. The Taliban maintain a published legal code, the layeha, which binds both Taliban units and populations to a set of standards enforced by local Taliban cells. In Kandahar and some other centers, the Taliban maintain a public safety hotline (akin to a 911 call center) that local people can call in an emergency, to confirm or deny Taliban involvement in an incident, or seek Taliban assistance. These behaviors, coupled with a moderate to high level of abuse by local officials and police, may indicate that the local population sees the insurgents as more legitimate and effective than the government in a given area.

Security Force Indicators

- Kill ratio. While raw body count is a poor indicator, kill ratio (the ratio between casualties inflicted and casualties suffered) can be a useful indicator of a unit's confidence, aggression and willingness to close with the enemy. However, in assessing this metric it is essential to control for civilian casualties, escalation-of-fire (EOF) incidents, and other possible indicators (discussed below) that a given unit is engaging in brutality or abuse. Kills resulting from indirect fires (artillery or mortars), air strikes, or kills by supporting coalition units also do not count. The only data relevant to this indicator are confirmed kills/captures, directly inflicted by the unit in question, on positively identified insurgents actually engaging in combat operations. Like many metrics, the absolute number of kills or captures at any given moment is less important than second-order data relating to trends over time. If a unit's kill ratio is improving, this may indicate greater confidence, better dominance over a given area and better intelligence, and possibly a closer relationship with local populations. But like other indicators, kill ratio must be interpreted in relation to other data before this can be known.

- Win/loss ratio. At the most general level, units that consistently win their engagements – inflicting more losses than they suffer, retaining possession of disputed ground and protecting key population groups – are usually performing better than units that consistently lose. In practice, however, most security force units win most engagements against insurgents, so that changes in the win-loss ratio over time are more significant than the absolute proportion of wins to losses. Again, in calculating this ratio, it is essential to control for engagements won due to artillery/air support or coalition force intervention, as these do not count in assessing the unit itself.

- Kill versus wound/capture ratio. In a standard combat engagement, for every one enemy killed, we expect to see 3 to 5 enemy wounded or captured. This is of course simply a general guideline, but some Afghan security force units consistently kill four or five enemy to one wounded or captured. This abnormal kill-to-wound ratio bears closer investigation. It may be that the enemy always fights to the death, or that Afghan units have a remarkably high level of marksmanship, though field observation and anecdotal evidence suggests neither of these is the case. It may also be that these units are relying on airpower and artillery and that this is generating this anomalous ratio. Alternatively, a kill-to-wound ratio of 4-5:1 (rather than the normal 1:3-5) may indicate that units are engaging in extra-judicial killings, or posthumously deeming dead civilians to be "enemy." There is insufficient evidence at this time to be certain, but as an indicator of possible security force brutality this needs to be closely tracked.

- Detainee guilt ratio. A unit's detainee guilt ratio is the proportion of individuals detained who, on subsequent investigation, turn out to be closely and genuinely linked to the insurgency. A unit that has a low detainee guilt ratio may be arresting lots of local military-age males, but if most of these are innocent it can be having a sharply negative effect on local support, and may even be producing insurgents as innocent detainees become radicalized in temporary detention. Conversely, a unit that has a high detainee guilt ratio is detaining mainly individuals who are genuinely linked to the insurgency, and this is a surrogate indicator that its intelligence is high quality, its methods are showing appropriate restraint, and it is probably gaining the confidence of the local population by developing a reputation for accuracy and effectiveness.

- Recruitment versus desertion rates. In order to grow Afghan security forces, huge efforts have been made in recruitment and retention. Yet desertion rates are also high – so high, for example, that in RC-South between June and September, total ANP numbers actually shrank when police killed, wounded, missing and absent without leave (AWOL) were taken into account. In general, when an organization's recruitment rates are higher than its desertion rates, morale can be said to be

functionally adequate. When desertion rates rise, along with other indicators like increased sickness rates and short-term AWOL, organizational morale is likely to be dropping. Short-term AWOL is not a reliable indicator in itself, however, because in countries like Afghanistan where recruits have little or no access to a banking system, they tend to go AWOL after payday to take their pay home.
- Proportion of ghost employees. Most Afghan military and police units have a proportion of "ghost employees" on their books. These are fictional employees whose pay the unit commander claims from higher headquarters, but then puts aside for his personal use. In most cases, these ghost employees generate corrupt income for senior officers. While this practice is unlikely to be stamped out any time soon, the proportion of ghost employees in a unit, and the way this number changes over time, may indicate the degree of corruption of the commanders concerned. It does not necessarily indicate poor morale – it may do so if unit members feel they are being exploited, but in some cases they see the practice as legitimate: in a society without robust social security or veterans pensions, some units use ghost employees to create a pool of funds that go to the welfare of incapacitated police or soldiers and the families of those killed in action.
- Location at start of firefight. Every firefight in Afghanistan is played out in front of an audience, and has a political and military meaning in the eyes of that audience. Afghan elders frequently call coalition commanders at the end of an engagement in order to offer their play-by-play commentary on a firefight that has just ended. One of the key elements in how the population interprets a firefight is the location of opposing forces. For example, if security forces are located in a population center, standing with the population at the start of an engagement, and the enemy attacks down from the hills, then the population frequently seems to interpret the insurgents as the aggressors and security forces as their protectors. Thus, even if the insurgents win the firefight, they may lose politically by pushing the population into our arms. Conversely, when security forces attack into a village or valley, even if acting on solid intelligence, the population sometimes perceives them as the aggressors, and may side with the insurgents. This is especially so in night attacks, surprise attacks, or engagements in remote terrain where rural populations are traditionally suspicious of strangers. If a unit is consistently located in close proximity to protected populations at the start of firefights, and consistently wins those firefights, this may indicate that the unit is gaining credibility and legitimacy in the eyes of the population.
- EOF incidents and CIVCAS. Units that consistently get involved in escalation-of-force incidents (where troops fire on civilians who fail to stop at roadblocks, drive too close to convoys or otherwise appear threatening), or inflict significant numbers of civilian casualties (CIVCAS) may have an overly aggressive attitude to the local population and may be placing too little emphasis on protecting civilians. They may also be overly nervous and frightened of their environment, making them trigger-happy. Almost certainly, units that frequently kill or wound civilians lack a close relationship with the local population, lack viable local partners and lack a good information network, making them more vulnerable to insurgent attacks.

- Duration of operations. Single-day operations, where a unit sleeps every night in its fortified base and only goes out in the daylight, tend to indicate lack of confidence, lack of energy, or the existence of a tacit (or possibly even explicit) live-and-let-live deal with the insurgents. Single day, large-unit sweep operations (daylight search operations, cordon-and-knock sweeps or short-duration raiding operations) may also be having a negative effect in their own right. A unit that consistently conducts multi-day operations, up to several weeks at a time, and lives in its area of responsibility rather than merely visiting it, tends over time to develop a closer rapport with the local population, becomes more familiar with local enemy groups, and protects its population while dominating its area more effectively.
- Night operations. If a given unit frequently operates by night, or stays out for several nights on operations, this may indicate that the unit is dominating its area of operations, is confident in its environment, and has the upper hand. In particular, if night operations tend to be protective (e.g. ambushing potential enemy routes used to infiltrate population centers and intimidate government-aligned population groups) then they may contribute to a popular feeling of safety and normality, and hence may bring the local population to the government side. On the other hand, if night operations are aggressive (raiding, hard-knock search operations, or use of air strikes and indirect fires to "deny" areas to insurgents) the same operations may actually contribute to a feeling of insecurity on the part of the population, and hence may have a de-stabilizing effect on the district.
- Small-unit operations. Units that mount a larger number of smaller unit operations (at squad, platoon or company level, depending on the local threat profile) tend to cover a greater area within their area of responsibility, with greater thoroughness. Willingness to conduct multiple small-unit operations also indicates a greater degree of confidence and an expectation of defeating the enemy if encountered.
- Combined action operations. Operations involving combined action – where coalition units intimately partner with local military, police, civilian authorities and coalition civilian agencies down to small-unit level – tend to indicate improved performance by all partners in the action. Coalition forces tend to perform better because they have access to local knowledge, language skills and situational awareness. Local military forces can access coalition fires, intelligence, mobility, medical support and other enablers, and have a constant professional exemplar in the presence of coalition troops. Local police are relieved of the burden of direct combat with main-force insurgents and can focus on their policing role, and they are constantly monitored, reducing the risk of corrupt or abusive behavior. Local and coalition civilian authorities and agencies are able to operate in higher-threat environments as part of a combined action team, giving them greater reach and endurance, better protection, and the ability to demonstrate responsible leadership and deliver essential services to the population.
- Dismounted operations. If a unit frequently operates on foot, this may be an indicator that it is more confident in its environment, has greater reach across its area of responsibility (much of which, in Afghanistan, may be out of reach of the road system), and has a better rapport with local populations. Anecdotal evidence and data from other campaigns suggests that units that operate dismounted may also be less vulnerable to roadside IEDs, though this is yet to be confirmed in the Afghan

context. Conversely, units that always operate from the supposed safety of road-bound armored vehicles may be predictable (due to always following a limited number of roads), may be easily ambushed, and may lack rapport with the population, which may see them as alien, strange or cowardly. The roadside IED is clearly a military weapon, but it is also a political weapon used by the insurgents to separate the security forces from the population. Dismounted operations can redress this separation. In practice, due to the size of Afghanistan and the lack of friendly troops, almost all operations commence with a road or air move to a jumping-off point, from which units may proceed dismounted. The positive effects of dismounted operations may improve the relationship between the unit and the population across its whole area of responsibility, however, not just in the actual areas where it operates dismounted.

- Driving technique. The driving style of a unit – whether drivers push civilian vehicles out of their way, whether they wait their turn in traffic, how aggressively they force civilian cars back from convoys, whether or not they illuminate passing traffic with laser sights, whether they hog the center lane of the road or drive in lane – is a good atmospheric indicator of a unit's attitude to the population, and hence of the population's likely attitude to that unit. Units that drive rudely, alienate the population and disrupt traffic and commerce with aggressive driving techniques usually have poor community rapport.
- Reliance on air and artillery support. If a unit relies too heavily on air strikes, artillery and mortar fire, and other forms of non-organic support in most of its engagements, this may indicate lack of confidence and unwillingness to engage with the enemy or the local population. It also creates conditions that may lead to increased CIVCAS or collateral property damage, as the unit is employing area weapons that it does not control, rather than organic direct-fire weapons. This tendency can be assessed by comparing the size of units engaged in a given series of combat actions with how often they call on non-organic fires: if a unit consistently draws on indirect fire even when engaging much smaller enemy groups, it may have a confidence problem. Conversely, if the unit regularly gets into situations where its small units encounter large enemy groups and have to be rescued by indirect fire, it may be over-reaching, or may be overmatched in its area of operations and require reinforcement.
- Pattern-setting and telegraphing moves to the enemy. Units that set patterns – always moving on set routes, always leaving or entering bases from the same direction at the same time, selecting the same overwatch positions on patrol after patrol, or developing standard ambush positions or observation posts – tend to become more vulnerable to insurgent ambushes, IEDs and attacks. Likewise, if a unit has a tendency to accidentally telegraph its moves to the enemy (say, by always massing helicopters in the same way before a raid) it may be more vulnerable to being out-maneuvered by the insurgents. On the other hand, telegraphing moves to the population is often appropriate in Afghanistan: even the Taliban rarely move from one valley or village to another without seeking community permission, and coalition units can message local populations – "we are coming into your valley next month, you have ten days to expel the enemy from your villages or we will be forced to mount a clearance operation" – in order to force the enemy to move without fighting.

This does not always work, but it is a technique that is familiar to Afghans as it is often used in their traditional forms of conflict, and may have a positive effect in some circumstances.
- Possession of the high ground at dawn. The Afghan campaign, in addition to being a counterinsurgency, a stabilization operation and a competition for governance, is also a classic mountain warfare campaign, especially in RC-North, RC-East and some parts of RCs-South, -West and -Capital. As such the basic tenets of mountain warfare tactics apply, including control of the high ground, maintenance of wide fields of observation from key terrain, dominance of peaks overlooking key routes, ability to bring plunging fire onto identified enemy positions and ability to move on the high ground at night. Units that consistently hold the high ground at dawn tend to demonstrate a mastery of this form of warfare, while units that are consistently overlooked by the enemy at first light tend to struggle in this environment.

Enemy Indicators

- High-technology inserts. The Taliban are generally a low-tech guerrilla force, but they do possess and deploy some high-technology capabilities: satellite phones, accurized weapons, sniper optics, and (in some parts of the country) high-tech components for improvised explosive devices. Presence of these high-tech inserts in a given insurgent group may indicate that it has access to better funding or greater support from external sponsors, and such a unit is more likely to be a full-time main force Taliban column, rather than a local (Tier 2) guerrilla group.
- Insurgent medical health. The health of individual insurgent detainees is also an indicator of the nature of the insurgent organization in a given area. Local guerrillas tend to suffer numerous health problems ranging from malnutrition through malaria, tuberculosis, leishmaniasis and other parasitic diseases, to diabetes, respiratory tract infections and other chronic health problems. Their health problems tend to track those of the local population in a given area. Main force units, on the other hand, often have a better general level of health and insurgents based in Pakistan or directly sponsored by external agencies may have received inoculations or other medical support – in both cases, the healthier an insurgent the more likely he is to have received external assistance.
- Presence of specialist teams and foreign advisers. Some Taliban main-force units work with specialist teams – snipers, heavy machine-gun and mortar teams, rocket teams, specialized reconnaissance teams, intelligence teams, media/propaganda teams, and so on. They also often include foreigners (i.e. of non-Afghan origin) and occasionally foreign advisors (usually Pakistani or central Asian in origin). The presence of these specialized teams, and especially of foreign advisers, in a given district may indicate that a main-force enemy column is working in the district.
- Insurgent village-of-origin. There is an extremely important difference between insurgents who originate from villages within the same district where they fight (local guerrillas) and insurgents who fight outside their district-of-origin. Local guerrillas are often part-time fighters, they frequently switch sides in the conflict

based on local (tribal or economic) motivation, and more generally are part of the fabric of local society. If a security force unit is to stabilize a given district, it needs to defeat these local guerrillas but it must also emphasize reintegration, reconciliation, and winning over these groups, which after all represent key members of society the unit is trying to stabilize. Thus, attempts to destroy local guerrillas outright can backfire by alienating communities, creating blood feuds that perpetuate the conflict. On the other hand, insurgents who operate outside their district-of-origin, or even originate from outside the country, can be deemed "foreign fighters" in the eyes of the community. They often lack tribal ties or rapport with the community, and should be targeted with maximum lethality, as ruthlessly as legally permissible. As a foreign body within local society, these fighters can be killed and captured intensively (as long as targeting is accurate and avoids innocent civilians) without disrupting our relationship with the locals. Indeed, local communities may actually feel safer and may partner more closely with units that ruthlessly target foreign- origin insurgents, while seeking to reintegrate and reconcile with local guerrillas.

- First-to-fire ratio. The first-to-fire ratio is a key indicator of which side controls the initiation of firefights, and is a useful surrogate metric to determine which side possesses the tactical initiative. If our side fires first in most firefights, this likely indicates that we are ambushing the enemy (or mounting pre-planned attacks) more frequently than we are being ambushed. This in turn may indicate that our side has better situational awareness and access to intelligence on enemy movements than the insurgents, and it certainly indicates that we have the initiative and the enemy may be reacting to us. Most importantly, the side that initiates the majority of firefights tends to control the loss rate, and this can be checked by mapping insurgent losses against which side fired first in the engagements where those losses were suffered – if the insurgents are losing most of their casualties in firefights they initiate themselves, then they are in control of their own loss rate and can simply stop picking fights if their losses become unsustainable, and re-start operations once they recover. If they are losing most of their casualties in engagements we initiate, then we control their loss rate and can force them below replenishment level and ultimately destroy the network in question.
- Price of black-market weapons and ammunition. Afghanistan has a substantial black market in weapons, ammunition, explosives and other military equipment. As in any other free market, the price of weaponry on this black market reflects supply (availability of weapons) and demand (the rate of arming or rearming among population groups and the insurgent requirements for weapons to support their operations). Thus price fluctuations over time – especially in standard weapons such as Chinese or Romanian AKs, or in commodities such as 7.62mm short AK rounds – can indicate changes in insurgent operational tempo, an increase in community demand (due to insecurity) or a drop in supply due to improved interdiction.
- Insurgent kill/capture versus surrender ratio. A larger number of defectors, deserters or surrenders on the part of an insurgent group may indicate a drop in that unit's morale. Conversely, unwillingness to surrender – fighting until killed or captured – on the part of insurgent fighters can indicate high motivation. Analysts can seek

- indications of an insurgent network's morale by comparing changes over time in the insurgent kill/capture rate with changes in the surrender/desertion rate. These ratios should also be considered in relation to the insurgent recruitment and retention rate – if a unit's loss rate is high but it has no difficulty obtaining local recruits then it is likely to be experiencing a high degree of local support.
- Mid-level insurgent casualties. The insurgents' loss rate is also a useful indicator, especially in relation to losses in the middle tiers of the insurgent organization – the level below the senior leadership group, comprising planners, operational facilitators, technical specialists, trainers, recruiters, financiers, and lower-level operational commanders. Killing senior leaders may not actually damage the insurgency particularly, especially if senior leaders who are killed are simply replaced by younger, hungrier, more radical and more operationally experienced leaders from the next generation. Likewise, the insurgents can (and do) expect to lose a significant number of foot-soldiers, and to replace them relatively easily with minimum disruption. On the other hand, killing or capturing the insurgent "middle management" tier can do significant damage to the organization, while leaving senior leaders intact and perhaps even convincing them over time that their campaign is futile, and without killing large numbers of lower-tier fighters and sympathizers who may be good candidates for reintegration. Thus the insurgent loss rate at the middle level of the network is an especially important indicator of the network's health and resilience.

APPENDIX E. METRICS USED BY INSURGENTS[50]

Metric 1: Victory Can Be Understood as the Perpetuity of Fighting

The influential Saudi militant, the late Yusuf al-'Uyayree, elucidates this long-term perspective in his works Meanings of Victory and Loss in Jihaad and The Future of Iraq and the Arabian Peninsula. This understanding is a cultural pillar of the global jihadi trend, which, based on its interpretation of the sacred sources, sees itself as the true, victorious sect that will fight until the end of days. This idea of victory is also apparent in the Creed of the Global Islamic Media Front, a primary outlet of the global jihadi movement: We believe that the victorious sect will be the sect of learning and jihad. We believe that jihad will continue until the Day of Judgment, with every pious man or wrongdoer, in every time and place, with an imam or without an imam. It will continue with a single individual or more. No tyrant's injustice or naysayer's discouragement will halt it. We believe that Jihad in God's way is the legitimate and sound way that will enable the Ummah to resume an Islamic life and establish a well-guided caliphate according to the program of the Prophet.

Metric 2: Victory Is Found in Obeying the Obligation to Fight Islam's Enemies, Not in the Outcome of Battle

Anwar al-Awlaki—formerly associated with an Islamic center in Falls Church, Virginia, and a past chaplain at George Washington University—delivered a lecture on al-'Uyayree's works in which he explained this understanding in poignant terms. In the transcription of his lecture, titled "Constants on the Path of Jihad," al-Awlaki stated: Victory is not what we are accountable for; we are accountable for whether or not we are doing what Allah commands. We fight Jihad because it is hard [obligatory] on us; we are not fighting to win or loose [sic]. If we broaden our perspective, we will come to realize that whoever rides the peak of Islam (Jihad) [parentheses and emphasis in original] can never loose [sic] and will always win but not always win in physical victory. This definition has implications for jihadis at the collective and individual levels. At the collective level, adhering to this duty results in overt obedience to and therefore guidance by Allah. When mujahideen (those who believe they are fighting in God's path) embrace this obligation and absorb this guidance, tangible strategic success for the ummah—the global Muslim community—is believed to follow. The establishment of the state of Israel and regional regimes is generally viewed by Jihadis as a byproduct of neglecting this obligation. At the individual level, a rational decision to exchange love for worldly comforts for the love of battle and to overcome Satan and those who hinder one from fighting represents more than simple obedience: it is a purifying, ennobling act. One hour of Jihad in Allah's path, according to a famous hadith beloved by Abdullah Azzam, architect of the Afghan jihad, is better than 60 years of praying. As case studies of jihadis in the United Kingdom and elsewhere attest, some young Islamists also see jihad as a social rite of passage.

Metric 3: The Institutionalization of a Culture of Martyrdom Is a Victory

According to exponents of global jihad such as Abu Ayman al-Hilali, martyrdom is the greatest victory a mujahid can have. Al-Hilali and others argue that martyrdom operations offer a direct route to Paradise, the most effective means to strike adversaries, and the loftiest form of witness. And as illustrated by West Point's Sinjar Records, a collection of nearly 700 foreign fighter biographies from Iraq, the idea that martyrdom is synonymous with victory for many jihadis goes well beyond theory. When al Qaeda in Iraq "bureaucrats" queried foreign fighters as to why they came to Iraq, or what duty they hoped to perform, 217 of the 389 who responded (56.3 percent) indicated a desire for martyrdom, whereas 166 projected their roles as "fighter" (or something similar).

Metric 4: Victory Comes by Pinpointing Islam's Enemies through the Refining Process of Jihad, and thus Maintaining Its Identity

Sayf-ad-Din al-Ansari, another online jihadi strategist, argued this point explicitly in a 2002 essay on the 9/11 attacks: Our Islamic community has been subjected to a dangerous process of narcosis. As a result, it has lost the vigilance that comes from faith and fallen into a deep slumber. The most dangerous consequence of this is that most Muslims can no longer distinguish between their enemies and their friends. The fallout from choosing peace and normalization has caused a great confusion of ideas. The resultant situation poses a genuine threat to our very identity. [The 9/11 attacks] came to move this war from the shadows out into the open, to make the community aware of the enemy. It revealed the perils that surround us in a way that everyone can understand. The attacks succeeded in laying bare the enemy's soul and talk of a new crusade with all the historical baggage the phrase entails. It became clear to everyone that this is a campaign against Muslims more than a war against the mujahidin. Islam itself is the target. The raid showed just how fragile is the supposed coexistence of Muslims and Crusaders. Fighting, al-Ansari argues, is equivalent to maintaining the ummah's identity against internal and external threats; it is the ultimate means to enjoin the good and forbid the evil. As the ever-popular jihadi author Muhammad al-Maqdisi contends in The Religion of Abraham, it is simply not enough to renounce tyrants verbally.

Metric 5: Establishing Pride, Brotherhood, and Unity in the Face of Threats to the Ummah Is a Form of Victory

Abu Ubayd al-Qirshi, another popular militant "strategist" who wrote a pseudo-scholarly essay complete with notes, "The Impossible Becomes Possible," advances this point forcefully: With the New York and Washington raids, al-Qa'ida established a model of a proud Islamic mentality. This outlook does not view anything as impossible. Al-Qa'ida embodies Islamic unity. Blood from all the countries of the Islamic community has mixed together in the Jihad that al-Qa'ida leads with no distinction between Arab and non-Arab. In and of itself, this is a step on the road to Islamic unity and the destruction of the colonialist treaties that have torn the body of the Islamic community apart. [W]ith absolute trust in God, a willingness to die in God's path, patience, and generosity of spirit these qualities undoubtedly lead to victory. While generally a pragmatic author concerned more with "jihadi strategic studies" than theology, al-Qirshi's view of brotherhood and unity echoes the perspectives of many salafis, militant or otherwise: preserving the integrity and purity of Islam in the face of contemporary intra-Islamic strife (fitnah), syncretistic practices, and external threats is of paramount importance. None of these can be confronted apart from a unified and self sacrificial methodology (the latter of which al-Qirshi and al Qaeda believe to be associated with violence and martyrdom).

Metric 6: Creating a Parity of Suffering with Islam's Enemies—Especially the Jews and Crusaders—is a Victory

According to Saudi cleric Nasr al-Fahd and al Qaeda spokesman Suleiman Abu Geith (among others), upholding the shari'a principle of "repayment in kind" (al-mu'amala bil-mithl) not only justifies but also demands the murder of millions of al Qaeda's enemies to avenge the millions of Muslims killed at their hands. Al-Fahd— whose well-known fatawa (religious opinions) concerning the "legitimacy" of the Taliban regime and the destruction of the Buddha statues in Afghanistan were widely circulated online—published on May 21, 2003, a fatwa justifying the use of nuclear weapons (as well as other weapons of mass destruction) against the "enemies of Islam." Al-Fahd wrote: The attack against it by WMD [which al-Fahd explicitly defined as "nuclear, chemical, or biological"] is accepted, since Allah said: "If you are attacked you should attack your aggressor by identical force." Whoever looks at the American aggression against the Muslims and their lands in recent decades concludes that it is permissible. They have killed about ten million Muslims, and destroyed countless lands. If they would be bombed in a way that would kill ten millions of them and destroy their lands—it is obviously permitted, with no need for evidence. Terrorism—including that involving WMD—is seen by authors such as Abu Geith and al-Fahd as being among the most expedient methods for achieving the reciprocal suffering (and thus, victory) for which their reading of Islamic law calls.

Metric 7: Victory Is Seen in the Maladies Afflicting God's Enemies, Especially Economic Recession and Natural Disasters

Al'Uyayree writes that economic hardships among Allah's enemies are sure signs of His favor upon the mujahideen and harbingers of their impending victory. Furthermore, we see in the writings of other extremists that natural disasters such as Hurricane Katrina are believed to foreshadow the imminent collapse of the West and victory for the Islamic vanguard over the unbelievers.

Metric 8: The Presence of Miracles in Jihad Foretells of Victory for the Mujahideen

Abdullah Azzam's book on miracles in the Afghan Jihad, The Signs of Rahmaan in the Jihaad of the Afghan—a "most viewed" publication on the extremist-leaning Makhtabah.net online bookseller—illustrates this point, as does a mountain of online jihadi writings covering the "miraculous events" of the battle of Fallujah, and the supernatural in contemporary Afghanistan.

Metric 9: The Promotion of the Heroic Template Is Itself Victory

The jihadi literature reminds us and nauseam that victory does not depend on individual leaders; those who trust in men rather than Allah will eventually suffer moral, if not material, defeat. Instead, victory comes by emulating the "heroes" of fighting—those who leave everything behind to make their blood cheap for the ummah— and by enduring the temporary and refining trial of their absence. We are reminded that jihadi leaders themselves aspire to martyrdom when Allah wills it. As a testament to this notion, we see the wills, elegies, and eulogies of jihadis published and distributed on an almost industrial scale. Their message is consistent: Obey Allah as I did, avenge the ummah, and enter Paradise. .

Appendix F. Selected Extracts Regarding Whole-of-Government Approach from "National Security Strategy, May 2010"[51]

"To succeed, we must balance and integrate all elements of American power and update our national security capacity for the 21st century. We must maintain our military's conventional superiority, while enhancing its capacity to defeat asymmetric threats. Our diplomacy and development capabilities must be modernized, and our civilian expeditionary capacity strengthened, to support the full breadth of our priorities. Our intelligence and homeland security efforts must be integrated with our national security policies, and those of our allies and partners. And our ability to synchronize our actions while communicating effectively with foreign publics must be enhanced to sustain global support."

Successful engagement will depend upon the effective use and integration of different elements of American power. Our diplomacy and development capabilities must help prevent conflict, spur economic growth, strengthen weak and failing states, lift people out of poverty, combat climate change and epidemic disease, and strengthen institutions of democratic governance. Our military will continue strengthening its capacity to partner with foreign counterparts, train and assist security forces, and pursue military-to-military ties with a broad range of governments. We will continue to foster economic and financial transactions to advance our shared prosperity. And our intelligence and law enforcement agencies must cooperate effectively with foreign governments to anticipate events, respond to crises, and provide safety and security.

Strengthening National Capacity—A Whole-of-Government Approach

To succeed, we must update, balance, and integrate all of the tools of American power and work with our allies and partners to do the same. Our military must maintain its conventional superiority and, as long as nuclear weapons exist, our nuclear deterrent capability, while continuing to enhance its capacity to defeat asymmetric threats, preserve access to the global commons, and strengthen partners. We must invest in diplomacy and development capabilities and institutions in a way that complements and reinforces our global partners. Our intelligence capabilities must continuously evolve to identify and characterize conventional and asymmetric threats and provide timely insight. And we must integrate our approach to homeland security with our broader national security approach. *We are improving the integration of skills and capabilities within our military and civilian institutions, so they complement each other and operate seamlessly.* We are also improving coordinated planning and policymaking and must build our capacity in key areas where we fall short. This requires close cooperation with Congress and a deliberate and inclusive interagency process, so that we achieve integration of our efforts to implement and monitor operations, policies, and strategies. To initiate this effort, the White House merged the staffs of the National Security Council and Homeland Security Council.

However, work remains to foster coordination across departments and agencies. Key steps include more effectively ensuring alignment of resources with our national security strategy, adapting the education and training of national security professionals to equip them to meet modern challenges, reviewing authorities and mechanisms to implement and coordinate assistance programs, and other policies and programs that strengthen coordination.

Defense: We are strengthening our military to ensure that it can prevail in today's wars; to prevent and deter threats against the United States, its interests, and our allies and partners; and prepare to defend the United States in a wide range of contingencies against state and non-state actors. We will continue to rebalance our military capabilities to excel at counterterrorism, counterinsurgency, stability operations, and meeting increasingly sophisticated security threats, while ensuring our force is ready to address the full range of military operations. This includes preparing for increasingly sophisticated adversaries, deterring and defeating aggression in anti-access environments, and defending the United States and supporting civil authorities at home. The most valuable component of our national defense is the men and women who make up America's all-volunteer force. They have shown tremendous resilience, adaptability, and capacity for innovation, and we will provide our service members with the resources that they need to succeed and rededicate ourselves to providing support and care for wounded warriors, veterans, and military families. We must set the force on a path to sustainable deployment cycles and preserve and enhance the long-term viability of our force through successful recruitment, retention, and recognition of those who serve.

Diplomacy: Diplomacy is as fundamental to our national security as our defense capability. Our diplomats are the first line of engagement, listening to our partners, learning from them, building respect for one another, and seeking common ground. Diplomats, development experts, and others in the United States Government must be able to work side by side to support a common agenda. New skills are needed to foster effective interaction to convene, connect, and mobilize not only other governments and international organizations, but also non-state actors such as corporations, foundations, nongovernmental organizations, universities, think tanks, and faith-based organizations, all of whom increasingly have a distinct role to play on both diplomatic and development issues. To accomplish these goals our diplomatic personnel and missions must be expanded at home and abroad to support the increasingly transnational nature of 21st century security challenges. And we must provide the appropriate authorities and mechanisms to implement and coordinate assistance programs and grow the civilian expeditionary capacity required to assist governments on a diverse array of issues.

Economic: Our economic institutions are crucial components of our national capacity and our economic instruments are the bedrock of sustainable national growth, prosperity and influence. The Office of Management and Budget, Departments of the Treasury, State, Commerce, Energy, and Agriculture, United States Trade Representative, Federal Reserve Board, and other institutions help manage our currency, trade, foreign investment, deficit, inflation, productivity, and national competitiveness. Remaining a vibrant 21st century economic power also requires close cooperation between and among developed nations and emerging markets because of the interdependent nature of the global economy. America—like other nations—is dependent upon overseas markets to sell its exports and maintain access to scarce commodities and resources. *Thus, finding overlapping mutual economic interests with other nations and maintaining those economic relationships are key elements of our national security strategy.*

Development: Development is a strategic, economic, and moral imperative. We are focusing on assisting developing countries and their people to manage security threats, reap the benefits of global economic expansion, and set in place accountable and democratic institutions that serve basic human needs. Through an aggressive and affirmative development agenda and commensurate resources, we can strengthen the regional partners we need to help us stop conflicts and counter global criminal networks; build a stable, inclusive global economy with new sources of prosperity; advance democracy and human rights; and ultimately position ourselves to better address key global challenges by growing the ranks of prosperous, capable, and democratic states that can be our partners in the decades ahead. To do this, we are expanding our civilian development capability; engaging with international financial institutions that leverage our resources and advance our objectives; pursuing a development budget that more deliberately reflects our policies and our strategy, not sector earmarks; and ensuring that our policy instruments are aligned in support of development objectives.

Homeland Security: Homeland security traces its roots to traditional and historic functions of government and society, such as civil defense, emergency response, law enforcement, customs, border patrol, and immigration. In the aftermath of 9/11 and the foundation of the Department of Homeland Security, these functions have taken on new organization and urgency. Homeland security, therefore, strives to adapt these traditional functions to confront new threats and evolving hazards. It is not simply about government action alone, but rather about the collective strength of the entire country. Our approach relies on our shared efforts to identify and interdict threats; deny hostile actors the ability to operate within our borders; maintain effective control of our physical borders; safeguard lawful trade and travel into and out of the United States; disrupt and dismantle transnational terrorist, and criminal organizations; and ensure our national resilience in the face of the threat and hazards. Taken together, these efforts must support a homeland that is safe and secure from terrorism and other hazards and in which American interests, aspirations, and way of life can thrive.

Intelligence: ***Our country's safety and prosperity depend on the quality of the intelligence we collect and the analysis we produce, our ability to evaluate and share this information in a timely manner, and our ability to counter intelligence threats.*** This is as true for the strategic intelligence that informs executive decisions as it is for intelligence support to homeland security, state, local, and tribal governments, our troops, and critical national missions. We are working to better integrate the Intelligence Community, while also enhancing the capabilities of our Intelligence Community members. We are strengthening our partnerships with foreign intelligence services and sustaining strong ties with our close allies. And we continue to invest in the men and women of the Intelligence Community.

Strategic Communications: ***Across all of our efforts, effective strategic communications are essential to sustaining global legitimacy and supporting our policy aims.*** Aligning our actions with our words is a shared responsibility that must be fostered by a culture of communication throughout government. We must also be more effective in our deliberate communication and engagement and do a better job understanding the attitudes, opinions, grievances, and concerns of peoples—not just elites—around the world. Doing so allows us to convey credible, consistent messages and to develop effective plans, while better understanding how our actions will be perceived. We must also use a broad range of methods for communicating with foreign publics, including new media.

The American People and the Private Sector: The ideas, values, energy, creativity, and resilience of our citizens are America's greatest resource. We will support the development of prepared, vigilant, and engaged communities and underscore that our citizens are the heart of a resilient country. And we must tap the ingenuity outside government through strategic partnerships with the private sector, nongovernmental organizations, foundations, and community-based organizations. Such partnerships are critical to U.S. success at home and abroad, and we will support them through enhanced opportunities for engagement, coordination, transparency, and information sharing.

APPENDIX G. DEFINITIONS

Irregular Warfare (IW) Operations and Activities *(Joint Operating Concept (JOC) v 1.0 (Sept 2007))*	
Irregular Warfare	A violent struggle among state and non-state actors for legitimacy and influence over the relevant population(s). Irregular warfare favors indirect and asymmetric approaches, though it may employ the full range of military and other capacities, in order to erode an adversary's power, influence, and will. *(Joint Publication (JP) 1-02; JP 1)*
Insurgency	1. An organized movement aimed at the overthrow of a constituted government through use of subversion and armed conflict. *(JP 1-02)* 2. An organized, armed political struggle whose goal may be the seizure of power through revolutionary takeover and replacement of the existing government. However, insurgencies' goals may be more limited. Insurgencies generally follow a revolutionary doctrine and use armed force as an instrument of policy. *(FM 100-20, 1990)* 3. An organized movement aimed at the overthrow of an established government or societal structure, or the expulsion of a foreign military presence, through the use of subversion and armed conflict. *(Proposed by U.S. Special Operations Command)* 2. The organized use of subversion and violence by a group or movement that seeks to overthrow or force change of a governing authority. Insurgency can also refer to the group itself. *(JP 3-24, 2009)*
Counterinsurgency (COIN)	See Table 1. Definitions of COIN.

Appendix G. (Continued).

Irregular Warfare (IW) Operations and Activities *(Joint Operating Concept (JOC) v 1.0 (Sept 2007))*	
Unconventional Warfare (UW)	A broad spectrum of military and paramilitary operations, normally of long duration, predominantly conducted through, with, or by indigenous or surrogate forces who are organized, trained, equipped, supported, and directed in varying degrees by an external source. It includes, but is not limited to, guerrilla warfare, subversion, sabotage, intelligence activities, and unconventional assisted recovery. Also called UW. *(JP 1-02; JP 3-05)*
Terrorism	1. The calculated use or threat of unlawful political violence against noncombatants, intended to coerce or intimidate governments or societies through fear. (Proposed) 2. The calculated use of unlawful violence or threat of unlawful violence to inculcate fear; intended to coerce or to intimidate governments or societies in the pursuit of goals that are generally political, religious, or ideological. (JP 1-02; JP 3-07.2)
Counterterrorism (CT)	Actions taken directly against terrorist networks and indirectly to influence and render global and regional environments inhospitable to terrorist networks. Also called CT. See also antiterrorism; combating terrorism; terrorism. *(JP 3-26)*
Foreign internal defense (FID)	Participation by civilian and military agencies of a government in any of the action programs taken by another government or other designated organization to free and protect its society from subversion, lawlessness, and insurgency. *(JP 3-22)*
Stabilization, security, transition, and reconstruction operations (SSTRO)	Stability Ops: 1. An overarching term encompassing various military missions, tasks, and activities conducted outside the United States in coordination with other instruments of national power to maintain or reestablish a safe and secure environment, provide essential governmental services, emergency infrastructure reconstruction, and humanitarian relief. (JP 1-02; JP 3-0) 2. Military and civilian activities conducted across the spectrum from peace to conflict to establish or maintain order in states and regions. (DODD 3000.05, Nov 2005)

	Irregular Warfare (IW) Operations and Activities
	(Joint Operating Concept (JOC) v 1.0 (Sept 2007))
	3. Stability Operations is defined as an overarching term encompassing various military missions, tasks, and activities conducted outside the United States in coordination with other instruments of national power to maintain or reestablish a safe and secure environment, provide essential governmental services, emergency infrastructure reconstruction, and humanitarian relief. (DoDI 3000.05, Sep 2009) 4. Leverage the coercive and constructive capabilities of the military force to establish a safe and secure environment; facilitate reconciliation among local or regional adversaries; establish political, legal, social, and economic institutions; and facilitate the transition of responsibility to a legitimate civilian authority. (FMI 3.07 Stability Operations, Oct 2008) Military Support to Security, Transition, and Reconstruction: Department of Defense activities that support U.S. Government plans for stabilization, security, reconstruction and transition operations, which lead to sustainable peace while advancing U.S. interests. (DODD 3000.05, 2005)
Psychological operations (PSYOP)	Planned operations to convey selected information and indicators to foreign audiences to influence their emotions, motives, objective reasoning, and ultimately the behavior of foreign governments, organizations, groups, and individuals. The purpose of psychological operations is to induce or reinforce foreign attitudes and behavior favorable to the originator's objectives. Also called PSYOP. (JP 3-13-2; JP 1-02)
Information operations (IO)	The integrated employment of the core capabilities of electronic warfare, computer network operations, psychological operations, military deception, and operations security, in concert with specified supporting and related capabilities, to influence, disrupt, corrupt or usurp adversarial human and automated decision making while protecting our own. Also called IO. See also computer network operations; electronic warfare; military deception; operations security; psychological operations. (JP 3-13; JP 1-02)

Appendix G. (Continued).

Stability Ops	
Stability operations are a core U.S. military mission that the Department of Defense shall be prepared to conduct and support. They shall be given priority comparable to combat operations and be explicitly addressed and integrated across all DoD activities including doctrine, organizations, training, education, exercises, materiel, leadership, personnel, facilities, and planning.	DoDD 3000.05 (Nov 2005)
Stability Operations is defined as an overarching term encompassing various military missions, tasks, and activities conducted outside the United States in coordination with other instruments of national power to maintain or reestablish a safe and secure environment, provide essential governmental services, emergency infrastructure reconstruction, and humanitarian relief.	DoDI 3000.05 (Sep 2009)
An overarching term encompassing various military missions, tasks, and activities conducted outside the United States in coordination with other instruments of national power to maintain or reestablish a safe and secure environment, provide essential governmental services, emergency infrastructure reconstruction, and humanitarian relief.	JP 1-02; JP 3-0 (revised March 2010):
Leverage the coercive and constructive capabilities of the military force to establish a safe and secure environment; facilitate reconciliation among local or regional adversaries; establish political, legal, social, and economic institutions; and facilitate the transition of responsibility to a legitimate civilian authority.	FMI 3 07 Stability Operations (Oct 2008):
Foreign Internal Defense	
Participation by civilian and military agencies of a government in any of the action programs taken by another government or other designated organization to free and protect its society from subversion, lawlessness, insurgency, terrorism, and other threats to its security.	JP 1-02; JP 3-22 Foreign Internal Defense (July 2010)

Foreign Internal Defense	
Participation by civilian and military agencies of a government in any of the action programs taken by another government or other designated organization to free and protect its society from subversion, lawlessness, and insurgency.	DoDD 3000.07 - Irregular Warfare (IW) (Dec 2008)
Participation by civilian and military agencies of a government in any of the action programs taken by another government or other designated organization to free and protect its society from subversion, lawlessness, insurgency, terrorism, and other threats to its security.	JP 1-02; Air Force Doctrine Document (AFDD) 2-3.1 Foreign Internal Defense (Sep 2007)
Classified.	FM 3-05.202 Special Force Foreign Internal Defense Operations (Feb 2007)
Unconventional Warfare	
A broad spectrum of military and paramilitary operations, normally of long duration, predominantly conducted through, with, or by indigenous or surrogate forces who are organized, trained, equipped, supported, and directed in varying degrees by an external source. It includes, but is not limited to, guerrilla warfare, subversion, sabotage, intelligence activities, and unconventional assisted recovery. Also called UW.	JP 1-02; JP 3-05 (Dec 2003)
Unconventional warfare is a broad spectrum of military and paramilitary operations, normally of long duration predominantly conducted through, with, or by indigenous or surrogate forces who are organized, trained, equipped, supported, and directed in varying degrees by an external source. It includes, but is not limited to, guerrilla warfare, subversion, sabotage, intelligence activities, and unconventional assisted recovery (JP 3-05). Within the U.S. military, conduct of unconventional warfare is a highly specialized special operations force mission. Special operations forces may conduct unconventional warfare as part of a separate operation or within a campaign.	FM 3-05 (Feb 2008)
Operations conducted by, with, or through irregular forces in support of a resistance movement, an insurgency, or conventional military operations.	FM 3-05.201, Special Forces Unconventional Warfare; FM 3-05.130 (Sep 2008)

Appendix G. (Continued).

Counterterrorism (CT)	
Actions taken directly against terrorist networks and indirectly to influence and render global and regional environments inhospitable to terrorist networks. Also called CT. (FM 3-24 references this	JP 1-02 (April 2001, amended 2010)
• Actions, including antiterrorism and counterterrorism (CT), taken to oppose terrorism throughout the entire threat spectrum. • Actions taken directly against terrorist networks and indirectly to influence and render global and regional environments inhospitable to terrorist networks. • Objectives - thwart or defeat terrorist attacks against the U.S., our partner nations (PNs), and interests; attack and disrupt terrorist networks abroad so as to cause adversaries to be incapable or unwilling to attack the U.S. homeland, allies, or interests; deny terrorist networks WMD; establish conditions that allow PNs to govern their territory effectively and defeat terrorists; and deny a hospitable environment to violent extremists	JP 3-26 (Nov 2009)
Operations that include the offensive measures taken to prevent, deter, preempt, and respond to terrorism.	Air Force Doctrine Document (AFDD) 2-3 - Irregular Warfare (August 2007)
Lead our nation's effort to combat terrorism at home and abroad by analyzing the threat, sharing that information with our partners, and integrating all instruments of national power to ensure unity of effort.	NCTC Strategic Intent 2009-2013
The primary mission of the Office of the Coordinator for Counterterrorism (S/CT) is to forge partnerships with non-state actors, multilateral organizations, and foreign governments to advance the counterterrorism objectives and national security of the United States. Working with our U.S. Government counterterrorism team, S/CT takes a leading role in developing coordinated strategies to defeat terrorists abroad and in securing the cooperation of international partners.	Office of the Coordinator for Counterterrorism Department of State

Intelligence	
The product resulting from the collection, processing, integration, evaluation, analysis, and interpretation of available information concerning foreign nations, hostile or potentially hostile forces or elements, or areas of actual or potential operations. The term is also applied to the activity which results in the product and to the organizations engaged in such activity.	JP 1-02 (April 2001, amended 2010); AFDD 2-9
The product resulting from the collection, processing, integration, evaluation, analysis, and interpretation of available information concerning foreign nations, hostile or potentially hostile forces or elements, or areas of actual or potential operations. The term is also applied to the activity which results in the product and to the organizations engaged in such activity.	JP 2-0 Joint Intelligence (June 2007)
Intelligence is the product resulting from the collection, processing, integration, evaluation, analysis, and interpretation of available information concerning foreign nations, hostile or potentially hostile forces or elements, or areas of actual or potential operations. The term is also applied to the activity that results in the product and to the organizations engaged in such activity (JP 2-0). The Army generates intelligence through the intelligence warfighting function.	FM 2-0 Intelligence (March 2010)
The intelligence warfighting function is the related tasks and systems that facilitate understanding of the operational environment, enemy, terrain, and civil considerations. It includes tasks associated with intelligence, surveillance, and reconnaissance (ISR) operations, and is driven by the commander. (See chapter 7.) Intelligence is more than just collection. It is a continuous process that involves analyzing information from all sources and conducting operations to develop the situation. The intelligence warfighting function includes the following tasks: Support to force generation. Support to situational understanding; conduct ISR; provide intelligence support to targeting and information capabilities.	FM 3-0 Operations (February 2008)

Appendix G. (Continued).

Intelligence	
COIN is an intelligence-driven endeavor. The function of intelligence in COIN is to facilitate understanding of the operational environment, with emphasis on the populace, host nation, and insurgents. Commanders require accurate intelligence about these three areas to best address the issues driving the insurgency. Both insurgents and counterinsurgents require an effective intelligence capability to be successful. Both attempt to create and maintain intelligence networks while trying to neutralize their opponent's intelligence capabilities.	FM 3-24 Counterinsurgency (Dec 2006)
Surveillance	
The systematic observation of aerospace, surface, or subsurface areas, places, persons, or things, by visual, aural, electronic, photographic, or other means.	JP 1-02 (April 2001, amended 2010)
Surveillance is the systematic observation of aerospace [sic], surface or subsurface areas, places, persons, or things, by visual, aural, electronic, photographic, or other means." (JP 1-02) The Air Force perspective emphasizes that surveillance operations are sustained operations designed to gather information by a collector, or series of collectors, having timely response and persistent observation capabilities, a long dwell time and clear continuous collection.	AFDD 2-9 ISR (July 2007)
Surveillance is the systematic observation of aerospace, surface, or subsurface areas, places, persons, or things by visual, aural, electronic, photographic, or other means (JP 3-0). Other means may include but are not limited to space-based systems and special CBRN, artillery, engineer, special operations forces, and air defense equipment. Surveillance involves observing an area to collect information.	FM 2-0 Intelligence (March 2010)

Surveillance is the systematic observation of aerospace, surface, or subsurface areas, places, persons, o r things, by visual, aural, electronic, photographic, or other means (JP 1-02). Surveillance involves observing an area to collect information.	FM 3-0 Operations (February 2008)
Reconnaissance	
Reconnaissance is a mission undertaken to obtain, by visual observation or other detection methods, information about the activities and resources of an enemy or potential enemy, or to secure data concerning the meteorological, hydrographic, or geographic characteristics of a particular area.	JP 1-02 (April 2001, amended 2010)
• Special Reconnaissance. SOF may conduct SR into insurgent strongholds or sanctuaries. Activities within SR include environmental reconnaissance, armed reconnaissance, target and threat assessment, and post-strike reconnaissance • Insurgent Reconnaissance and Surveillance. Insurgents have their own reconnaissance and surveillance networks. Because they usually blend well with the populace, insurgents can execute reconnaissance without easily being identified. They also have an early warning system composed of citizens who inform them of counterinsurgent movements. Identifying the techniques and weaknesses of enemy reconnaissance and surveillance enables commanders to detect signs of insurgent preparations and to surprise insurgents by neutralizing their early warning systems. Thus, sophisticated counter ISR efforts may be required.	JP 3-24 COIN Operations (Oct 2009)
Reconnaissance is a mission undertaken to obtain, by visual observation or other detection methods, information about the activities and resources of an enemy or potential enemy, or to secure data concerning the meteorological, hydrographic, or geographic characteristics of a particular area." (JP 1-02) The Air Force perspective emphasizes that reconnaissance operations are transitory in nature and generally designed to collect information for a specified time by a collector that does not dwell over the target or in the area.	AFDD 2-9 ISR (July 2007)

Appendix G. (Continued).

Reconnaissance	
Reconnaissance is a mission undertaken to obtain, by visual observation or other detection methods, information about the activities and resources of an enemy or adversary, or to secure data concerning the meteorological, hydrographic, or geographic characteristics of a particular area (JP 2-0). Other detection methods include signals, imagery, and measurement of signatures or other technical characteristics. This task includes performing chemical, biological, radiological, and nuclear (CBRN) reconnaissance. It also includes engineer reconnaissance (including infrastructure reconnaissance and environmental reconnaissance).	FM 2-0 (March 2010)
Units performing reconnaissance collect information to confirm or deny current intelligence or predictions. This information may concern the terrain, weather, and population characteristics of a particular area as well the enemy. Reconnaissance normally precedes execution of the overall operation and extends throughout the area of operations. It begins as early as the situation, political direction, and rules of engagement permit. Reconnaissance can locate mobile enemy command and control assets—such as command posts, communications nodes, and satellite terminals—for neutralization, attack, or destruction. Reconnaissance can detect patterns of behavior exhibited by people in the objective area. Commanders at all echelons incorporate reconnaissance into their operations.	FM 3-0 (Feb 2008)

APPENDIX H. ACRONYMS

AAA	American Anthropological Association
ABI	Activity-based Intelligence
ACTD	Advanced Concept Technology Demonstration
AFDD	Air Force Doctrine Document
AFPAK	Afghanistan/Pakistan
AJP	Allied Joint Document
ANA	Afghan National Army

ANP	Afghan National Police
ANSF	Afghan National Security Forces
API	Application Program Interface
ASD	Assistant Secretary of Defense
ASD(SO/LIC&IC)	Assistant Secretary of Defense for Special Operations/Low-Intensity Conflict and Interdependent Capabilities
ASWORG	Antisubmarine Warfare Operations Research Group
AWOL	Absent Without Leave
BA	Battlespace Awareness
BICES	Battlefield Information, Collection, and Exploitation System
CAP	Combat Air Patrol
CCDR	Combatant Commander
CDCs	Community Development Councils
CENTCOM	United States Central Command
C-IED	Counter Improvised Explosive Device
CIVCAS	Civilian Casualties
CJCS	Chairman of the Joint Chiefs of Staff
CJTF	Combined Joint Task Force
COIN	Counterinsurgency
COMINT	Communications Intelligence
CONOPS	Concept of Operations
CT	Counterterrorism
DARPA	Defense Advanced Research Projects Agency
DCGS	Distributed Common Ground Systems
DI2E	Defense Intelligence Information Enterprise
DIA	Defense Intelligence Agency
DNI	Director of National Intelligence
DOCEX	Document Exploitation
DoD	Department of Defense
DoS	Department of State
DSB	Defense Science Board
ELINT	Electromagnetic Intelligence
EO	Electro-optical
EOF	Escalation-of-fire
F3	Find, Fix, and Finish
FAO	Foreign Area Officer
FID	Foreign Internal Defense
FININT	Financial Intelligence
FISINT	Foreign Instrumentation Signals Intelligence
FM	Field Manual
FMV	Full Motion Video
GEOINT	Geospatial Intelligence
GMTI	Ground Moving Target Indicator
HSCB	Human Social, Culture and Behavior Modeling Program

HTS	Human Terrain System
HUMINT	Human Intelligence
I&W	Indications and Warnings
IC	Intelligence Community
ICD	Intelligence Community Directive
ICEWS	Integrated Crisis Early Warning System
IEDs	Improvised Explosive Device
IMINT	Imagery Intelligence
INFORMS	Institute for Operations Research and the Management Sciences
INT	Intelligence
IPB	Intelligence Preparation of the Battlefield
IPT	Integrated Product Team
IR	Infrared
ISAF	International Security Assistance Force
ISR	Intelligence, Surveillance, and Reconnaissance
JOG	Joint Operations Guidance
JP	Joint Publication
JS	Joint Staff
LiDAR	Light Detection And Ranging
MASINT	Measurement and Signature Intelligence
MC&G	Mapping, Charting, and Geodesy
MCO	Major Combat Operations
MIP	Military Intelligence Program
MOD	Ministry of Defense
MOI	Ministry of the Interior
NGA	National Geospatial-Intelligence Agency
NGO	Non-Governmental Organization
NIM	National Intelligence Manager
NIP	National Intelligence Program
NRO	National Reconnaissance Office
NSA	National Security Agency
NSC	National Security Council
ODNI	Office of the Director of National Intelligence
OEF	Operation Enduring Freedom
OGC SWE	Open Geospatial Consortium's Sensor Web Enablement
ONR	Office of Naval Research
OR	Operations Research
OSINT	Open Source Intelligence
OUSD(I)	Office of the Under Secretary of Defense for Intelligence
PCPAD	Planning and direction; Collection; Processing and exploitation, Analysis and production; Dissemination
PED	Processing, Exploitation, Dissemination
PIR	Priority Intelligence Requirement
PRT	Provisional Reconstruction Team
R&D	Research and Development

RC	Regional Command
RF	Radio Frequency
S&T	Science and Technology
SAR	Synthetic Aperture Radar
SIGINT	Signals Intelligence
SO	Stability Operations
SOF	Special Operations Forces
SWaP	Size, weight, and power
TCPED	Tasking, Collection, Processing, Exploitation, and Dissemination
TOR	Terms of Reference
TTP	Tactics, Techniques, and Procedures
UAVs	Unmanned Aerial Vehicle
UCDMO	Unified Cross Domain Management Office
U.S.	United States
USA	United States Army
USAF	United States Air Force
USAID	United States Agency for International Development
USCENTCOM	United States Central Command
USD(AT&L)	Under Secretary of Defense for Acquisition, Technology, and Logistics
USD(C)	Under Secretary of Defense Comptroller
USD(I)	Under Secretary of Defense for Intelligence
USD(P&R)	Under Secretary of Defense for Personnel and Readiness
USD(P)	Under Secretary of Defense for Policy
USG	United States Government
USMC	United States Marine Corps
USN	United States Navy
USSOCOM	United States Special Operations Command
UW	Unconventional Warfare
VV&A	Verification, Validation, and Accreditation
WAPS	Wide Area Persistent Surveillance

APPENDIX I. BIBLIOGRAPHY

Afghanistan's Security Environment. Washington, DC: Government Accountability Office, 5 May 2010.

Allen, Patrick. "Understanding Local Actor Bases of Power." *IO Journal*. August 2010.

Batson, Douglas E. "Napoleonic Know-how for Stability Operations" In *Modern Military Geography*, ed. Francis A. Galgano and Eugene J. Palka. New York, NY: Routledge, 2010.

Best, Richard A. Jr. "Intelligence, Surveillance, and Reconnaissance (ISR). Acquisitions: Issues for Congress." *CRS Report for Congress*. Washington, DC: Congressional Research Service, June 2010.

Brannen, Kate. "Draft of U.S. Army Ops Concept Continues Break from Past Doctrine." *Defense News* (July 7, 2010).

Bunker, Robert. "The Ugly Truth: Insurgencies are Brutal." *Small Wars Journal* (2010).

Burchard, John. *Q.E.D.: MIT in World War II*. Cambridge, MA: The MIT Press, 1948.

CJCSM 3500.04E: Universal Joint Task Manual. Washington, DC: Department of Defense, Joint Chiefs of Staff, 25 August 2008.

Clapper, James. "Leading the IC: A Re- Set." Washington, DC: Office of the Director of National Intelligence, August 2010.

Cohen, Raphael S. "A Tale of Two Manuals." *PRISM* Vol. 2 No. 1 (2010): 87- 100.

Condra, Luke N., Joseph H. Felter, Radha K. Iyengar, and Jacob N. Shapiro. "The Effect of Civilian Casualties in Afghanistan and Iraq." Washington, DC: National Bureau of Economic Research, July 2010.

Cooper, Helene and Mark Landler. "Targeted Killing is New U.S. Focus in Afghanistan." *The New York Times* (31 July 2010).

Cordesman, Anthony H. "The Afghan War: Metrics, Narratives, and Winning the War." Washington, DC: Center for Strategic and International Studies, 7 June 2010.

Counterinsurgency FM 3-24. Washington, DC: Department of the Army, December 2006.

Cozzens, Jeffrey B. "Victory from the Prism of Jihadi Culture." *Joint Force Quarterly* No. 52 (Winter 2009): 86-91.

Defense Acquisitions: Opportunities Exist to Achieve Greater Commonality and Efficiencies among Unmanned Aircraft Systems. Washington, DC: Government Accountability Office, July 2009.

Defense Intelligence Strategy. Washington, DC: Department of Defense, 2010.

Demarest, Geoff. "Let's Take the French Experience in Algeria Out of U.S. Counterinsurgency Doctrine." *Military Review* (July-August 2010).

Department of Defense Directive 3000.07: Irregular Warfare. Washington, DC: Department of Defense, 1 December 2008.

Diehl, Jackson. "A Surge of Problems in Afghanistan." *The Washington Post* (14 June 2010).

Dilanian, Ken. "Study Says Rules Aimed at Curbing Afghan Civilian Casualties Also Reduce Attacks on U.S. Troops." *The Los Angeles Times* (3 August 2010).

Donovan, G. Murphy. "Signals and Noise in Intelligence." *Small Wars Journal* (27 August 2010).

Douglas, Ian A. "Law Enforcement Technology in Counterinsurgency Operations: Is CLEAR the Right Tool?" Graduate thesis, Georgetown University, 16 April 2010.

Ehrhard, Thomas P. "Air Force UAVs: A Secret History." Portland, ME: The Mitchell Institute: July 2010.

Eikenberry, Karl and Stanley McChrystal. *U.S. Government Integrated Civil Military Campaign Plan for Afghanistan*. Washington, DC: Department of Defense, 27 July 2010.

Felter, Joseph H. III. "Taking Guns to a Knife Fight: A Case for Empirical Study of Counterinsurgency." Ph.D. diss., Stanford University, June 2005.

Final Report of the American Anthropological Association Commission on the Engagement of Anthropology with the U.S. Security and Intelligence Communities. Arlington, VA: American Anthropological Association, 4 November 2007.

Final Report on the Army's Human Terrain System Proof of Concept Program. Arlington, VA: American Anthropological Association – Commission on the Engagement of Anthropology with the U.S. Security and Intelligence Communities, 14 October 2009.

Available on the Internet at: http://www.aaanet.org/cmtes/commissions/CEAUSSIC/upload/CEAUSSICHTSFin alReport.pdf.

Fitzsimmons, Michael F. "Governance, Identity, and Counterinsurgency Strategy." Ph.D. diss., University of Maryland, 2009.

Flynn, Michael T., Matt Pottinger, and Paul D. Batchelor. *Fixing Intel: A Blueprint for Making Intelligence Relevant in Afghanistan.* Washington, DC: Center for a New American Security, January 2010.

Flynn, Michael T., Rich Juergens and Thomas L. Cantrell. "Employing ISR Special Operations Forces Best Practices." *Joint Force Quarterly* No. 50 (Fall 2008): 56- 61.

Francis, David. "Want to Know How the War in Afghanistan is Going? Watch Kandahar."

The Christian Science Monitor (21 October 2010).

Fussell, Christopher, Trevor Hough, and Matthew Pedersen. "What Makes Fusion Cells Effective?" Monterrey, CA: U.S. Naval Postgraduate School, 2010.

Gabbay, Michael. "Mapping the Factional Structure of the Sunni Insurgency in Iraq." *CTC Sentinel* (March 2008).

Gorka, Sebastian L.v. and David Kilcullen. "An Actor-centric Theory of War: Understanding the Difference Between COIN and Counterinsurgency." *Joint Force Quarterly* No. 60 (Winter 2011): 14-18.

Hughes, Patrick M. "Guerilla War...Back Again?" Mobil Riverine Force Association, 22 July 2003. Available on the Internet at: http://www.mrfa.org/article4.htm. Last accessed 25 January 2011.

Ignatius, David. "Petraeus Rewrites the Playbook in Afghanistan." *The Washington Post* (19 October 2010).

Intelligence Community Directive Number 503: Intelligence Community Information Technology Systems Security, Risk Mangement, Certification and Accreditation. Washington, DC: Office of the Director of National Intelligence, September 15, 2008.

Intelligence, Surveillance, and Reconnaissance: DOD Can Better Assess and Integrate ISR Capabilities and Oversee Development of Future ISR Requirements. Washington, DC: Government Accountability Office, January 2010.

Intelligence, Surveillance, and Reconnaissance: Overarching Guidance is Needed to Advance Information Sharing. Washington, DC: Government Accountability Office, March 2010.

"Intel Under Fire: Can OR Help Win the Afghan War?" *ORMS Today* (June 2010).

Irregular Warfare (IW) Joint Operating Concept (JOC) Version 1.0. Washington, DC: Department of Defense, Joint Chiefs of Staff, 11 September 2007.

Jones, Seth G. "The Rise of Afghanistan's Insurgency: State Failure and Jihad." *International Security* Vol. 32 No. 4 (Spring 2008): 7-40.

JP 1-02 DOD Dictionary of Military and Associated Terms. Washington, DC: The Joint Staff, April 2010.

JP 3-24 Counterinsurgency Operations. Washington, DC: The Joint Staff, 5 October 2009.

Kagan, Frederick. "We're Not the Soviets in Afghanistan." *The Weekly Standard* (21 August 2009).

Kaplan, Edward H., Moshe Kress and Roberto Szechtman. "Confronting Entrenched Insurgents." *INFORMS Operations Research* (March- April 2010).

Kaplan, Fred. "A New Plan for Afghanistan: Less Counterinsurgency, More Killing and Capturing." *Slate* (13 October 2010).

_____. "The Transformer." *Foreign Policy* (September-October 2010).

Katzman, Kenneth. "Afghanistan: Politics, Elections, and Government Performance." *CRS Report to Congress*. Washington, DC: Congressional Research Service, 29 June 2010.

Key Challenges and Solutions to Strengthen Interagency Collaboration. Washington, DC: Government Accountability Office, 9 June 2010.

Kilcullen, David. "Measuring Progress in Afghanistan." Kabul, Afghanistan: December 2009. Available on the Internet at: http://hts.army.mil/Documents/Measuring%20Progress%20 Afghanistan%20(2).pdf.

Kress, Moshe, and Roberto Szechtman. "Why Defeating Insurgencies is Hard: The Effect of Intelligence in Counterinsurgency Operations – A Best- Case Scenario." *INFORMS Operations Research* (May- June 2009).

Latif, S. Amer. "An Analytical Study of the Kurdish Worker's Party. PKK) as an Insurgent Movement." Graduate thesis, Catholic University of America, 1999.

Le Sage, Andre. "Africa's Irregular Security Threats: Challenges for U.S. Engagement." *Strategic Forum* (May 2010).

Litchfield, John D. Unconventional Counterinsurgency: Leveraging Traditional Social Networks and Irregular Forces in Remote and Ungoverned Areas. Ft. Leavenworth, KS: U.S. Army School of Advanced Military Studies, 2010.

Mattis, James. "Feedback on the DSB Report on Understanding Human Dynamics." (12 June 2009).

McChrystal, Stanley A. and Michael T. Hall. *ISAF Commander's Counterinsurgency Guidance*. Kabul, Afghanistan: International Security Assistance Force/U.S. Forces- Afghanistan, August 2009.

Murphy, Kate. "Web Photos that Reveal Secrets, Like Where You Live." *New York Times* (August 11, 2010): B6.

The National Military Strategy of the United States of America: Redefining America's Military Leadership. Washington, DC: Chairman of the Joint Chiefs of Staff, 8 February 2011.

National Security Strategy. Washington, DC: The White House, May 2010.

O'Brien, Sean P. "Crisis Early Warning and Decision Support: Contemporary Approaches and Thoughts on Future Research." *International Studies* Review Vol. 12 No. 1 (March 2010): 87- 104.

Olsen, Eric T. "Context and Capabilities in Irregular Warfare." *Special Warfare* (September- October 2010).

Orem, John and Hugh Chen. "A New Strategic Balance: The Implications for ISR."

Paul, Christopher, Colin P. Clarke, and Beth Grill. *Victory Has a Thousand Fathers: Sources of Success in Counterinsurgency*. Santa Monica, CA: The RAND Corporation, 2010.

Petraeus, David H. "CENTCOM Update." Washington, DC: The Center for a New American Security, 11 June 2009.

_____ *COMISAF's Counterinsurgency Guidance*. Kabul, Afghanistan: International Security Assistance Force/U.S. Forces - Afghanistan, 1 August 2010.

"Political Military Policy Planning Team." Program Overview. Washington, DC: U.S. Department of State, 2010. Available on the Internet at: www.state. Last Accessed January 24, 2011.

"The QDR in Perspective: Meeting America's National Security Needs in the 21st Century." Washington, DC: QDR Independent Review Panel, 2010.

Rempe, Dennis M. "Counterinsurgency in Colombia: A U.S. National Security Perspective, 1958-1966." Ph.D. diss., The University of Miami, May 2002.

Report of the Defense Science Board 2004 Summer Study on Transition to Hostilities. Washington, DC: Defense Science Board, December 2004.

Report of the Defense Science Board Advisory Group on Defense Intelligence Operations Research Applications for Intelligence, Surveillance, and Reconnaissance (ISR). Washington, DC: Defense Science Board, January 2009.

Report of the Defense Science Board Task Force on Defense Biometrics. Washington, DC: Defense Science Board, March 2007.

Report of the Defense Science Board Task Force on Defense Biometrics – Modalities Matrix. Washington, DC: Defense Science Board, March 2007.

Report of the Defense Science Board Task Force on Intelligence – Operations Research Applications to Intelligence, Surveillance, and Reconnaissance. Washington, DC: Defense Science Board, January 2009.

Report of the Defense Science Board Task Force on Time Critical Conventional Strike from Strategic Standoff. Washington, DC: Defense Science Board, March 2009.

Report of the Defense Science Board Task Force on Understanding Human Dynamics. Washington, DC: Defense Science Board, March 2009.

Rubin, Alissa J. "French General Mixes Formula for a Bit of Afghan Calm." *The New York Times* (13 October 2010).

Schmitt, Eric, Helene Cooper, and David Sanger. "U.S. Military to Press for Slower Afghan Drawdown." *The New York Times* (11 August 2010).

Sepp, Kalev I. "Best Practices in Counterinsurgency." *Military Review* (May-June 2005): 8-12.

Shane, Scott, Mark Mazzetti and Robert F. Worth, "Secret Assault on Terrorism Widens on Two Continents." *The New York Times* (14 August 2010).

Shanker, Thomas, and Eric Schmitt. "U.S. Intelligence Puts New Focus on Afghan Graft." *The New York Times* (12 June 2010).

Shilling, Adam. *Nation-Building, Stability Operations and Prophylactic COIN*. Ft. Belvoir, VA: Center for Army Analysis, 5 May 2010.

Silber, Mitchell D. and Arvin Bhatt. *Radicalization in the West: The Homegrown Threat*. New York, NY: NYPD Intelligence Division, 2007.

Sirak, Michael C. "ISR Revolution." *Air Force Magazine* (June 2010): 36- 42.

"SOCOM Commander Concerned Over Direction of Pentagon COIN Strategy." *Inside the Navy* (31 May 2010).

Stein, Jeff. "GAO Again Slams U.S. National Security Agencies." *The Washington Post* (9 June 2010).

Sticha, Paul J. Dennis M. Buede and Richard L. Rees. "It's the People, Stupid: The Role of Personality and Situational Variables in Predicting Decisionmaker Behavior." Presentation to the 73rd Symposium of the Military Operations Research Society, 4 January 2006.

Tactical Persistent Surveillance. Washington, DC: U.S. Army Intelligence Center, 25 September 2007.

Thomas, Jason. "The Cognitive Dissonance of COIN: Right Doctrine, Wrong War." *Small Wars Journal* (13 August 2010).

Thompson, Gary H. and David W. Muench. *UnityNet: A Globally Deployable Sensor for 'White' Information.* Washington, DC: Defense Intelligence Agency, 5 May 2010.

Tirpak, John A. "Beyond Reachback: New ISR Systems and Techniques Put Awesome Intel at the Fingertips of Practically any Warfighter." *Air Force Magazine* (March 2009).

United States Government Counterinsurgency Guide. Washington, DC: USG, January 2009.

United States Government Integrated Civilian- Military Campaign Plan for Support to Afghanistan. Kabul, Afghanistan: Embassy of the United States of America and U.S. Forces- Afghanistan, August 10, 2009.

Unmanned Aircraft Systems: Additional Actions Needed to Improve Management and Integration of DOD Efforts to Support Warfighter Needs. Washington, DC: Government Accountability Office, November 2008.

Unmanned Aircraft Systems: Advance Coordination and Increased Visibility Needed to Optimize Capabilities. Washington, DC: Government Accountability Office, July 2007.

Unmanned Aircraft Systems: Comprehensive Planning and a Results- Oriented Training Strategy Are Needed to Support Growing Inventories. Washington, DC: Government Accountability Office, March 2010.

Worobec, Stephen F. "International Narcotics Control in the Golden Triangle of Southeast Asia." Ph.D. diss., The Claremont Institute, 1984.

End Notes

[1] Michael T. Flynn, Matt Pottinger, and Paul D. Batchelor, *Fixing Intel: A Blueprint for Making Intelligence Relevant in Afghanistan* (Washington, DC: Center for a New American Security, January 2010): 7. Emphasis added.

[2] *Report of the Defense Science Board 2004 Summer Study on Transition to and from Hostilities* (Washington, DC: Defense Science Board, December 2004).

[3] Ibid., v. Emphasis added.

[4] Robert Gates, Speech to the United States Military Academy, West Point, NY (Washington, DC: Office of the Assistance Secretary of Defense for Public Affairs Press Release, February 25, 2011).

[5] *United States Government Counterinsurgency Guide* (Washington, DC: USG, January 2009).

[6] *Report of the Defense Science Board 2010 Summer Study on Enhancing Adaptability of U.S. Military Forces* (Washington, DC: Defense Science Board, January 2011): 66.

[7] Ibid.

[8] *United States Government Integrated Civilian- Military Campaign Plan for Support to Afghanistan* (Kabul, Afghanistan: United States Embassy – Kabul/USFOR, August 2009).

[9] Christopher Paul, Colin P. Clarke, and Beth Grill, *Victory Has a Thousand Fathers: Sources of Success in Counterinsurgency* (Santa Monica, CA: The RAND Corporation, 2010): xiii.

[10] The Task Force reviewed 53 case studies of insurgencies. In every case the actions taken were reactive and occurred after the insurgency had taken hold. See Kalev I. Sepp, "Best Practices in Counterinsurgency," *Military Review* (May-June 2005): 8-12.

[11] *Report of the Defense Science Board 2004 Summer Study on Transition to and from Hostilities.*

[12] Ibid., v. Emphasis added.

[13] See Appendix F for a more detailed explanation of the whole-of-government concept from the 2010 National Security Strategy.

[14] *United States Government Counterinsurgency Guide.*

[15] Ibid.

[16] Ibid., v.

[17] *The National Military Strategy of the United States of America: Redefining America's Military Leadership* (Washington, DC: Chairman of the Joint Chiefs of Staff, 8 February 2011): 7.

[18] Flynn, et al., *Fixing Intel*, 7.

[19] *JP 1- 02 Department of Defense Dictionary of Military and Associated Terms* (Washington, DC: The Joint Staff, April 2010).

[20] Sebastian L.v. Gorka and David Kilcullen, "An Actor- centric Theory of War: Understanding the Difference Between COIN and Counterinsurgency," *Joint Force Quarterly* No. 60 (Winter 2011): 17.

[21] *Department of Defense Directive 3000.07: Irregular Warfare* (Washington, DC: Department of Defense, 1 December 2008): 2.

[23] *United States Integrated Civilian- Military Campaign Plan for Support to Afghanistan*, 5.

[24] Stanley A. McChrystal and Michael T. Hall, *ISAF Commander's Counterinsurgency Guidance* (Kabul, Afghanistan: International Security Assistance Force/U.S. Forces-Afghanistan, August 2009), 2.

[25] *The National Military Strategy of the United States of America*, 6.

[26] *United States Government Integrated Civilian- Military Campaign Plan for Support to Afghanistan*.

[27] The Task Force observes that "group" can denote different entities. For example, while groups in Iraq are often characterized in terms of religious and ethnic affiliation, village groups in Afghanistan appear more relevant to population analysis.

[28] *Report of the Defense Science Board Task Force on Intelligence – Operations Research Applications for Intelligence, Surveillance, and Reconnaissance* (Washington, DC: Defense Science Board, January 2009).

[29] See Appendix E for examples of such metrics.

[30] See Appendix F for some examples of insurgent metrics.

[31] *Report of the Defense Science Board 2006 Summer Study on 21st Century Strategic Technology Vectors* (Washington, DC; Defense Science Board, 2006), xii.

[32] Ibid., 13.

[33] *Final Report on the Army's Human Terrain System Proof of Concept Program* (Arlington, VA: American Anthropological Association – Commission on the Engagement of Anthropology with the U.S. Security and Intelligence Communities, 14 October 2009), 4.

[34] China area studies are the typical exception to this rule.

[35] AFPAK Hands (APH) program is located within the Joint Staff Pakistan-Afghanistan Coordinating Cell (PACC). The purpose of the program is to develop a cadre of AFPAK subject matter experts.

[36] Andreas Tolk and Lakhmi C. Jain, eds., *Studies in Computational Intelligence*, Vol. 168, *Complex Systems in Knowledge- Based Environments: Theory, Models and Applications*, "Principles for Effectively Representing Heterogeneous Populations in Multi-Agent Simulations," by Daniel T. Maxwell and Kathleen M. Carley (New York, NY: Springer, 2009): 199-228.

[37] Greg L. Zacharias, Jean MacMillan, and Susan B. Van Hemel, eds., *Behavioral Modeling and Simulations: From Individuals to Societies* (Washington, DC: The National Academies Press, 2008): 3.

[38] Michael Maybury, "Social Sensing," *Human Social Culture Behavioral Modeling Program* (Summer 2010): 6.

[39] *Intelligence Community Directive Number 503: Intelligence Community Information Technology Systems Security, Risk Management, Certification and Accreditation* (Washington, DC: Office of the Director of National Intelligence, September 15, 2008).

[40] The 2004 Summer Study dedicated an entire chapter to identification, location, and tracking in asymmetric warfare (153), which noted that surveillance of people, things, and activities required to populate the databases needed for identification, location, and tracking will require persistence beyond that typical of many of today's ISR sensors.

[41] For a summary of operations research as a field of practice, see: http://www.informs.org/AboutINFORMS/About-Operations-Research.

[42] John Burchard, *Q.E.D: MIT in World War II* (Cambridge, MA: The MIT Press, 1948): 92.

[43] *Report of the Defense Science Board Task Force on Intelligence – Operations Research Applications to Intelligence, Surveillance, and Reconnaissance*, 3.

[44] *Report of the Defense Science Board 2010 Summer Study on Enhancing Adaptability of U.S. Military Forces*, 66.

[45] Ibid.

[46] Paul, et al., *Victory Has a Thousand Fathers*.

[47] See Kalev I.Sepp, "Best Practices in Counterinsurgency," *Military Review* (May- June 2005).

[48] The Task Force also considered the recommendations of the 2009 DSB study on human dynamics. See: *Report of the Defense Science Board Task Force on Understanding Human Dynamics* (Washington, DC: Defense Science Board, March 2009).

[49] David Kilkullen, "Measuring Progress in Afghanistan," (Kabul, Afghanistan: December 2009): 6- 18, http://humanterrainsystem.army.mil/Documents/Measuring%20Progress%20Afghanistan%20%282%29.pdf

[50] Jeffrey B. Cozzens, "Victory from the Prism of Jihadi Culture," *Joint Forces Quarterly* No. 52 (Winter 2009): 86-91.

CHAPTER SOURCES

Chapter 1 - This is an edited, reformatted and augmented version of a Congressional Research Service publication, R41284, dated January 20, 2011.

Chapter 2 - This is an edited, reformatted and augmented version of a United States Government Accountability Office publication, GAO-11-465, dated June, 2011.

Chapter 3 - This is an edited, reformatted and augmented version of a Department of Defense, Defense Science Board Task Force on Defense Intelligence publication, dated February 2011.

INDEX

A

Abraham, 126
abuse, 76, 77, 117
access, 6, 8, 11, 14, 15, 20, 42, 76, 77, 85, 92, 93, 105, 113, 119, 120, 122, 123, 128, 129
accessibility, 115
accountability, 36, 41, 42, 43, 45, 77
accreditation, 94
acquisitions, 15, 16, 19, 20, 22, 33
adaptability, 21, 129
adaptation, 87
adaptations, 18
adjustment, 9
advancement, 96
advisory body, 8
aerospace, 70, 138, 139
Africa, 64, 146
age, 118
agencies, vii, 3, 5, 7, 8, 9, 13, 15, 20, 21, 25, 26, 27, 28, 29, 30, 31, 32, 33, 34, 36, 37, 38, 39, 40, 45, 50, 56, 58, 69, 75, 80, 82, 84, 86, 90, 102, 105, 107, 120, 122, 128, 132, 134, 135
aggregation, 69
aggression, 117, 127, 129
agility, 52, 55, 60
Air Force, 8, 9, 11, 12, 13, 17, 22, 23, 33, 34, 35, 45, 67, 68, 110, 135, 136, 138, 139, 140, 143, 144, 147, 148
Algeria, 79, 144
alienation, 76
ambivalence, 87
anthropology, 64, 87, 90, 98
APL, 109, 110
appetite, 105
appropriations, 8, 9, 11, 17, 18, 19, 20, 21, 31, 34, 38, 39
Appropriations Act, 19, 23

Arabian Peninsula, 124
architect, 125
armed conflict, 57, 71, 103, 131
armed forces, 29, 39, 72
arms control, 2, 3
articulation, 79
assassination, 115
assessment, 11, 12, 13, 28, 36, 37, 40, 54, 63, 71, 73, 84, 88, 139
assessment tools, 73
assets, 17, 20, 26, 27, 30, 32, 34, 41, 42, 58, 68, 69, 70, 78, 80, 83, 84, 96, 97, 99, 106, 116, 117, 140
audit, 28, 46, 86
authentication, 99
authorities, 30, 120, 129
authority, 2, 8, 13, 26, 31, 33, 34, 35, 40, 69, 98, 102, 115, 131, 133, 134
automation, 85
awareness, 42, 58, 85, 88, 95, 106, 120, 123

B

baggage, 126
bandwidth, 85, 91, 96, 100, 106
banking, 119
base, 6, 7, 11, 17, 31, 96, 120
behaviors, 73, 86, 117
benchmarks, 20
benefits, 78, 86, 93, 99, 130
black market, 123
blood, 123, 127
blueprint, 54
border security, 77
Bosnia, 4
bribes, 113
brutality, 117, 118
budget line, 116

bureaucracy, 4
business model, 9
businesses, 77, 114

C

Cabinet, 13
cabinet members, 3
cables, 11
campaigns, 70, 86, 87, 90, 105, 120
candidates, 99, 124
CAP, 141
career prospects, 90, 103
case studies, 125, 148
challenges, vii, viii, 1, 2, 5, 12, 14, 16, 18, 20, 31, 35, 39, 40, 41, 44, 45, 54, 55, 61, 62, 63, 72, 76, 86, 92, 94, 95, 97, 98, 99, 100, 129, 130
chemical, 127, 140
Chief of Staff, 22, 112
China, 149
CIA, 3
cities, 5, 114
citizens, 131, 139
civil war, 117
clarity, 26, 35, 41, 69
classes, 95
classification, 92, 98
cleavage, 114
climate, 63, 71, 128
climate change, 63, 71, 128
climates, 59, 106
clustering, 99
coalition troops, 78, 120
coercion, 76
Cold War, 3, 6, 12, 57, 65, 72, 103
collaboration, 37, 81, 90, 107
collateral, 79, 93, 121
collateral damage, 79, 93
colleges, 87
Colombia, 57, 104, 147
commerce, 14, 121
commercial, 6, 7, 9, 13, 14, 16, 23, 96, 107
communication, 9, 54, 59, 85, 95, 106, 130
communities, 9, 16, 26, 27, 32, 40, 76, 96, 100, 105, 123, 131
community, vii, 2, 9, 13, 14, 15, 16, 20, 21, 25, 29, 30, 31, 32, 34, 43, 53, 55, 56, 70, 71, 72, 78, 83, 84, 90, 91, 92, 97, 98, 102, 105, 114, 117, 121, 123, 125, 126, 131
competition, 16, 122
competitiveness, 129
complement, 8, 128
complexity, 2, 7, 9, 34, 78, 82, 98

compliance, 43, 114
complications, vii, 1, 20
composition, 5
computer, 84, 96, 133
computing, 97, 106, 107
conditioning, 42, 43
conference, 9
conflict, 10, 58, 61, 62, 78, 79, 85, 86, 88, 94, 106, 122, 128, 131, 132
connectivity, 92
consensus, 1
construction, 113, 114, 116
consumers, 2
contingency, 18, 26, 31, 52
controversial, 55
cooperation, 2, 21, 54, 76, 77, 128, 129, 136
coordination, 4, 16, 20, 21, 30, 72, 77, 82, 92, 100, 101, 103, 104, 106, 128, 131, 132, 133, 134
correlations, 54
corruption, 76, 77, 113, 114, 116, 117, 119
cost, vii, 1, 3, 4, 7, 12, 15, 16, 18, 21, 25, 28, 36, 41, 45, 54, 86, 87, 92, 96, 100, 107, 113
cost constraints, 21
cost controls, 7
cost saving, 36, 41, 100, 107
counterterrorism, vii, 1, 2, 5, 53, 55, 60, 78, 129, 136
covering, 83, 127
creativity, 131
creep, 16
criminality, 113, 114
criminals, 76, 117
crises, 55, 63, 71, 95, 128
criticism, 75
crop, 95, 113
crops, 116
cultural beliefs, 73
culture, 57, 59, 79, 84, 85, 87, 88, 91, 104, 106, 130
currency, 129
curricula, 88
customers, 6, 7, 52, 55, 60, 61, 70, 75, 84, 102
cybersecurity, 92
cycles, 20, 129

D

data center, 107
data collection, 66
data processing, 21, 31, 32
database, 84, 90
decision makers, 15, 30, 39, 44, 68

deficiencies, 19
deficiency, 91
deficit, 129
democracy, 130
democratization, 87
denial, 75
Department of Defense, v, vii, viii, 2, 19, 21, 22, 23, 24, 25, 27, 44, 46, 49, 50, 51, 52, 53, 54, 66, 69, 133, 134, 141, 144, 145, 149
Department of Homeland Security, 130
deployments, 102
deposits, 95
depth, 89, 91, 101
destruction, 126, 140
detainees, 118, 122
detection, 70, 78, 84, 139, 140
detention, 118
deterrence, 83
developed nations, 129
developing countries, 130
development assistance, 57, 104
diabetes, 122
diplomacy, 128
direct observation, 83
directives, 26, 28, 35, 45
disappointment, 18
disclosure, 92
disposition, 43
distress, 95
diversity, 60, 78, 113
DNA, 99
dominance, 118, 122
downlink, 96
draft, 42, 84

E

early warning, 139
echoing, 15
economic development, 56, 75, 87, 88, 102
economic growth, 114, 128
economic institutions, 129, 133, 134
economic power, 129
economic relations, 129
economics, 54, 90
economies of scale, 7
education, 67, 86, 88, 129, 134
educational psychologists, 88
elders, 89, 115, 119
e-mail, 44
emergency, 71, 117, 130, 132, 133, 134
emergency response, 130
emerging markets, 129

employees, 119
employment, 9, 68, 133
encoding, 98
endurance, 11, 120
enemies, 10, 126, 127
enemy combatants, 79
energy, 120, 131
engineering, 15, 97
enrollment, 99
environment, 3, 5, 20, 52, 59, 62, 65, 71, 76, 77, 82, 85, 89, 90, 92, 95, 98, 107, 119, 120, 122, 132, 133, 134, 136, 137, 138
environmental aspects, 73
environmental stress, 95
epidemic, 128
equipment, 4, 21, 123, 138
ethics, 87
everyday life, 6
evidence, 28, 46, 84, 118, 120, 127
evil, 126
evolution, 4, 9, 54, 59
execution, 69, 84, 91, 94, 96, 97, 98, 116, 140
executive branch, 4, 5, 14, 20, 21
exercise, 31, 63
expenditures, 100
expertise, 10, 15, 53, 73, 79, 87, 88, 90
exploitation, 14, 29, 53, 56, 68, 69, 70, 74, 79, 84, 91, 96, 115, 142
explosives, 123
exports, 129
exposure, 92
expulsion, 131
extraction, 99
extremists, 127

F

facilitators, 124
failed states, 71
faith, 125, 129
families, 119, 129
fatwa, 127
fear, 132
federal government, 2
Federal Government, 50
Federal Reserve Board, 129
fiber, 15
fidelity, 6
fights, 118, 123
financial, 14, 26, 31, 34, 35, 41, 42, 73, 84, 128
financial data, 34, 41, 42
financial regulation, 34
financial resources, 26, 31

fingerprints, 99
fires, 117, 120, 121, 123
fishing, 95
flaws, 14
flight, 10
fluctuations, 113, 115, 123
force, 14, 15, 27, 31, 32, 33, 52, 53, 57, 60, 62, 69, 75, 78, 79, 83, 97, 103, 118, 119, 120, 121, 122, 123, 127, 129, 131, 133, 134, 135, 137
foreign intelligence, 130
foreign investment, 129
foreign language, 91
formation, 114, 117
foundations, 129, 131
fruits, 113
funding, 2, 3, 8, 11, 13, 16, 18, 19, 22, 25, 26, 28, 31, 33, 34, 35, 37, 38, 39, 40, 41, 42, 43, 45, 56, 62, 88, 90, 101, 122
funding authorization, 38, 39
funds, 6, 9, 14, 18, 20, 26, 28, 30, 43, 45, 116, 119
fusion, 55, 60, 85, 91, 97, 107

G

GAO, vii, 8, 9, 12, 16, 22, 23, 25, 26, 27, 29, 32, 33, 34, 38, 44, 49, 50, 111, 147
geography, 56, 59, 74, 90, 94, 97, 101, 106
geolocation, 74
global communications, 72
global economy, 129, 130
global scale, 72
global security, 71
God, 124, 125, 126, 127
governance, 56, 63, 67, 71, 73, 75, 80, 87, 89, 90, 102, 113, 122, 128
governor, 116
GPS, 6
grants, 116
gravity, 80
growth, 3, 7, 12, 18, 26, 27, 36, 91, 92, 129
guidance, viii, 25, 26, 27, 28, 30, 34, 35, 36, 37, 40, 45, 53, 61, 66, 71, 72, 101, 125
guidelines, 66, 90
guilt, 118

H

hazards, 130
health, 58, 106, 122, 124
health problems, 122

Hezbollah, 79
history, 10, 12, 57, 71, 104
homeland security, 20, 38, 39, 128, 130
homes, 77
host, 59, 112, 138
hostilities, 52, 54, 58, 59, 73, 105
House, 9, 12, 13, 14, 16, 18, 19, 20, 22, 23, 24, 30, 37, 39, 40, 42, 44, 45
House of Representatives, 22, 23, 24, 37, 39, 42, 44
House Report, 45
housing, 114
human, 21, 29, 56, 57, 62, 64, 69, 72, 74, 79, 86, 88, 90, 93, 94, 96, 97, 98, 101, 103, 130, 133, 149
human behavior, 88, 94
human resources, 64
human right, 130
human rights, 130
Hunter, 18
Hurricane Katrina, 127
hybrid, 71, 79, 81
hypothesis, 66, 94

I

identification, 14, 43, 54, 59, 99, 149
identity, 99, 126
image, 15
imagery, 7, 10, 13, 14, 15, 18, 38, 79, 96, 97, 140
images, 15
immigration, 130
improvements, 35, 52, 76, 92, 105
inattention, 94
income, 119
incompatibility, 87
indexing, 97
India, 88
individual differences, 88
individuals, 59, 72, 77, 78, 86, 93, 106, 118, 133
Indonesia, 88
induction, 87
industry, 7, 10, 23, 53, 55, 95, 99
inflation, 129
information processing, 29
information sharing, 31, 52, 55, 60, 85, 92, 100, 107, 131
information technology, 105, 107
infrastructure, 6, 64, 67, 71, 72, 77, 90, 91, 99, 105, 107, 132, 133, 140
initiation, 123
insecurity, 76, 113, 120, 123
institutions, 90, 103, 128, 129, 130

insurgency, 57, 58, 63, 64, 66, 67, 68, 70, 72, 76, 78, 79, 83, 86, 87, 94, 95, 103, 104, 107, 118, 124, 132, 134, 135, 138, 148
Insurgency, 51, 57, 69, 103, 131, 145
integration, 14, 26, 27, 30, 31, 36, 37, 38, 39, 40, 41, 68, 70, 85, 128, 137
integrity, 126
international financial institutions, 130
International Narcotics Control, 148
interoperability, 15, 30, 40, 68, 77, 92, 99
intervention, 55, 58, 87, 104, 107, 118
investment, 11, 14, 18, 19, 26, 27, 31, 33, 37, 38, 39, 40, 41, 42, 43, 52, 59, 84, 85, 88, 90, 93, 94, 98, 100, 107, 116
investments, vii, 3, 7, 25, 27, 30, 32, 36, 38, 40, 43, 55, 60, 64, 85, 87, 90, 91, 94
Iraq, 3, 4, 10, 12, 15, 17, 18, 21, 27, 30, 64, 71, 79, 85, 92, 105, 124, 125, 144, 145, 149
Iron Curtain, 7
Islam, 125, 126, 127
Islamic law, 127
isolation, 10, 14
Israel, 125
issues, vii, 1, 4, 14, 16, 17, 18, 19, 26, 27, 37, 55, 56, 58, 61, 68, 77, 83, 85, 89, 99, 100, 101, 104, 129, 138
iteration, 40

J

Jews, 126
jihad, 124, 125, 126, 127
jurisdiction, 18

K

kidnapping, 113, 115
kill, 96, 117, 118, 119, 123, 127
kinship, 116
Kosovo, 4

L

lack of confidence, 117, 120, 121
landscape, 5, 98
language processing, 99, 107
language proficiency, 91
language skills, 88, 91, 120
languages, 88, 91, 93, 99
law enforcement, 67, 93, 128, 130
lead, 2, 16, 27, 30, 31, 40, 77, 86, 88, 89, 121, 126, 133

leadership, 6, 57, 76, 86, 100, 104, 120, 124, 134
learning, 74, 86, 124, 129
learning environment, 86
Lebanon, 10, 64, 71, 79
legislation, 4, 9, 17, 18, 20, 42, 43
leishmaniasis, 122
light, 58, 87, 92, 104, 105, 122
local community, 114, 117
local government, 77, 113, 116
logistics, 76, 77
love, 125
LTC, 111

M

majority, 13, 18, 71, 123
malaria, 122
malnutrition, 122
man, 12, 124
management, viii, 9, 25, 26, 27, 28, 30, 33, 34, 36, 37, 39, 40, 41, 42, 43, 58, 69, 74, 78, 80, 81, 83, 92, 97, 98, 105, 124
manpower, 56, 62, 101
mapping, 123
Marine Corps, 31, 46, 84, 90, 143
market economics, 113
Maryland, 145
mass, 63, 85, 105
materials, 113
matter, iv, 11, 42, 43, 63, 64, 149
measurement, 99, 140
media, 7, 10, 12, 64, 93, 122
mediation, 113
medical, 93, 120, 122
membership, 39
mentor, 76, 77
mentoring, 76
messages, 130
methodology, 28, 37, 126
Mexico, 64
Miami, 147
Middle East, 62
Military Order, 74
militias, 117
mineral resources, 59, 95, 106
MIP, 5, 14, 69, 103, 142
mission, 12, 39, 52, 55, 60, 68, 69, 70, 75, 78, 79, 80, 82, 85, 87, 92, 96, 97, 99, 134, 135, 136, 139, 140
missions, 2, 4, 7, 9, 12, 15, 16, 17, 20, 21, 22, 32, 33, 34, 39, 40, 75, 76, 77, 79, 80, 82, 86, 88, 89, 93, 129, 130, 132, 133, 134
models, 72, 88, 94, 96, 100

modules, 88
momentum, 36, 41, 64
moral imperative, 130
morale, 118, 119, 123
motivation, 123
multiple nodes, 9
murder, 126
Muslims, 126

N

nation states, 20
National Aeronautics and Space Administration, 13
National Defense Authorization Act, 22, 23, 24, 26, 27, 37, 38, 39, 40, 42, 45
national interests, 72
national policy, vii, 1, 5, 18
national security, 8, 9, 14, 16, 19, 21, 54, 55, 58, 59, 61, 63, 69, 87, 88, 98, 104, 128, 129, 136
National Security Agency (NSA), 3, 28, 29, 30, 45, 46, 101, 110, 111, 112, 142
National Security Council, 5, 21, 101, 128, 142
national strategy, 56, 101
NATO, 67
natural disaster, 127
natural disasters, 127
natural resources, 95
NCTC, 136
negotiating, 84
new media, 130
next generation, 124
NGOs, 61, 72, 75, 86, 92, 113
nodes, 85, 140
nuclear weapons, 127, 128

O

Obama, 4, 11, 17, 22, 23
Obama Administration, 4, 11, 17
obedience, 125
Office of Management and Budget, 18, 21, 129
officials, 2, 9, 14, 15, 28, 33, 34, 35, 36, 37, 40, 44, 45, 50, 52, 55, 56, 69, 78, 101, 114, 115, 116, 117
operating costs, 7, 37
Operation Enduring Freedom, 142
operations research, 82, 92, 149
opportunities, 7, 41, 81, 91, 93, 116, 131
orbit, 6, 9
organize, 89, 91
outreach, 76

overlap, 4, 6, 11, 14, 28, 31, 32, 35, 36, 37, 41, 44, 45, 81
oversight, vii, 1, 2, 4, 6, 7, 12, 16, 18, 21, 26, 27, 31, 34, 35, 40, 77, 91
ownership, 115, 116

P

Pakistan, 111, 122, 140, 149
PAN, 73
parallel, 13, 89
parasitic diseases, 122
peace, 4, 126, 132, 133
peacekeeping, 4
Pentagon, 13, 21, 23, 147
permit, 12, 18, 85, 140
personnel costs, 35, 36
phenomenology, 78, 82, 96
Philippines, 88
physical phenomena, 94
physical sciences, 65, 66
platform, 80, 81, 85, 96, 97
playing, 66
police, 77, 112, 113, 114, 115, 117, 118, 119, 120
policy, 6, 17, 19, 26, 29, 31, 34, 35, 36, 53, 61, 66, 69, 70, 71, 72, 92, 97, 100, 101, 130, 131
policy instruments, 130
policy makers, 29
policymakers, 2, 3, 4, 5, 14, 55, 58, 69, 101, 104
political leaders, 57, 104
political system, 88
polling, 98
popular support, 113
population group, 76, 85, 89, 118, 120, 123
portfolio, 5, 27, 28, 30, 32, 35, 36, 37, 42, 43, 81, 82, 85
portfolio management, 28, 30, 43, 81
poverty, 128
preparation, iv, 3, 86
president, 99
President, 3, 5, 13, 19, 23
prevention, 83
primacy, 67
principles, 17
probability, 27
professional development, 64
professionals, 13, 88, 129
profit, 53, 55
programming, 8
project, 116
proliferation, 15, 64
propaganda, 122
prosperity, 128, 129, 130

protection, 53, 57, 60, 62, 69, 75, 77, 78, 79, 83, 103, 117, 120
psychology, 90
public health, 57, 103
public safety, 117
punishment, 117
purity, 126

Q

qualifications, 13

R

radar, 95
reading, 127
real terms, 57, 103
real time, 97
reality, 6
reasoning, 133
recall, 99
recognition, 86, 107, 129
recommendations, iv, 17, 20, 23, 25, 36, 42, 51, 52, 53, 54, 55, 56, 59, 62, 63, 82, 85, 100, 107, 149
reconciliation, 123, 133, 134
reconstruction, 54, 59, 93, 132, 133, 134
recovery, 68, 132, 135
redundancy, 98
reform, 115
Reform, 23, 76
regional problem, 87, 88
regions of the world, 95
regulations, 14
reinforcement, 121
relatives, 116
relevance, 67
reliability, 12, 28
relief, 71, 116, 132, 133, 134
remote sensing, 95
reputation, 117, 118
researchers, 90
resilience, 124, 129, 130, 131
resistance, 86, 135
resolution, 10, 96, 97, 98, 113
resource allocation, 16, 40, 81, 82
resources, 13, 16, 26, 34, 35, 36, 38, 40, 43, 52, 53, 55, 60, 62, 66, 70, 72, 75, 81, 82, 83, 85, 89, 90, 92, 95, 99, 101, 103, 116, 128, 129, 130, 139, 140
response, 30, 36, 37, 42, 54, 59, 82, 88, 138
restoration, 71

restrictions, 92
retention rate, 124
retina, 99
rewards, 90
risk, 14, 57, 91, 104, 113, 120
risks, 7, 17, 41
root, 66, 85, 86, 88
roots, 87, 130
routes, 120, 121, 122
rule of law, 67, 76, 113
rules, 92, 140
rural areas, 114
rural population, 119

S

sabotage, 132, 135
safe haven, 71
safe havens, 71
safety, 66, 117, 120, 121, 128, 130
sanctuaries, 64, 139
satellite service, 6
satellite technology, 8
savings, 10, 41, 107
scaling, 59, 107
scarcity, 63, 71
science, 53, 56, 57, 59, 62, 66, 69, 72, 73, 87, 88, 90, 93, 98, 101, 102
scientific knowledge, 93
scientific method, 57, 66, 103
scope, vii, 25, 26, 28, 31, 32, 33, 34, 35, 36, 41, 43, 45, 60, 66, 94
Secretary of Defense, 4, 8, 11, 13, 15, 17, 18, 19, 22, 23, 26, 27, 29, 30, 32, 34, 36, 41, 42, 43, 44, 45, 49, 51, 54, 59, 72, 90, 100, 101, 103, 110, 111, 112, 141, 142, 143, 148
security, 5, 13, 39, 56, 57, 61, 67, 71, 75, 76, 77, 78, 80, 81, 85, 89, 92, 95, 100, 102, 104, 112, 113, 114, 115, 118, 119, 121, 123, 128, 129, 130, 132, 133, 134, 135
security assistance, 67
security forces, 67, 71, 76, 78, 112, 113, 114, 115, 118, 119, 121, 128
seizure, 131
semiotics, 87
Senate, 8, 9, 12, 16, 19, 22, 24, 44
sensors, 7, 9, 12, 14, 15, 55, 60, 68, 70, 80, 85, 91, 96, 98, 149
SES, 102
settlements, 85
shape, 20, 57, 86, 104
Sharia, 113
shortage, 91

shortfall, 89, 91, 94
showing, 118
signals, 3, 18, 19, 29, 38, 72, 79, 84, 89, 140
signs, 127, 139
simulation, 72, 85, 94
simulations, 94
social change, 56, 102
social control, 89
social network, 74, 93, 105
social relations, 93
social relationships, 93
social sciences, 60, 64, 65, 66, 79, 82, 86, 87, 88, 93, 103, 107
social security, 119
social structure, 93
society, 65, 84, 87, 119, 123, 130, 132, 134, 135
sociology, 64, 90
solution, 9, 14, 90, 96
Somalia, 88
Southeast Asia, 111, 148
specialists, 124
specialization, 74, 90, 103
specifications, 15, 99
Spring, 4, 145
stability, 4, 5, 6, 55, 58, 60, 64, 66, 71, 75, 78, 92, 104, 115, 129
stabilization, 4, 54, 59, 95, 122, 133
stakeholders, 9
state, 5, 18, 34, 57, 61, 64, 69, 71, 72, 80, 88, 89, 104, 125, 129, 130, 131, 136, 146
states, 63, 71, 128, 130, 132
statistics, 114
statutes, 14
storage, 97, 99
strategic planning, 4, 32
stress, 87, 95
structure, 13, 17, 32, 39, 55, 67, 74, 94, 97, 131
style, 74, 121
supernatural, 127
surveillance, vii, 2, 5, 8, 12, 15, 17, 18, 19, 20, 21, 25, 27, 44, 55, 68, 69, 71, 74, 84, 95, 96, 137, 138, 139, 149
synchronization, 68
synchronize, 9, 40, 128

T

tactics, 79, 94, 122
takeover, 131
Taliban, 83, 113, 114, 115, 116, 117, 121, 122, 126
tanks, 1, 129

target, 4, 6, 8, 13, 65, 72, 79, 80, 81, 84, 85, 86, 123, 126, 139
target population, 65
target populations, 65
taxation, 114
taxes, 114
teams, 93, 122
technical comments, 42
techniques, 1, 53, 73, 87, 90, 92, 94, 96, 121, 139
technologies, vii, 1, 2, 3, 6, 7, 9, 10, 11, 14, 16, 17, 18, 20, 52, 53, 59, 79, 96, 99, 100, 105, 106, 107
technology, 10, 16, 39, 59, 66, 93, 95, 96, 97, 99, 105, 122
telecommunications, 72
telephone, 6
tempo, 123
tension, 6
tensions, 89
terminals, 140
territory, 66, 71, 136
terrorism, 52, 130, 132, 134, 135, 136
terrorist groups, 2, 20
terrorists, 58, 75, 76, 104, 136
testing, 14, 85
threats, 71, 72, 77, 83, 126, 128, 129, 130, 134, 135
time constraints, 16
trade, 6, 34, 36, 37, 38, 40, 41, 57, 104, 107, 129, 130
trade-off, 6, 34, 36, 37, 38, 40, 41
training, 58, 67, 84, 86, 88, 90, 92, 94, 106, 129, 134
transactions, 73, 74, 99, 128
transcription, 125
transparency, 131
transportation, 113
Treasury, 82, 129
treaties, 126
trial, 127
tuberculosis, 122
turnover, 115

U

U.S. policy, 61, 64
unit cost, 23
United, v, 2, 4, 5, 21, 23, 24, 25, 44, 54, 56, 63, 64, 66, 71, 75, 76, 83, 84, 85, 102, 125, 129, 130, 132, 133, 134, 136, 141, 143, 146, 148, 149
United Kingdom, 125

United States (USA), v, 4, 5, 13, 21, 23, 24, 25, 44, 54, 56, 63, 64, 66, 71, 75, 76, 83, 84, 85, 102, 111, 112, 129, 130, 132, 133, 134, 136, 141, 143, 146, 148, 149
universities, 87, 88, 129
Unmanned Aerial Vehicles, 79
urban, 5, 85, 96, 114
urban areas, 5, 114

V

validation, 94
variations, 113
vegetables, 113
vehicles, 1, 11, 12, 78, 85, 96, 121
vein, 76, 86
velocity, 91, 106
Vietnam, 10, 57, 64, 103
violence, 69, 76, 114, 115, 116, 117, 126, 131, 132
violent extremist, 5, 136
vision, 27, 36, 66
vulnerability, 88

W

war, 9, 79, 100, 115, 126
warning systems, 139
Washington, 2, 9, 22, 23, 24, 49, 50, 56, 102, 125, 126, 143, 144, 145, 146, 147, 148, 149
waste, 10
water, 95, 116
weapons, 2, 10, 29, 64, 114, 121, 122, 123, 127
weapons of mass destruction, 2, 127
web, 98
web service, 98
welfare, 119
White House, 22, 128, 146
windows, 18
withdrawal, 62
WMD, 127, 136
workers, 54
World War I, 65, 144, 149

Y

yield, 3, 6, 74, 93